ANTHOLOGY OF
CATALAN LYRIC POETRY

ANTHOLOGY

OF

CATALAN LYRIC POETRY

SELECTION AND INTRODUCTION
BY
JOAN TRIADÚ

EDITED BY JOAN GILI

UNIVERSITY OF CALIFORNIA PRESS
BERKELEY AND LOS ANGELES 1953

Published in the U. S. A. by the
University of California Press, Berkeley and Los Angeles

OXFORD, BY TIPOGRAFÍA MODERNA, VALENCIA

INTRODUCTION

I: BACKGROUND

Fundamental considerations

THE field of Catalan lyric poetry is wide and varied, and its history has been a long one. This particular anthology was compiled in order to bring together its essentials rather than to provide a representative selection; my criterion was personal throughout, my choice being based upon my own reactions to the poems I read. When any poem succeeded in imposing its self-sufficiency upon me, then I felt that it had proved the perpetuation of its motive force. A poem at rest contains, just like a stone or a metal, latent energy which can be freed by the intervention of the reader. Once this has been released, its static framework should vanish, and its essence become as alive as it was when the poem was first composed. If any poem is to continue to be valid "poetry", then its powers of enchantment must persist in just that way. When properly approached such poems can resurrect their poets and revive a world which had seemed lost. A passion, a sorrow, silence —or a darting glance— come back into existence as they were at the moment when the poet abstracted them from reality to endow them with another, more enduring, life. That transfiguration was what I sought when making my selection, because I felt that no poem could lack it and still be effective poetry today.

I therefore excluded such whole periods and genres as could make no contribution to the essential message which any poetry contains for all mankind, in so far as it is the synthesis of any people's personality. Much that I omitted was by no means lacking in poetic merit nor, still less, in art; but I was concerned with something else, and it was essential that nothing should be allowed to confuse the issue. This anthology became more homogeneous as a result of my approach. It gained, indeed, a certain timelessness, for a living community of experience became apparent in poems from every age. Arbitrary divisions into epochs had to disappear because they seemed absurd, and all that was left was a subtle process of internal evolution, embodied —with all its surprises, its sorrows, its feelings, and its disillusionments— by successive schools of style. One gains a composite vision of Man-upon-Earth at the heart of it all, an Adam growing up and growing older with Mankind; when centuries in the life of a people are seen as though they were decades in the life of this single Man, his growth is slow but steady, devoid of any seemingly abrupt upheavals. The poetry which I have brought together constitutes a synthesis of man's experience, and seeks to present the reader with nothing more nor less than the history of humankind in Catalonia at its deepest, at its most significant, and at its least refutable.

When used to designate the area where Catalan is spoken, "Catalonia" reaches from the French plains at the foot of the Pyrenees down to the coastal plains on the South-Eastern edge of the Iberian Peninsula. It is a narrow and a hilly land, which pivots upon the Balearic Isles, and has been bountiful throughout its history. The Greeks barely touched upon its shores, nor did the Carthaginians leave much impression, but Catalonia was drawn into the Roman empire when this was at the height of its glory. After the Romans left, the latinised inhabitants had to resist Barbarian incursions from the North, and later they succumbed before the Moors, yet these left little trace north of the Ebro. Levantine traders were also amongst the diverse elements which formed the Catalan race, whilst Goths and Franks —who had come to raid but stayed to be assimilated— linked Catalonia firmly to Carolingian Europe as the centre of culture withdrew from Rome towards the North and West to make the continent which we now know. The Catalan people and their language assumed their personality together. The greatest civilising force was the Church, which sponsored the first attempts at literature and dominated all the decorative arts; the growing splendour of the monasteries led, in its own way, towards the growth of the courtly institutions which evolved around the earldoms of which Catalonia was composed.

Catalonia faced the sea, with islands and coast protecting it against the Moorish corsairs. Landwards it was linked to Aragon, in whose expanse the force of kingdoms which evolved upon the central tableland was spent before it could impinge upon the Catalans. They held both sides of the Pyrenees, which enabled them to contribute to the diffusion of Provençal culture, and they fought a losing battle to incorporate the entire heritage of all the "langue d'Oc". When they were obliged to give up this attempt by the death of King Pere "the Catholic" at the battle of Muret, in 1213 the Catalans turned their attention to the sea. They made the Mediterranean their fief by unremitting conquests which led them to Greece, island by island, during the course of the Thirteenth and Fourteenth Centuries. Landwards, however, the relentless pressure of the Peninsula weighed heavily on Aragon, and the Catalans were unable to dissociate themselves from Castile after royal marriage had linked them together in 1469. The people of this land, which had been so rich in its own being, so noble and firm in its laws, became a silent, sullen folk. They punctuated their prolonged subjection by fierce revolts, often provoked by very minor aggravations of their lot when greater ones had been ingenuously accepted; once up in arms they proved tenacious in resistance, however hopeless their case might seem to be.

By the time the full Renaissance came, the Catalans were too spent to recognise the changes afoot in Europe. They had been ousted from the Mediterranean by the Ottoman power, and denied free access to the New World beyond the ocean by Castile. The great nations were formed without their participation, and Catalonia's art and speech —its very being— lay dormant. Only the humbler folk stood by their language, keeping its spirit alive. Once the Bourbon monarchy was on the wane, the Catalan tongue rediscovered its tradition and its soul. Catalonia had regained free access to sea trade, commerce flourished, and as the Catalans found their rightful place amongst progressive peoples great men were born amongst them once again, men of genius and of action, law-givers, and poets with a message to convey. It took less than a century for Catalonia to regain all the vigour it had had before the decadence began, three centuries before. Poetry, voice as always of a people's soul, has revealed this reawakening far more fully than tangible achievements, and more truly than the fluctuations of Catalonia's freedom and material prosperity.

Such is the matter of this book, which also deals with the birth, life, death, and resurrection, of a literature whose history has been distinct in several ways from that of all the other Romance languages. Rarely has a country's decadence involved its literature to such a great extent, and yet the *Renaixença* has been one of the most remarkable revivals in literary history. This vitality can only be explained by the latent persistence of essential values, precisely those things which had been involved in the apparent disappearance of Catalan personality. The language proved stronger than the circumstances which had brought it so near to annihilation. All this can most clearly be seen when studying the lyric poetry of Catalonia, which is the purest and most transcendental embodiment of its tongue.

Language and themes

Catalonia's poets have always tended towards theocentric humanism, appealing constantly to a standard of values which, being high above the surface turmoil of events, enabled them to view this in perspective. At times they have been well in advance of their day, groping towards future truths which they could not know they were prefiguring; at other moments they have looked backwards, spanning a gap of centuries to re-evoke tradition. During those dark years anonymous bards had kept that flame of poetry alive, embodying their bitterness in songs which had an inner, vital meaning for the folk who treasured them. The poets have consistently exemplified that Catalan ability to bring order out of strange, dispersed, conflicting elements —the best defence for such a frontier people—, but in this they have merely played their part in the collective task of keeping a firm foothold in space and in time. Their theocentric humanism, their vision and their genius were merely facets of the national soul. They were facets which assisted its survival, by furthering Catalonia's capacity for a constant and organic evolution in which essentials have been renewed, but never lost, because it has always proved adaptable without becoming subject to distortion. This constant "Humanism" has always been the most decisive mark of the Catalan poetic outlook; it is a force which has moved the people as much as it has moved creative artists, although it may have moved them in different ways when for a time the two pursued two separate paths.

Catalonia's culture is wholly Mediterranean; it is due in part to the natural reactions of a people confronted with such a country, robust yet delicate, and infinitely varied even in the immediacy of its appeal. Whenever her poets have endeavoured to convey this landscape directly —without confusing its reality by intellectualising it away— they have been moved so deeply by it that they transformed it into a very real constituent part of life. Man has always been their protagonist, yet they have found him as much in the fullness of surrounding nature —in its sober elegance and clear-cut knowledge of the Golden Mean— as in Mankind itself. Both the form and content of Catalan poetry have constantly been marked by these same traits, and the precious approach has been as rare as the wilfully capricious one, or as the pursuit of intricate elaboration as an end in itself. There has always been something virginal about the Catalan tongue, something of a wholly artistic rapture which has sought to create a poetic language not to be applied to mundane ends. It is perhaps true to say, of course, that no tongue save Ancient Greek has ever had such a natural predisposition towards poetry, and it is as a consequence of this that Catalan poets have generally remained unhampered by any formal rhetoric, since they never required one in order to achieve a "poetic" form of expression. Furthermore, its banishment from all official usage, and lack of cultivation by uninspired professionals of verse for centuries, preserved it from that standardisation of topics, phrases and *clichés* to which both those employments lead. This demanded a constancy of the creative urge from which poets might otherwise have been exempt but it did so without obliging them to seek the recondite, since words in daily use had never been devalued by professional abuse. The possession of such a vehicle —a vital and a vivifying tongue moulded by an alert and intelligent people— has meant that Catalan poets have never been under any need to seek individualisation through the mere differentiation of technique. Instead, they have tended to cultivate a very limited gamut of poetic forms throughout long periods of their creative lives, if not throughout a whole career. They would achieve perfection in these forms quite early, but rather than change them, they would constantly repeat them, without remission, because they wished to stress the message and not some novelty in their technique. Form and content have always been kept in equilibrium, and a constant stress upon the need to justify the former by the latter has avoided the superficiality which attends upon the exaltation of words for their own sake. These three characteristics, extreme economy in use of words, sobriety, and simplicity of structure, have persisted in Catalan poetry down to the present day.

A constant impulse towards universality of appeal has also been at work alongside those three deep-rooted stylistic aspects of the tongue; it corresponds to other facets of the organic growth of Catalan. Complete romanisation served not merely to contribute towards the amalgam which became a national temperament, but also to pave the way for the appearance of Christianity and to intensify the fervour with which it was welcomed when it came. Religious sentiments are a theme which broadens the appeal of poets, and since there has rarely been a land in which Christianity became so deeply part of a people's soul, religious inspiration has been responsible for much poetry in Catalonia. The devotion of the poets has been, at heart, that of the people as a whole, a healthy and a popular devotion, realistic, resilient and full of hope. Theirs is a Franciscan vision of Christianity, whose devotion is part source and part product of a loving communion with nature, and of a frank admiration for the beauty of a world which has endeared itself to them from childhood. A graceful and a noble piety, part of their Latin heritage, becomes apparent in every aspect of their life. Few of the major poets have failed to turn to God; they have sought His aid when confronted by the mysteries of existence, turning to Him as much for an explanation of phenomena as for help when troubled by doubt. Yet they have rarely risen to mystic heights; they seem bound down by their humility, and by a certain restraint which is almost a sense of shame. Far from seeking God by the abstruse paths of metaphysical speculation, or by turning their imagination inward, they have sought Him in the Beauty and in the Reason of Nature. Seen in divine tranquillity, the world is very beautiful; and the loveliness of their own land led them to prayer. Llull (1233?-1315?) and Verdaguer (1845-1902), both Catalans, were two of the greatest religious poets of the Western World. Although six centuries apart, they spoke with God in the same tongue, not just with the selfsame God but in the selfsame way. Theirs was no abstract mysticism, because their preoccupation with humanity linked them too closely to the earth for them to forget their own condition. This tense limitation on transcendence underlies all their most significant poems.

Religious inspiration has also led the Catalans to meditate on death, and to write much poetry about its transcendental aspect; they have never seen it as an event which ends with itself. Because of the vital urge of their communion with external nature, death proved the most painful of all subjects; yet their sincerity, and the realism of their cult of life, prevented lapses into mock heroics or vain evasions of the issue. The elegiac mood, with all the grave loveliness contained in that nostalgic sentiment, was born of this conflict, and grew with it.

There was also human love under its many aspects. Conjugal and paternal love, and patriotism, proved sources of valid poetic inspiration thanks to the simplicity with which they were expressed and the intensity with which the poet viewed his feelings. This intensity made their formulation strangely intimate, as intimate as that of lovers' love itself. The great poets of the Middle Ages phrased that sentiment with violence, as though their verses were the outcome of some sombre and heart-rending progress of the soul. Their protest was majestic, full of grandeur, devoid of pettiness, magnificent in an autonomous nobility which already held something of the Renaissance. They sought no sublimation of their feelings by theology or by romanticism, but endeavoured to convey the impact of their passion by the fullest possible assertion of the Beloved. She was always a very real person, loved for her defects as much as for her virtues, because the mediaeval lyricist knew no cleavage between his ideal and a woman of flesh and blood such as marks the passion of the modern Catalan poet. Modern love lyrics may be coloured by the physical or by the spiritual aspect of love, but have never handled both these aspects of the Beloved at once since the romantic period began. Nevertheless, Woman exerts an even deeper influence today than in the Middle Ages. It is a subtler one, less explicitly confessed, responsible for a strange purposiveness within the poet, which seems to disquiet him obscurely at every level on which his vision moves. Modern Catalan lyricism holds an element of mystery which it had lacked before, and which derives from this fresh consciousness of woman. The troubling immanence of death in life, apprehended in those partial glimpses of Truth which form the total vision of the poet, now overshadows love with a sense of doom.

The modern Catalan poet is also confronted by fresh problems. Poets elsewhere have met them, but perhaps they assail the Catalan with even greater force as a result of the peculiar history which poetry has had in Catalonia. The answers to these problems are generally implicit in the questions they pose, but the answers themselves are such that the problems cannot be resolved in spite of this. There is a basic conflict between the poet and society, at every level —from that of the family to that of mankind as a whole. This conflict cannot be understood without analysing the modern poet's vision. This is coloured by a far clearer sense of personal solitude in the face of Creation than ever there was amongst the mediaeval poets, which may be the result of the lack of any stable sense of values or of the materialistic way in which Western civilisation has recently developed. A clear-cut consciousness, reasoned as much as intuitive, of what the poet's aims should be, and of conflict between these and the tangible frustrations he encounters, have intensified the anguish of such solitude. Poets will often soliloquise as though there was no-one to hear, tending more and more to escape into the lyrical joys of sheer word-magic and the suggestiveness of images and moods. Yet this holds none of that Northern fancy which fills its dreams with metaphysical figures conjured up from its imagination.

The Catalan poet's creative experience results from the impact of the concrete world upon his sensibility; still impeding ascent to heights of mysticism, it pervades him whenever he encounters love or senses that immanence of death in life. Far from conflicting with the older modes of vision, this new perspective has joined the earlier themes as though it were their complementary. This violent reaction against solitude has created a new, but parallel, poetic attitude which blends life and poetry together. It is the attitude of a poet moving subjectively, in a world of dreams within his mind, striving to understand himself as much as external reality. Modern Catalan poetry is very conscious of the discovery of this additional dimension in the poet's world.

Foreign influences

One can, in part, explain Catalan poetic development in terms of foreign influence. Whenever free, Catalonia proved the channel whereby this entered the Peninsula. Whenever subject to Castile, however, the schools of thought and movements of opinion which flourished in the rest of Europe could produce none save a very delayed reaction. The various phases through which this poetry has passed thus correspond to the changing circumstances of Catalan history. Of the three major influences before the *Renaixença*, the first and most powerful was that of Provence, the second that of Italy, and the third, the Castilian which coincided with the decadence.

Catalan poetry was evoked by Provençal; the earliest verses written in Catalonia were in provençalised Romance, and in two centuries approximately thirty salient poets born in Catalonia wrote only in Provençal. This was, for them, an artificial language, but they considered it to be the poetic tongue *par excellence* because it had been evolved as a poetic medium by a great school of poets. Other fashions from the North —from France— were blended with the Provençal by these Catalans, who made important contributions to the splendour of the greatest school of poetry which Europe had know since Virgil and Horace. The political influence which Catalonia exerted on Provence was as great as the linguistic influence of Provençal on Catalan, so that when Provence was destroyed by Simon de Montfort the lands were firmly linked not merely by their poetry and by the kinship between their languages but also by strong ties of blood and of tradition. As a result of this, the influence of the troubadours persisted longer in Catalonia than in any other literature which had encountered it, although Provençal had become almost as much a universal tongue in poetry as Latin was for every other purpose, reaching as far afield as England when at the height of its power.

All except the religious genres of Catalan poetry were once wholly subject to Provence. Italian influence reigned as supreme, in its turn, but this did not inhibit individuality in any way. Italian trends displaced the Provençal with the coming of the Renaissance, ending the dull traffic which mediocre poets made out of a dead tradition, and Petrarchan Humanism was the first renaissance current to be felt. It also left the deepest mark upon the Catalans, influencing all the greatest fifteenth century poets.

They displayed so vigorous a personality in their developments that they themselves influenced the whole Peninsula and Western European culture. These outstanding figures were the men from Valencia, in the South. They were the best exponents of their innovations, and the influence of Italy which they incorporated and transformed died only with the decadence of Catalonia.

The Castilian influence, which first began to be generally felt in literature at about that time, was an effect of that decadence, not a fresh source of inspiration. It met no resistance, it brought no new vitality, and its results are of no value now whether they be viewed from Catalonia or Castile. Matters would have been quite different had the case been similar to that of Provençal, and had poets writing in Castilian formed a school which could contribute to Castilian literature, but this time a foreign influence led to virtual silence. The impact of another language on the mere remnants of a literature proved overwhelming, and the Catalans made no valid use of the new medium. Poetry only survived amongst the humbler people, who always wrote in Catalan.

Apart from the anonymous ballads, whose corpus forms the *Cançoner*, no truly great poem was written by a Catalan from the end of the Italian phase until the influence of Castilian had begun to recede: Aribau's *La pàtria* (1833), in Catalan once more, heralded the *Renaixença*. This was to be the consequence of many interacting factors, some of which came into being when Catalan autonomy was first suppressed. The movement really began when Barcelona surrendered to the French and Spanish armies in 1714, after a lengthy siege; subjection gave Catalonia that strength which those who have been wronged and humbled can derive from their suffering. Although these feelings are reflected in the ballads, they had to wait for full poetic expression until the *Renaixença*, in the Nineteenth Century. The weakening of the central power, improved economic conditions which enriched Catalonia, the impact of Romanticism, and the encyclopaedic tendencies of learned thought, all helped to renew the vitality of a language preserved by the people and the Church. Combining with that sense of community in suffering, these produced the *Renaixença* itself. The reappearance of poetry gave the *Renaixença* its self-confidence, becoming the very symbol of its strength.

The poets of the new Catalan renaissance were influenced by Sir Walter Scott, by French Romantics like Chateaubriand, and by such Italians as Manzoni, Alfieri and Fascolo, and subsequently by Carducci and Leopardi. All these were apt sources for a romantic cult of the past which fostered Catalonia's longing for a return to freedom and past greatness. The Castilian influence was soon eliminated, because the substitution of Catalan for Spanish was the first requirement of this new poetry, but it did exert a certain braking effect upon development during the early years. Even so, the last few major figures to write in Castilian contributed towards the preparation for the *Renaixença* in other ways; some of them were men of great personality, like Cabanyes, and not even the use of a foreign medium could mask the wholly Catalan orientation of what they had to say. Although this fact may earn them praise as true precursors of the *Renaixença*, it reduced the intrinsic merit of their works; these no longer lay within the true channel of Castilian development but yet belong to Castilian literature by virtue of their medium. Had these men but lived a few years later and written in Catalan, their works would then have gained them the fame which their abilities deserved.

Although Provençal was re-asserting its own independence, it had little influence on the *Renaixença* because the movement of the *Felibrige* lagged behind. French and Italian influences on the other hand continued to be fruitful sources of inspiration throughout the first phase, and do still play their part in Catalan development today. Once the revival had achieved stability, then individuals were able to examine foreign literature with a more critical approach. The major German poets were then discovered one by one, and each made his own contribution towards the growth of the new Catalan poetic consciousness. The first to be read were Nietzsche and Novalis, and then Goethe. The latter's influence was to remain, even after the first two had been superseded by Rilke, and Rilke, in turn, by a deepening interest in Hölderlin. A complementary of this Germanic trend was a revived interest in the Classical World, which wove Horatian and Virgilian themes and attitudes into the reborn humanism of the Catalans.

Greece came into prominence more recently, but stirred the poets far more deeply. The vigour of this Hellenism, and its fruitfulness as a source of modern poetic inspiration, appears to be a unique phenomenon today; at no time since the original New Learning of the Renaissance has such a classical phase proved so stimulating. Modern Catalan poetry required such a phase of classicism after its romantic period, although restraint is so instinctive to the Catalan that one can perceive a certain innate classicism of form throughout romanticism. The Hellenistic influence was indirect at first, being drawn from Italy; but the next steps were easy and one found romantic content being gradually canalised by an increasingly classical logic of thought and form. The best productions of this phase are far from dead or second-hand; their Hellenism is less a matter of details than an atmosphere which filters through and in between the more characteristic features of modern verse without distorting them or minimising their significance, and it has thus proved to be one of the most beneficial influences which Catalan poetry has ever undergone.

There is still something virginal and serene about Catalan poetry today which is a direct fruit of this interaction of the Greek and the Germanic during the Nineteenth Century; Goethe, for whom the Mediterranean held so romantic an appeal, had led the way with Winckelmann towards this rediscovery of the Greek world—although the Catalans were a Southern people they yet had to view their sea through Northern eyes before they could apprehend its full poetic message. Once the new poets had found some self-reliance and reincorporated the classical heritage, they began to return to their own Catalan predecessors, the poets of the Middle Ages and the Fifteenth Century. They were most deeply influenced by these in their love lyrics and in the forms and general tone of their verse, but the religious and mystical production of the Middle Ages has also played a considerable part in the development of modern religious poetry. The popular ballads have had more influence upon the form of modern verse than on its content.

As the perspective shortens so does the scene become less easy to portray with clarity. Stabilisation of the new Catalan poetic vision has given it a greater capacity for understanding foreign movements and making an apt choice amongst them, bringing very diverse reactions. This was only to be expected in a land which had always been sensitive to foreign influences; but its result has been a bewildering eclecticism whose major sources have included not only modern English poetry but Shakespeare, Keats, and Pater, the more recent Castilians like Jorge Guillén and Federico García Lorca, and all the French schools of poetry since Mallarmé. Germanic and Hellenic influences have not, however, ceased to play their part. It must also be borne in mind that none of these latest fashions has had so marked an effect as any of those which were felt in the course of the Nineteenth Century, or during the Middle Ages, Renaissance, and Decadence. There is less of a communal subservience to fashion than of a series of personal debts to individual foreign poets, and specific poems have had a greater impact than specific abstract doctrines. Each modern Catalan has come under influences which he has made his own and has contributed towards the general vision of his day. Modern Catalan poetry has shown sufficient vitality to maintain its independence, selecting such elements as it found meaningful and incorporating these without degenerating into a mere reflection of some foreign source. It also displays certain markedly national characteristics which have survived in spite of wars and centuries of decadence, and all the major facets of the earlier poetry are still to be discerned. There is that same sincerity and humanising zeal, that same economy of words, that same classical —yet intimate— austerity which moulds the poet's thought and is the secret of that magical Catalan poetic atmosphere.

The survival of these qualities is a tribute to the vitality of the language. Exiled from official usage for whole centuries, often persecuted, it has nevertheless maintained its unity and its linguistic area, if one includes Valencian and Majorcan. Writers and grammarians could take up the language as they found it and adapt it to meet all modern needs, including the translation of Greek, Latin and Biblical texts and foreign literatures. They gave it an elegance, a solidity and yet a flexibility which have made it as fine a vehicle for all forms of literary expression as any other language of today. Thanks to the survival of the medium employed, Catalan poetry was able to regain continuity despite the decadence.

II: THE MIDDLE AGES AND THE RENAISSANCE

The Catalan Troubadours and the School of the Jocs Florals

THE first Catalan lyric was written almost nine hundred years ago. Based upon a Latin poem which had itself been written in Catalonia, the *Cançó de Santa Fe* was composed between 1054 and 1076 in a language still so primitive and fluid that critics long held it to be Provençal. They have now adjudged it Catalan, however rudimentary the differentiation of the two may have been, but the fact that such a controversy could arise shows how closely Catalan poetry was related to that of the tongues beyond the Pyrenees from its inception. The religious nature of the subject marks the first appearance of one of the major streams of Catalan poetic inspiration. This poem displays a remarkable degree of perfection in both form and content, yet it probably antedates the Castilian *Cantar del Mío Cid* by a century at least.

If certain obscure references are accepted, then the first Catalan troubadours also belonged to the second half of the Eleventh Century, but what we now know as the Catalan School of Troubadour Poetry can be more accurately said to have begun towards the end of the Twelfth. Some thirty noteworthy poets of very varied character and genius wrote in Provençal, but the stream of anonymous poems on popular and on religious themes continued to develop in the vernacular amongst the people. Had the case been one of two neighbouring tongues which differed widely and had developed side by side, then this peculiar position could never have come about, but —strange though this dichotomy may seem— it can be explained by the close kinship between Catalan and Provençal. The latter was bound to exert a strong influence over the cultured poets of the other land in view of its more advanced development as a medium of civilised expression. Such samples of popular and religious poetry as have survived, and they are very few and far between, are hard to date precisely. There is a charming straightforwardness about the timidity with which these anonymous poets sought to express their emotions in such works as the *Plany de la Verge*, the *Plant de Sant Esteve* and the *Balada de la Verge Maria*, and in the more vigorous and forceful *Virolai de Montserrat* (or *de Madona Santa Maria*). About the beginning of the Fourteenth Century this popular religious genre came under the influence of the troubadours, most notably that of Cerverí de Girona, and its pristine sincerity succumbed to an excessive cultivation of the artificialities of troubadour technique during the transitional stage between the decadence of Provençal and the birth of a truly national literature in Catalonia. Not merely the host of anonymous poets but also such figures as Dalmau de Castellnou, Pere de Vilademany, Fra Ugó (the Prior of Ripoll), King Jaume II, Jofre de Foixà, the Chaplain of Bolquera and Queen Constança of Mallorca, displayed a certain vacillation in their style which marked the uneasy gropings of Catalan in search of lyrical autonomy.

There were two major influences in this phase: the religious strain of popular verse on the one hand, and the markedly profane inspiration of the troubadours on the other. Many of the Catalan courtiers who wrote their verse in Provençal right up to the end of the Thirteenth Century, although with an ever increasing number of Catalan elements intruding as the years went by, were highly vigorous and vital personalities. They made their own original contributions to poetry throughout the uninterrupted progress from pure Provençal towards a language which was Provençal only in so far as certain terms and words were still part of the Catalan poetic lexicon.

At one time or another the Catalan troubadours employed the whole range of metres invented by those of Provence, but they displayed a greater tendency towards uniformity of pattern, coupled with a more natural approach to content and a more marked desire to be sincere. They preferred the *trobar plan*, a clear uncomplicated style derived from common usage, to that cultivation of obscurantist exclusiveness which was embodied in the *trobar clus*, and they were also distinguished by a deeper preoccupation with the meaning of what they wrote. Furthermore, they first made patriotism as important as religion in their poetry. Although they cannot be numbered amongst the Catalan poets because they wrote in Provençal, there are some who should be mentioned here because they stood out amongst the finest of the troubadours, such as Count Ramon Berenguer V of Barcelona (King of Aragon as Alfons II), who lived in the second half of the Twelfth Century, his contemporaries Guillem de Cabestany and Guerau de Cabrera, Guillem de Bergadà, who probably died at the beginning of the Thirteenth Century, Arnau the Catalan, Pere the Great, and Cerverí de Girona. Guillem de Bergadà was one of the most popular of troubadours, yet one of the most Catalan of those who wrote in Provençal. The death of Cerverí de Girona in 1280 marked the beginning of the decay of Provençal as a poetic medium in Catalonia. North of the Pyrenees, this decay had begun more than half a century before with the death of King Pere, the Catholic, who had been both an ardent Catalan and a poet in his own right.

The influence of Provence and France gained a

fresh lease of life during the Fourteenth Century as a result of the foundation of the "Sobregaia Companyia dels Set Trobadors" at Toulouse. A group of Catalans who frequently competed at its Jocs Florals gathered round King Pere the Ceremonious to foster a similar but autonomous movement in Catalonia. This achieved its own expression in the Floral Games of Barcelona, modelled upon those of Toulouse, but the school of poets which grew up around these did not produce much work of great poetic merit. The historical importance of these Jocs Florals is considerable, because they kept Catalan poetry alive during the fifty years preceeding the Italian influence of the Renaissance. Religious in their inception, the Games soon became no more than a tourney of poetic art whose rich prizes (jewels, set in the shape of flowers) provoked an intensive cultivation of technique without evoking much true inspiration. The Jocs Florals also established the linguistic autonomy of Catalan as a poetic medium so securely that even translations from the Provençal were sometimes made. The refinement of technique may have been gained at the expense of sincerity, but at least it had attained a high degree of polish before the influence of Italy reached Catalonia. Towards the end of this period the poetic influence of the French provided a bridge between Provence and Italy which greatly helped Catalan comprehension of the new Italian measures, and it was these which were to be the primary factor in the next phase of Catalan poetic evolution.

The charter authorising the institution of the Games had been signed by Joan I, who earned the title of Patron of Courtliness —*Amador de la Genti-*

lesa— by this act, and he had granted it to Jaume March (1335?-14...?). Already past the prime of life Jaume was to share the tasks of Master and Maintainer of the Games with another nobleman of note, but he continued as Maintainer well into the reign of Martí the Humane. His own poetry was almost completely impersonal —little more than a series of technical exercises upon the standard themes of Provençal tradition— and as much can be said of almost everything written by this school. The works of his cousin Pere March (1338-1413?) reveal a forceful mind, but he valued reasoning more highly than poetic qualities, and the bulk of what he wrote is only poetry because in verse, and only lends itself to formal criticism. Guillem de Masdovelles was also one of a family of poets. He himself belonged completely to the schools of Barcelona and Toulouse, but his nephew Joan Berenguer de Masdovelles (14...-1467?) was already a man of the Renaissance; uncle and nephew held prolonged discussions upon literary topics. Another interesting figure of the period was Llorenç Mallol, of the Tolosan School, because one of the religious poems which he presented at Toulouse bears an apparently remarkable resemblance to a love lyric by Petrarch. Both Catalan and Italian owed debts to a common source, a poem by the troubadour Bertran de Born; but Mallol's poem is nonetheless the first sign of the passing of an age, in spite of Provençal sensuality and its lack of Petrarchan subtlety.

In the course of time, French influence displaced the Provençal in the Jocs Florals. This can be clearly seen from the works of Lluís de Vilarrasa and Arnau March (who was either an uncle or a cousin of Ausiàs), both deeply indebted to Guillem de Machaut. Their poetry became more agile in consequence, and a little more sincere; Lluís de Vilarrasa introduced the ballade and employed it with heightened lyricism, whilst Arnau March gained a new sense of variety by introducing lines of different length into a single poem. Grave at all times, but at his gravest in religious verse, the latter always burnished his lines to perfection. These two were the last poets of note belonging to that Northern school which had persisted, under one form or another, from the first inception of literary Catalan well into the Fifteenth Century; with the Renaissance the centre of cultural activity shifted Southwards to Valencia.

In the meantime the popular cultivation of poetry had continued, still chiefly on religious themes. It was more closely related to the growth of other literary genres in the vernacular than the cultured poetry of the Jocs Florals could ever be because the men who produced it had obtained their direct experience of "literature" through attendance at the Mystery Plays, through social satires and political invective, songs of every kind, and the gay or solemn chants of the liturgical calendar, and through their cultivation of the art of story-telling. This art preserved poems, legends and fables, transmitting its vitality to all prose-writers, most especially to those who cultivated the popular genres. The Catalan poetry which we can study is chiefly that of cultured circles, due to the problems of transmission and survival; this continued to evolve apart from popular taste and unaffected by its fluctuations, but the forcefulness and rich variety of prose written with a popular appeal proves how deeply the life of the people was affected by mediaeval literature. Poetry grew from the people and gave them a means of self-expression, whilst clergy and aristocracy alike participated in the tempestuous interplay of passions which marked the later Middle Ages. As much literature was written in this troubled atmosphere as in the tranquillity of cloistered cells or by ascetic Scholars.

Ramon Llull

Ramon Llull (1233?-1315?) does not fit into this picture. He is an isolated figure who must be considered on his own, with just the bare framework of ideas needed to fit him into the pattern of his age. Outstanding in every way, he cannot be placed in that strict line which leads uninterruptedly from the first troubadour to the last poet of the decadence, and yet he is perhaps the finest example of that fusion between literature and populace characteristic of the Catalan genius. The decline of Provence had already begun in Ramon Llull's day; Jaume I had abandoned the rights of his line to Languedoc and to Provence itself, and had turned instead to strengthen Catalonia by the reconquest of Mallorca and Valencia from the Moors. The Occitanian phase of Catalan foreign policy was over and the literary influence of Provençal was on the wane; Catalan nationalism produced its own literature, and this grew up around the Chronicles and around the works of Ramon Llull himself. Llull's isolation enhances the merits of his work; he neither followed nor founded a school, although he began his poetic career as a courtier in Mallorca, cultivating verse as a mere exercise of wit. After his conversion he destroyed his earlier work, to use poetry as a medium for passionate self-expression; his subsequent works (and none of the earlier ones survives) are all so personal and so bound up with his immediate aims that all he wrote or did came from within himself. Such influences as can be traced in his works do not represent the results of conscious selection but the inescapable climate of opinion in which he lived, imposed upon him in the same way as the history and actual climate of the land where he was born. They were all facts not his to choose or to disown, but he was forceful in his adaptation of them to further his own ends. The insignificance of the influence which he exerted compared with the vastness of his output and the universality of all his aims is probably due to this very individualism; his legacy was never treated as it deserved to be, and although echoes of his philosophic thought can be distinguished up to the present day, his influence has always been a partial one, and only indirectly apprehended. Subsequent thinkers have never faced up to the full import of his reasoning, neither to refute it nor to take it further, almost as though they shrank away from the fieriness of all he did or wrote.

He has two claims to poetic greatness. Firstly, unpoetic though this may seem, having made effective use of poetry to further his own high aims. Secondly, having served the ends of poetry although such was not his purpose. Poetry sums up both these complementary facets of his grandeur, synthesizing a vital unity by its transcendence of the paradox.

To state this is to affirm that Ramon Llull was a true and valid poet, small though the quantity of verse may be within the huge accumulation of his writings and in spite of the fact that his poetry remains quite on one side of the normal Catalan poetic evolution. The works of Ausiàs March (that other great mediaeval poet) and even those of certain secondary figures, on the other hand, represent definite stages in that evolution which cannot be ignored if it is to be understood. In his own day, Ramon Llull was never viewed as a poet, and this may have something to do with the neglect which his verse was accorded; vastly talented, he seemed an intruder into literary fields because he was the complete antithesis of the poetic academicians, with all their "laws" and treatises and formal gatherings, fashions and rigid schools. This unconventional freedom which he displayed sprang from the immense vitality behind his life and works, a dynamism which enabled him to remain untrammelled by shackles which would have fettered any normal writer.

The quality of his verse demands a greater emphasis than merely quantitative assessment of the place it holds amongst his works would gain for it. The division between his lyrical and his didactic writings is far from being a clear and simple one. Neither branch of his production can be readily defined in terms of a neat and orderly series of characteristics, because all aspects of his life appear inextricably mixed in every part of his work. His poetry preserves its spontaneity, however dry the subject may occasionally be, thanks to the fact that his feeling for problems which are normally solved by reason alone was largely intuitive. Even in logic he was less a scholar using a technique than a vehicle for this poetic intuition of reality. Lacking in artistry because he lacked the artist's concentration upon art, his complex genius lacked nothing essential to the poet. His internal conflict led him into reasoned folly, and he could curse as well as love; he hated himself, as man, because he loved mankind. He was as much the poet in this as was Ausiàs March when inspired by Woman or a woman, or Verdaguer inspired by the poet's lyre or the priest's chalice. Llull felt himself marked out by the finger of God from the time of his visions of Jesus on the Cross, which led to his conversion and remained without parallel even in his long and turbulent and holy life; marked out by God, and henceforth unable to be a man just like any other. Nothing else could matter any more, and not even such external circumstances as lay at the heart of his age or formed the very framework of his life could move him greatly, and when all is said and done his place in time left very little mark on him.

Granted that the influence of Provence was already declining, in politics and in the realm of poetry, but Ramon Llull was nonetheless contemporaneous with Cerverí de Girona; no poet other than Llull was to be free from France or Provence for a further century after his death in 1315. Nor does it matter very much that his verse-forms and style, and even much of the conventional poetic imagery which he employed, were Provençal, nor even that provençalisms do at times appear in the language he employed for verse, because Llull not only enriched the forms he used but put them to very different ends, and used them in a greater variety than any other poet prior to the *Renaixença*. Provençalism of form had no effect upon the content of his verse, he was merely employing the only metres which had yet been elaborated in any Romance tongue. His use of Catalan, on the other hand, was a remarkable innovation; the Catalan he used for verse was very often wholly free from Provençal contamination thanks to the very precise use which he had learnt to make of it in prose. He transposed the whole world of poetic imagery which he derived from Provence into another key, to use it on the plane of mysticism. This was, perhaps, a seemingly simple transposition, but it was a work of genius which left its mark upon all subsequent mystical writing in the Iberian Peninsula. Paradoxical though it may seem, such writings do thus owe a significant, if an indirect, debt to that world of courtly gallantry and overwrought profane frivolity for which the troubadours had written.

Llull's best poetry was embodied in the three hundred and fifty-six versicles of which his *Llibre d'amic e amat* consists. Produced when he was at the height of his powers, this book was written during one of the periods in which he felt himself to be in closest touch with God; influences derived from Moslem Sufi mystics, from the Hebrew Song of Songs and from the Courtly Love of the Provençal troubadours, are fused into one transcendent paean upon this divine communion. Terms and images derived from these varied sources gained a new meaning and a fresh validity when they had been transfigured by his "folly of love", and he achieved that almost naive simplicity which marks the highest reaches of religious poetry. His lyricism transcended the specific climate of belief within which he wrote because its magic was derived from eternal and undenominational poetic values, and he produced a work of universal import. His Christian inspiration was closely akin to that of St Francis of Assisi, and in being the first great Catalan exponent of Franciscanism, Ramon Llull was introducing a theme whose cultivation by Catalan poets was to grow progressively more fruitful. Its background was a landscape as ingenuous, as simple and as enchanting as his theme, and as pure as the Garden of Eden before the Fall. He succeeded in infusing the sentiment of Nature with a fresh and vibrant life which truly anticipated the vitality of the renaissance vision of the world. Nature is neither a background nor an allegory here, but has its own perspective, and the characters —God and the Soul— move inside it, not in front of it.

The dramatic intensity of his desire for clear and perfect union with God produced a work whose deep sincerity has never been surpassed. Every thought appears to have been refined by his love before it reached the surface, to be embodied in phrases whose words are, for the most part, very short but which become extraordinarily effective in their context. They are blent into simple rhythms such as require to be learnt by heart, and once these had reached the paper his poet's task was done, and universal poetry achieved. But Llull himself took further agonising years in dying, torn by the anguish of his desire to save and to be saved whilst in this world. He died without knowing that what would save him here on earth would be the supreme poetry which he had written.

Jordi de Sant Jordi and Ausiàs March

There was no figure comparable to that of Ramon Llull in all the period from the Eleventh to the Fifteenth Centuries; neither the schools of Toulouse and Barcelona nor even the school of Catalan troubadours produced a single poet of his stature. When a great prose-writer, Bernat Metge (1350?-1412), wrote the first truly Renaissance work in Catalonia, *Lo somni*, at the very end of the Fourteenth Century, the works of Ramon Llull were fittingly amongst its many sources. Bernat Metge was a humanist, and the humanism of Italy which he introduced brought with it a renovation of old forms and a fresh vitality which proved so powerful that the transition from the poetry of the Jocs Florals to the school of Dante and of Petrarch took very few years. Andreu Febrer and the Valencians Jordi de Sant Jordi (1395?-1430?) and Ausiàs March (1397-1459) were courtiers and soldiers, and Andreu Febrer's translation of the *Commedia* (which preserves the *terza rima*) was written in intervals between the wars in which they fought. Between them they created what is now known as the Renaissance School, the last —but by far the most important— of the schools of poetry before the decadence, and one which yet owed much to its native predecessors in spite of its italianising. Somewhat later came Roiç de Corella (142.-1500) whose noble gravity marked the last important facet of the period; he too was a Valencian.

Jordi de Sant Jordi's varied but scanty poems survive in the anthologies which he compiled. Their universal appeal is due to the delicacy of his restraint and to the subtle way in which his language blended the distant with the passionate in his love-lyrics. He was the first great poet to come decisively under the influence of the Petrarchan mode of thought—until lately scholars had even maintained that the debt was one of Petrarch to Jordi de Sant Jordi. The power of his personality and his own intellectual stature combined to save him both from the danger of being dwarfed by the greatness of his master and from being the residuary legatee of the decaying Provençal school, although he still employed much which was in the manner of the earlier fashions. He was far from being servile in his imitations, and took the troubadour Montaudon for model in his *Enuigs* with a deliberate maliciousness which was extremely humanistic in its freedom. He similarly modified the lines he borrowed for his *Passió d'amor* to fit them better to his purpose, avoiding naming sources which erudite readers would be expected to perceive. This particular work attests once again to the importance of the Provençal tradition by the way in which it draws upon the fund of troubadour poetry as though upon the classics; this did indeed then take the place the classics held in other European literatures, and Jordi de Sant Jordi neither rejected it nor succumbed to it.

Both the form and content of his poems embodied things which were new to Catalonia. Much of his technique was Petrarchan, and he was a Petrarchan in the way in which he derived from his own experience all the poetry which it might hold. The sequence of his few remaining poems gives one an abstract of his life and the love-lyrics dedicated to Isabel are indeed amongst the most moving and sincere of the genre. He tells us little about her —only such details as emerge from the few references made to the ideal which she embodied for him— because he never attempted to record the vision which he always carried in his mind. Yet this figure of a woman is not an abstraction but a very concrete point of reference to which he related all he had to say, an ideal whose presence permeates his poetry as though foreshadowing some imminent revelation. His deliberate self-effacement has an underlying violence which makes each rigidly controlled avowal peal through the grave atmosphere in which his poems move. They are free from worn philosophies, drawing their strength instead both from eternal themes —which he expressed with classical simplicity— and from the matter of his daily life: the anguish of love, farewells, absence and longing, the chastening realities of circumstance, and the intrusiveness of death. When he addressed the king from an Italian prison to which the war had brought him, he did so in a spirit of high chivalry which enabled him to draw comfort from his very sufferings—but none from the prospect of becoming reconciled to Catalan defeat. He also wrote his *Estramps* to his beloved there, basing one of the richest and most moving of all Catalan poems on an appeal to past experience shared, exalting love until his personal emotions attained not only dignity and greatness but truly universal meaning. He wrote in lines whose clarity would half delude one into thinking it simplicity but which were always polished until their definitive form appears inevitably just; he had a technique of ennobling words by isolating them in order to employ the fullness of their meaning, placing them where that would be driven home by the measures of his verse. Its tone was grave in its warmth and vehemence, endowing the very pauses it imposed between the lines with vibrant life until the whole seems elegiac in its stateliness.

One would take Jordi de Sant Jordi for a forerunner of Ausiàs March rather than for his contemporary because of the way in which the latter's genius makes his poetry stand out. Ausiàs March is not only the most renowned Catalan lyric poet but also the one whose works have most deeply influenced the moderns. The most important element in his poetry is thought. He reached a point at which, as he says himself, he seemed to have been stripped of every other human faculty and left as mere stark naked intellect; all the vigour of his humanity and his poetic genius, all the strength of his passion, became canalised with frightening intensity into sheer intellection. The vigour and fecundity of the thought he embodied in patterns inherited from a monotonous tradition served to transfigure them. His learning, his temperament, and his experience blended together, and he became a tragic poet whose *Cants* form one vast but single work. Its clarity is fired with the ardour of a mystic's passion, and it is one of the strangest and finest poems which any man has ever written.

Ausiàs March drew upon his wide and varied reading for themes, patterns, and allusions, but the strength of his personality was such that there was no subservience in this. Not only did he derive fresh poetry from old subjects and time-honoured situations, but he was sufficiently eclectic to avoid submission to the Renaissance trends of the age in which he lived, though without denying the values which it had discovered. His intellection fitted within that framework thanks to his instinctive taste for such harmonious concord, but one could not strictly describe him as a "man of his age". He never subscribed to its fullness, although he did adapt himself to live in it, remaining instead a solitary genius whose life and vision transcended his environment. The past of Christendom weighed upon him with all its Aristotelian scholasticism; his intimate sense of sin awakened his intellect and transmuted it into conscience. His poetic conflict lay in the doubts surrounding eternal life—salvation or damnation. One might almost call him a Mediaeval poet conscious of having sinned with the Renaissance, vividly ashamed of this as converts always are of sin. His analysis has a renaissance subtlety in which the influence of Petrarch gives an anguished chiaroscuro to the poet's world. Yet he owed even more to Dante than to Petrarch: traces of Dante can be found throughout his work, although received as part of the full current of his Christian heritage, whereas he is Petrarchan only in his intellectual processes, not in his attitude. The most intense conflict with which this world confronted him was produced by a love worthy of his genius, as strange and powerful in its dominion as his own poetic vision of the world. He had to formulate all this in verse. This experience brought him face to face with death, in giving him the most intense desire for life, and if he had never had this love the poet in him would have been obliged to forge it. The mental processes which it involved were very similar to those of Petrarch, but there was less of the literary impulse about Ausiàs March, less of the conscious desire to achieve artistic creativity. They were two totally different men, and since they were both sincere as poets their poetry remains just as essentially different, in spite of all the things their works have in common.

Ausiàs March owed as much of his technique to the troubadours as he did to Petrarch; he was deeply acquainted with their poetry but saw them in sufficient perspective to avoid their defects and to be able to reject their language and vocabulary almost completely, whilst still employing the metres they had used. He even has something of their thought and of their courtly world, although there is more which is Italianate about him. This is largely because his career as a soldier took him to Italy, as it took Jordi de Sant Jordi and Andreu Febrer, for he was a courtier and a warrior of the old nobility, a man of culture and great learning whose patrons were the dukes and kings he served.

He first saw his lady, Teresa, at church in Lent. That perspective of an anguished populace oppressed by grief and darkened walls was suddenly foreshortened till nothing was left in focus except a woman standing by a crucifix. The poet in Ausiàs March fell on his knees before them, and never ceased to worship that twin image of God who loved him and the Woman whom he loved, whom he had found intent in meditation on that same God's passion. These two symbols were to haunt him all his life, and he had time for pondering upon them when travelling back and forth to the Court of Aragon at Naples, or in the tedious intervals which punctuate campaigning. The conflict between them gradually matured, to be projected into a poetry which was shot through and through with doubts, sorrow and passion. His humanistic learning had given him access to the wisdom of previous thinkers; themes and doctrines culled from poets, theologians, saints, philosophers, and mediaeval theorists on love were daringly fused into the substance of his personal experience. His poetry soon became widely known and gained him a great reputation even in his lifetime; he too, like Jordi de Sant Jordi, was long erroneously thought to have influenced Petrarch, but his influence upon Peninsular poetry is undeniable. It was recognised by Castilians of the stature of the Marqués de Santillana, Garcilaso de la Vega, Gutierre de Cetina, and Herrera, whilst he became the avowed model for the later Catalan poets of the Fifteenth Century and decadence. He has also influenced a number of salient modern poets, but he is even more important for his own achievements than as the creator of a school; his love poetry stands far above that of all previous mediaeval lyricists.

Ausiàs March's originality lay less in the substance of his thought or the technique of its formulation, or even in his imagery, than in the gravity and the intensity which he displayed in self-analysis and in the subtlety with which he expounded and anatomised all the facets of his intellectual progress. Life had given him everything required to make him a poet. He had been born with a gift for the apt choice of words and structure, unmarred by any innate love of artifice, and with a mind capable of piercing every aspect of human nature, dissecting both body and soul. He was granted Teresa, completely human in the blend of good and evil which he found in her, and then she died early—thus becoming yet more deeply and less forgettably his. The rest of his rich and varied life by land and sea was spent in ceaseless pondering upon salvation, an issue which her death brought home to him. Moved throughout by ardent, very human passions, his voice gained from their depth something of the power of choral chant, to beat into his poems with full solemnity and vigour. The *Cants d'amor* were his earliest poems and the finest, perhaps because they came the closest to experience; those which mourned Teresa, styled by posterity the *Cants de mort*, were their inevitable sequel; then face to face with the imminence of his own death, he wrote the *Cants morals*, which led up to his final *Cant espiritual* — a general confession, a prayer and a lament. Looked at in their entirety his writings form a balanced, architectonic whole based upon the poetry of love. When death had intervened, the poet built another storey out of his perplexed and agonised remorse. This was a pain which could only be resolved in God, in God's good time and through His grace and love; Ausiàs March's life and works drew to their close as these were finally attained. His last confession stands on the summit of that edifice, and it is a prayer for death because he was weak and feared not death but sin. He had unravelled and shed, line by line, that intricate web of living and loving, of doing good and doing evil, which had grown more intricate and more intense throughout his life. There was nothing left to shed save life itself; he begged for deliverance in that one final poem which crowns his works sublimely, gaining him eternity as a great poet where all he had sought was to achieve a man's eternal life, through God's great mercy.

The Valencian School in the Fifteenth Century

Dante's translator, Andreu Febrer, was a contemporary of Ausiàs March and Jordi de Sant Jordi, but he was more deeply influenced by France and by Provence than by the Italians; even in his frequent imitations of Petrarch there is much that is Provençal. A poet of passionate love, he tended towards an undue artificiality in its expression. Lleonard de Sors was a subtler man, of the same period and the same court; his lyrics are denser and more difficult, highly intellectualised, and sometimes didactic in their aim. Joan Berenguer de Masdovelles (14...-1467?), on the other hand, was a poet of rare and vivacious charm, although his verses reflect the political preoccupations of his day. Instinct with the spirit of his age, they form a larger body of poetry than has survived from any of his contemporaries. He was the most prominent member of a whole family of minor poets of his name, and was in his work a follower of Jordi de Sant Jordi. Hug Bernat de Rocaberti is more important; Andreu Febrer and he were the two Catalans most influenced by Dante, and he was heir to all that was Italian in his century. Although his technique was refinedly literary, his *La comèdia de la glòria d'amor* contains some truly lyrical passages. He, too, was a soldier, and a typical example of the courtly warriors of the Renaissance, well-read, refined, agreeable, and a man of good taste with a taste for good living.

Febrer's friend, Pere Torroella, brought up abroad, marked the beginnings of an annihilatory transition by writing both in Catalan and in Castilian. This bilingualism appears to have been associated with the general southwards shift of Catalan poetry and literature corresponding to the shifting of emphasis away from Provence, towards Italian culture. Although the Renaissance had begun at Barcelona, with Bernat Metge, it flowered more fully in Valencia; since Valencia was less Catalan, this flowering could suffer a swifter although less spectacular transition from splendour to decay under the impact of Castile. The second half of the Fifteenth Century witnessed that transition. It was a gradual process; in the case of Romeu Llull, who died at Barcelona in 1484, the Catalan portion of his work remained the vital one — writing in Castilian and Italian was merely a pastime. A man of parts —he was the Governor of Barcelona when he died, and one of the most influential men of his day— Romeu Llull was the last poet of that city before the decadence set in. His poems have survived in a manuscript called the *Jardinet d'orats* (Orchard of Fools), which also incorporates the work of Joan Roiç de Corella (142.—1500). The latter was the third great Valencian lyricist of the period, and it is interesting to observe that even after Romeu Llull had died at Barcelona, Valencia could produce a major poet, and that there was indeed still time for a whole school to grow up around him before the decadence overwhelmed Valencia too. Many of its works are to be found in that same manuscript, and a number of anonymous poems amongst them assist in the definition of this final phase by showing that the debt to the troubadours was still a fundamental one even after the full flowering of the Valencian Renaissance.

Joan Roiç de Corella was the poetic successor of Ausiàs March and Jordi de Sant Jordi, but as a prose-writer he stands in the direct line of two great humanists, Bernat Metge and Antoni Canals, the Valencian (d. 1419). The final phase before decay was thus dominated by a humanist, as it had been begun by one a hundred years or so before. He died, as far as we know, during the first year of the Sixteenth Century. Aragon, which had been the most powerful maritime state in the Mediterranean, warden of the Pyrenees and feared in the heart of the Peninsula, had ceased to be an independent kingdom. The Aragonese prince who had married the heiress to Castile now ruled his territories from the latter kingdom, in a way which responded to other needs than those of his inheritance. Coming at this time, the works of Roiç de Corella were the last flickering of a dying torch, not a flame to lead the way to greater glory, despite their brilliance and their clarity.

A great and a subtle poet, brutal at times yet verging upon manneristic artifice at others, he owed a greater debt to the Renaissance than any of his predecessors or contemporaries. He possessed a very personal mode of feeling, marked by that spontaneous irony which has come to be associated with Valencian poetry of this and later, modern, phases. His works move in an atmosphere of solemn artistry and almost ritual decoration, with occasional flashes of bright light. Although his most important works are perhaps his religious lyrics, he was also inspired by love for a lady called Caldesa. Scholar, courtier and theologian, the major characteristics of his life can all be argued from the evidence of his surviving works, although his personality is blurred in history by the confusion amongst a number of men of his name who lived at that time. The early *Tragèdia de Caldesa*, a work in prose and verse, already displayed the vigour of his artistry and of his knowledge of formal rhetoric; in it he analysed the alternate adoration and repulsion which he felt for a woman in whom baseness and refinement seemed to blend. Although described with a certain affectation and an undue emphasis upon the ingenuities of wit, Caldesa almost attains the stature of a myth — but a myth very close to reality, never a symbol or a mere abstraction. All Roiç de Corella's love poetry has an air of coming from a mundane cleric who adopts something of the preacher's tone when he mentions death; Valencia was very close to the Rome of the half-century before the Sack in 1525 just then. Ecclesiasticism appears in a purer form in his religious poetry, where he seemed to seek a liturgical embodiment for his aesthetic attitude towards existence. Most of it relates to Passiontide, and lays a highly coloured, vibrantly descriptive emphasis upon visualisation of the scene. In one great prayer to Our Lady, for instance, he requires that she be viewed as in a Pietà, with her dead Son's head in her lap; Joan Roiç de Corella painted such pictures as though he saw them in a richly ornate church, depicted boldly in stained glass transfigured by the rising sun, or wrought into an ornate and gilded reredos which has been struck into relief against the darkness by a single shaft of blinding, golden light. His imagery is full of the ornaments of ritual, incense and vestments, myrrh and perfumes, but his lines remain sincere in spite of being so eruditely wrought. Roiç de Corella's apt use of polished rhetoric places him amongst the craftsmen of the Renaissance.

His collaboration with other Valencians of his day leads one to a consideration of their independent works. Some of these already displayed a marked leaning towards Castilian. Bernat de Fenollar (1435?-1526?), Jaume Gaçull, Joan Escrivà, and Francesc de Castellví are four of the most prominent of these, and Fenollar and Castellví collaborated with yet another poet, Narcís de Vinyoles, in a curious work entitled the *Escacs d'amor*. Its very deft virtuosity and openly plebeian taste were the marks of this school. The lengthy anonymous *Col·loqui de dames*, for instance, contains one of the most daring dialogues in any literature. A certain spritely and malicious joy led these Valencian poets to perform intricate verbal dances in their abundant satires. The sunlight and the vivid colours of their landscape have something of this same frank, shameless vivacity, but it is a quality which unfortunately limits the appeal of a great deal of their work. One can still read certain lively pieces by Jaume Gaçull with pleasure, nonetheless, or the religious works and *cobles* upon the Passion by Escrivà. These all died during the first quarter of the Sixteenth Century, and though Valencia was still to produce important writers they were to write in the alien Castilian tongue.

The poets of the Decadence

The first bilingual poet of note had died a little earlier in Barcelona. Pere Torroella (1430?-1501?) was among the earliest Catalan nobles to be brought up in Castile and to live there. This Castilian environment was the decisive factor in his life; the transfer of the Court to Castile was to have a similar effect upon Catalan culture in general. He was an alert and cultured man, so well-schooled in the traditional techniques of poetry that he could write a poem in which several speakers expressed themselves in their own tongue and after their own manner, in Provençal, French, Castilian, Galician, and Catalan. He was also deeply influenced by Italy, as was natural for a man of his age, and he wrote one poem in sonnet form. His most obvious debt is to Ausiàs March; mainly derivative though his art may be, his own feelings sometimes glitter through his borrowings in his Catalan verses. These include a number of good lyrics, whereas his famous lines in Castilian against womankind display no more than a considerable virtuosity.

As the Sixteenth Century opened out, Catalan literature almost ceased to exist. A general weakening of spirit had been leading towards decadence, and literature now merely held the mirror up to nature. No further prose was written, except in the historical field. Valencian became an increasingly castilianised dialect, whilst Majorcan and *Rosellonès* drew apart from the mother tongue. Occasional Catalan poems continued to be written in Catalonia itself, but only five poets appeared in the course of three centuries; none was of great merit, and two, moreover, wrote only in Castilian. The first of these was Joan Boscà i Almogàver (1500-1544), known as Boscán in Castile, who was a contemporary of Pere Torroella; the second, Manuel de Cabanyes (1808-1833), lived some three centuries later and was a contemporary of Aribau and Rubió i Ors, and witnessed the beginnings of the *Renaixença.* The other three have achieved significance more for their isolation than for any virtues of their work; Pere Serafí and Joan Pujol (d. 1626) were chiefly influenced by Ausiàs March, whereas Francesc Vicenç Garcia (1582-1623) followed the Castilian school of Góngora.

Pere Serafí, who was still alive about 1563, copied Boscà by using the Italian metres which he had introduced into Castile. His works are chiefly intellectual curiosities. His own life was peaceful and undisturbed and very limited in scope, and when he tried to write on themes which had moved Ausiàs March and in the latter's style, he was merely performing a literary exercise which held no feeling whatsoever. He also wrote popular songs, modelled upon the works of the troubadours, whose facility gained him considerable fame in his own day. They have a certain grace and charm, but their lyrical value is reduced by the artificiality and affectation of his style. Joan Pujol was more sincere, though less capable. He was another follower of Ausiàs March, whom he made the protagonist of the *Visió de somni*, using traditional metres in a courageous attempt to write an epic on the battle of Lepanto — largely won by the Catalan mariners who took part in it.

Francesc Vicenç Garcia lived at the beginning of the Seventeenth Century, wrote copiously, and died young. He had fully assimilated the influences of Castile, and only the mere mechanics of his Catalan medium keep his work apart from Castilian literature. The Catalan he used was empty and spiritless, purely a form of speech. This may have been the reason why his superficial wit was so well thought of at the Court — his poetry would seem familiar there, or indeed anywhere in the Peninsula except in Catalonia. His conceits and affectations were those of the Castilian schools, and this subservience to their conventions marked the ultimate degradation of Catalan literature. Skilful versifier though he was — amongst the most skilful in Catalan—, Garcia failed completely in his attempt to adapt one language to another and to say in Catalan (but in Castilian metres) what other poets were then saying in the Castilian tongue. Had he followed the traditional simplicity of the language in which he chose to write he might have made a noble contribution to Catalan literature. His courtly pretensions, and the superficiality of his brilliance, led him to perpetrate a series of ridiculous and arid mannerisms which were essentially provincial in the intellectual context of the day. Francesc Fontanella, who followed Garcia, had even less of Catalan about him; he was no more than a Castilian poet writing in a Catalan dialect. With his appearance, Catalan can be said to have vanished as a valid literary medium.

III: THE RENAIXENÇA AND THE TWENTIETH CENTURY

The Cançoner

ALTHOUGH Catalan disappeared from literature for three centuries, it continued to be used by anonymous poets. They wrote in ballad-form, producing the *Cançoner*, but such ballads as survive are hard to date, and it is almost as hard to determine what part learned contributions played in their development. The realistic attitude of these anonymous poets attained an equilibrium between Castilian influence and the Catalan traditions such as the courtly poetasters never reached. The people continued to create a very vital form of poetry in spite of the lack of literary craftsmen. The corpus of ballads steadily increased, and was preserved by oral tradition until its presence was noted by the scholars of the *Renaixença*, who were swift to collect and record what had survived. Apart from its undeniable lyrical importance, the persistence of this body of popular poetry constituted one of the major justifications of the *Renaixença*; it attested both to the vigour of the instinctive urge for such autonomous survival and to the great achievements of which that urge was capable even under the most adverse circumstances. Any survey of Catalan lyric poetry must therefore pause to analyse and to evaluate these ballads.

Many are very lyrical, having a nobility and grandeur which is all their own. The most popular have been preserved with innumerable variants, and their origins lie many stages back from the versions which survive, frequently belonging to the common fund of European folklore; one in a hundred proves to be a perfect poem. Even in this genre the metres became castilianised, yet the vigour of the national personality persisted in spite of this and of Castilian accretions to the lexicon. Passed on and bettered by word of mouth throughout the centuries of decadence, these songs became part of the daily life of cities, villages, and fields, and almost one with the cycle of the seasons. They reflect the feelings of the people, and partially make up for the lack of epic poetry by glorifying the courage of minor local heroes — bandits, rebels, or partisans. They rarely deal with the old days of chivalry under the Counts and the Kings, or with major victories, defeats, or sieges, such as history records. The three chief characteristics of these poems are their dramatic intensity, an expressive but extremely brutal vocabulary, and themes in which love and death are tragically blended. They have a direct and realistic vividness which leaves no room for mystery; such marvels and fancies as they hold are ingenuous and naive. They were songs which sprang from the collective genius of a restrained but highly sensitive people, alive to every facet of the human tragedy in which they were involved.

The beginnings of the Renaixença

The last poet of the decadence was the greatest Catalonia gave to Castile; Manuel de Cabanyes died in 1833, three centuries after Roiç de Corella, and everything about his work was Catalan except the language in which he wrote. His work foreshadowed the most fruitful sources of the early *Renaixença*, drawing upon the Latin classics and contemporary Italian poets. Cabanyes sought to express the ideals of his land and its thirst for a return of glory, and wrote austere and robust verse untrammelled by artificialities or mannerisms. His high purpose represented a return to the direct line of Catalan tradition. It was due to this that his poetry seemed out of place in the Castilian tongue and in Castile, and therefore gained him no fame nor approbation outside Catalonia. The year Cabanyes died, Bonaventura Carles Aribau (1798-1862) published his ode *La Pàtria*, which would still have been the best poem written in Catalan since the Fifteenth Century even if it had been devoid of any wider meaning. Its importance for us is even greater because it became the point of departure for the *Renaixença.* When the humanistic zeal of Catalonia was revived by the impact of Romanticism, it sought expression in Catalan once more; even if Aribau's nostalgia is romantic, the stress he laid upon the significance of the mother tongue was classical in its appeal. *La Pàtria*, never meant to be more than a circumstantial ode, became the living revelation of the strength and potency of Catalan as a literary language. Its greatness lay in the brilliance with which Aribau phrased his appeal in a Catalan which had no direct antecedents. It appeared in a newspaper, fittingly so because it brought the first news of Catalan revival.

Once under way, the *Renaixença* was sponsored by the people, by the erudite, and by philologists alike. It drew on the literary past, the continuous religious tradition of the *goigs*, sermons and catechisms in the vernacular, and on more recent Catalan translations of the Bible. There had been previous attempts to use the language again, failures such as the *Càntics catalans* (published at Perpignan in 1826), *Lo Temple de la Glòria* by Ignasi Puigblanch, which was probably written even earlier, or the *dècimes* in the direct tradition of Garcia and Fontanella written by Josep Robreño, but Aribau's *La Pàtria* was the decisive contribution. It is an attractive poem in its own right, its words well chosen and its phrases turned with a pleasant grace which reverted to an archaic alexandrine harmony of form. It had an elegiac note of mourning for the past, and it contained an uncompromising affirmation of loyalty to his mother tongue. This duality of subject, in which its humanistic and romantic sources intertwined, was the secret of its immense success as a source of inspiration for the *Renaixença;* this success immortalised it in a way which not even its intrinsic merits could have done.

A whole literary movement soon came into being. Joan Cortada (1805-1868) and Miquel Anton Martí (d. 1864) were led by their desire for erudite divulgation to prepare a dictionary and to translate Grossi, Tasso and Costi. They were also creative poets, and published *La noia fugitiva* and *Llàgrimes de la viudesa.* The second of these exerted a strong influence upon Martí's contemporaries, including Rubió i Ors (1818-1899), the first significant figure of the *Renaixença.* Rubió was conscious of the importance of what he was doing, and proclaimed the literary independence of Catalan in a manifesto which appeared as the prologue to his first book of poems. A poetic school soon grew up around him; his example had played a far more impressive part than the somewhat ingenuous poems of *Lo gaiter del Llobregat* (1841) might lead one to expect, because they united the aspirations of the intellectuals with those of popular feeling. When these poems first appeared as a regular feature of a Barcelona newspaper, they caused a great sensation, provoking repercussions in Valencia and in Mallorca. Each district soon discovered its own bard, who sang of its river to the tune of whatever his chosen instrument might be, in imitation of Rubió's piper and his Llobregat. Although he had drawn upon the troubadours for his romantic inspiration, he had come under a far more direct influence from Pere Serafí and from Garcia, and his language and metres remained very Castilian. The *Renaixença* might have been retarded had it not been for him, but certain aspects of the decadence would certainly have frustrated its vitality had it continued to follow his line, instead of that which Aribau had indicated in *La Pàtria*. Rubió i Ors also wrote an epic poem on the adventures of the Catalans in Greece. This gained him a prize from a learned society, establishing a precedent for such awards. In 1859, he organised the restoration of the Jocs Florals, which were first presided over by a scholar who was to prove an extremely important figure in the *Renaixença*: Manuel Milà i Fontanals (1818-1884). Poets from Valencia and Mallorca also entered the lists at Barcelona, and poets from Provence (headed by Frederic Mistral) later paid homage to the institution. The wheel had turned full circle, but save for very rare exceptions, the poetry of the Jocs Florals gave the clearest proof that such a return to the earliest source of inspiration was an error.

That attitude fortunately changed to something more alive, and closer to the earth, after the first two anthologies *Els trobadors nous* and *Els trobadors moderns* appeared; their very titles had mirrored the eruditely picturesque approach of the forty-four poets whose works they contained. The Valencian Tomàs Villaroya (1812-1856) had begun to follow Aribau. His follower Teodor Llorente (1832-1911) surpassed him in this vein, whilst a great Majorcan, Marià Aguiló (1825-1897), also joined the *Renaixença* at about this time. Aguiló, however, was a scholar above all. The first true poet of the movement was Josep Lluís Pons i Gallarza (1823-1894), who came from Barcelona, but whilst Manuel Milà i Fontanals fostered it in Barcelona itself — acting as its doyen and writing erudite poetry which was highly classical yet popular in feeling—Pons i Gallarza lived and wrote in Mallorca. Such men continued the *Renaixença* from the point to which it had been brought by Rubió i Ors, roughly grouped around the Jocs Florals, but they returned to the inspiration of Aribau and Cabanyes. These had both credited poetry with a transcendent function, and had seen the poet as a man destined to interpret the inner meaning of things. Those who best fulfilled this ideal were the poets of the Majorcan School, and it was they who —together with that greater figure, Verdaguer— revivified Catalan poetry by getting right away from all the trends which had led to its decadence. Good poets continued to pass through the Jocs Florals, bringing that institution into as high a repute as it had ever enjoyed in all its history, but as a school, the Jocs Florals attained no plane of universal value. During the past ninety years it has taken on more and more of the status of a dignified society, and latterly its meetings have had to be held in different foreign capitals as a result of the Spanish Civil War.

The expansion of the Renaixença

The past hundred years have witnessed one of the most interesting poetic revivals of European history. There has been no lack of Catalan lyric poets since Pons i Gallarza, Llorente and Verdaguer. Pons i Gallarza was responsible for the first important work, *L'olivera mallorquina*, which perpetuated the depth, clarity, and easy sonorous flow of the alexandrines used by Aribau. The appearance of such balanced and profound poetry after three and a half centuries of literary decadence is very striking, and one is tempted to attribute it to the resurgence of a whole people's spirit finding its embodiment through one man's mind. Pons i Gallarza, like all the Majorcan poets who succeeded him, was a classicist in the movement of his verse and the human way in which he saw the island landscape. He rediscovered those universal values which Catalan poetry needed, by reflecting on an instinctive love of nature and mankind. The high level he reached was not unworthy of his models: Horace and Virgil.

In Valencia, Teodor Llorente replaced the over-sentimental affectations of Villaroya with delicately rendered songs which hold the exultant light of that warmer and more southerly land. Their graceful images enter by the eyes, like the landscape he depicted. Unduly facile versification weakens his poetry, just as it had tended to mar that of the Sixteenth Century Valencian School. The most noteworthy of his contemporaries and successors have been Constantí Llombart (1848-1893), Vicenç Boix (1812-1880) and —best of the three—, Vicenç Wenceslau Querol (1836-1889). This school has continued to develop up to the present day, and is now headed by Xavier Casp (b. 1915).

The *Renaixença* had spread to all the Catalan-speaking lands when Verdaguer (1845-1902) began to write the most important epic poem of modern times, some thirty years after the publication of *La Pàtria.* The Jocs Florals sponsored much epic poetry. From the very beginning, there had been many long narrative poems, on subjects more or less heroic, starting with *Lo Temple de la Glòria* and *Joan Garí, ermità de Montserrat*—which extends to sixteen thousand lines. Rubió had written his *Roudor*, Damàs Calvet (1838-1891) his *Mallorca cristiana*, and there had been works of the same nature by Pelai Briz, Picó i Campamar, Bofarull, Balaguer, Aguiló, Milà, and Angel Guimerà— all of which were well known in their own day. It was by no means strange that Verdaguer should also write an epic, having had so many predecessors in the genre, but none possessed his dominion over the language in which he wrote. Even with the vigour of his Catalan inspiration it required great poetic genius to bridge the gap between his predecessors and his own high standards. Verdaguer's isolation amongst his own contemporaries is as great as that of Ausiàs March had been; his genius rose from the confusion of schools and movements with *L'Atlàntida*, in 1877.

Born in 1845, he had chosen the priesthood as the result of a natural vocation, with no prior mental conflict. The fundamental crisis of his poetic life came after his ordination as a country cleric in 1870. His ecclesiastical training had attempted to tranquillise the violence of his poetic energy and to canalise it into a given stream, but whilst it taught him about God and gave him the rudiments of the humanities—which blended in with his own Catalan inheritance—it wrecked his health. From being a sturdy lad he became an ailing man with a precarious hold on life, and the sharp contrast between sickness and health resulted in a mental crisis in which he seemed to find himself faced with an agonising choice between his priesthood and his poetry. When he put poetry before his priesthood, as his life's primary vocation, he clutched at its blinding flame till he was burnt to a mere cinder of a man. Subjectively, his life from then onwards was a long struggle illuminated by the clear, hard light of poetry. Priesthood and environment denied him the use of his youthful vigour. His pride in physical strength became a pride in intellectual capacity which found its outlet in poetry. His inner life was in addition complicated by profound spiritual misgivings. Verdaguer was sure that he knew God directly, but the conviction of his worthlessness, when measured against an infinite divinity, was a very humbling one. At times he tried to get closer to God than poetry could take him, and he found that he was far too near to the earth to be a mystic. As he grew older he found death more terrifying; although he believed in a future life he shrank away from it. When his own death drew near, he renounced his attempt to rise to God unaided, clutching at human forgiveness in the hope that mankind itself held something of divinity. There is a constant and direct connection between his life and poems; through the poems one can find the man, with all his terrors and his anguish and his supernatural rejoicing.

His works were richer and more varied than those of any other poet since Ramon Llull. He revived forgotten words, coined many himself, and created modern literary Catalan out of hardly anything at all. He treated the themes of popular poetry, using a more apt and subtle imagery than that of his predecessors. In his religious verse, which was the most important contribution to that genre for over five centuries, he concentrated the previously diffused Franciscan atmosphere to create a highly personal style of contemplation. His most original poems were those which came from his own tragedy, transfused with passion, surging with leashed strength, and some were truly magnificent creations. He gave free rein to his taste for grandeur and fantastic imagery in the *Atlàntida*.

Verdaguer was born on an age-old plain, which was torrid and intractable in summer, ashen and fey in misty wintry weather, enclosed by a great bend of a slow, meandering river whose waters sometimes rose to flood the lower ground, and the Pyrenees towered on the horizon. *L'Atlàntida* grew from childhood contemplation of that landscape and the folk-tales he had loved to hear, and from his reading during long Atlantic voyages undertaken on the orders of his doctors. This had included Plato and the classical epics. His first major work is a strange medley, passages of very forceful poetry come between lines of inappropriate language or false rhetoric, and the plot is of scant importance. The real protagonist is abstract strength; Hercules becomes a Catalan hero, incarnating the warrior-spirit of the race. Verdaguer embodied the passions of the primitive inhabitants with a brutal energy, hankering after the days when the whole world was new and still to conquer.

Just as Hercules was treated as a Catalan, so were the saints, angels and the Holy Family in his other works. He consistently identified himself with the Catalan people in his religious verse. Verdaguer wrote much poetry in the traditional Franciscan line of inspiration, following and guiding the religious feelings of the humble folk whom he admired. *Jesús Infant*, for instance, is one of the most moving and most "popular" books in Catalan literature. Some of the shorter poems are amazingly graceful, built up around very simple images of country life and the childhood of Christ, transfigured till there is nothing left save poetry. He was also indebted to Ramon Llull and to the Song of Songs.

In his maturity Verdaguer wrote another major poem, which aimed as high as *L'Atlàntida* but in a different way. In *Canigó* he used a wholly Christian medium for patriotism. It represented a fresh phase in his cult of the Pyrenees, singing of a Catalonia in whose great hills the faith of the humble had found a refuge as calm and quiet as Bethlehem. *Canigó* is undoubtedly his most successful poem because of the depth of its psychological insight, the perfection of its varied forms and the dramatic energy which animates it as a whole. The epic, the legendary, and the human, blend in a complex pattern endowed with multiple facets, relevances and validities. Love, one of its essential themes, is handled with great dramatic skill despite the lack of concrete images; it is present as tangibly when unexpressed as when explicit. Woman was a negative element in both his life and his work, felt rather through absence than through specific formulations. The hundreds of masterly stanzas of which *Canigó* consists are clear proof of Verdaguer's fondness for the panoramic view in landscape as in history.

Verdaguer turned to sadder poems which embodied the conflict between pride and trammelling circumstance —the essence of his tragedy— towards the evening of his days. They would not have gained him immortality; they mirror a spiritual surrender. That experiential vision of the world for which he became renowned, so personal and yet so universal in its alchemy, came from his earlier works.

The full flowering of the Renaixença

Costa i Llobera (1854-1922) and Joan Alcover (1854-1926) were Verdaguer's contemporaries. These two Majorcans had continued in the classicising vein, influenced not merely by antiquity but also by the French Parnasse, by the Italians and —above all— by the clear light of their own island. Like Verdaguer, Costa i Llobera was in holy orders; his classical sense of harmony with nature fused into an intensely Christian longing for transfiguration of the soul. His was a mystique which strove for perfection within the contingent universe because it was too humble to ascend to God. His works have the vigour apparent in those of all the major poets of the *Renaixença*, right through to Maragall, and he, too, displays that tendency to formulate the yearnings of his own people in prophetic visions or elegiac evocations of the past. In style and form, Costa i Llobera was a classicist from the first; his words were chosen with a view to their fullness of meaning and isolated to fulfil it. He was striving for a harmony through which he might realise himself; his polished, balanced lines, often modelled upon classical metres, are perfect examples of controlled intensity. Yet this harmonious aspect was never allowed to overlay the gravity of what he had to say; the formulae which he employed refined an innate romanticism into something higher and nobler and more universal. His passionate nature was canalised in a similar way by rigid subordination of his internal world to the requirements of his priesthood. Troubled by his love of formal beauty, he was worried when he wrote his *Horacianes* lest his love for Horace might give his poetry an unduly pagan character, but later works succeeded in blending his Christian and his pagan piety. Costa i Llobera's metrical contributions to the new Catalan poetic medium link his endeavours to those of Verdaguer. Joan Alcover wrote comparatively little. The death of his son was the fundamental experience which gave rise to a series of perfect elegies whose inevitability holds no doubts or vacillation, nor vagueness of meaning or form. Deep acquaintanceship with suffering and contemplation of a world devoid of love has muted their music without stifling it.

Miquel dels Sants Oliver (1864-1919) contributed to the decisive influence which the works of Costa and Alcover and the Majorcan school exerted upon the growth of Catalan poetry by the refinement of his lyricism. So did Maria-Antònia Salvà (b. 1869) by her presentation of the Majorcan countryside, in poems as noble and intense in form as in their matter, and by the graceful humility and charm of her songs. Gabriel Alomar (b. 1873) and, subsequently, Miquel Ferrà (1885-1947) were even greater as guides to others than as poets in their own right. These Majorcans have been as important in recent years as the Valencians in the Renaissance, and rich though the Fifteenth Century was, the scene was even richer at the close of the Nineteenth century, when Verdaguer was still alive and Maragall was at the height of his powers.

Angel Guimerà (1845-1924) was born in the same year as Verdaguer, and long dominated the circle of the Jocs Florals with narrative poems in a romantically passionate and —occasionally— melancholy vein. He was a dramatic rather than a lyric poet and his tragedies are his most important works. Largely autobiographical, his lyrical verse has little to recommend it other than the nobility of the sentiments expressed. Minor poets helped him to lead the Jocs Florals away from their dependence upon the rhetorical fashions of Castile by effective, if sporadic, borrowings from Leopardi, Heine and Musset. No one tried to imitate or follow Verdaguer; he had been too outstanding in his own field. Even if he inspired no followers, his example stimulated a major poet of quite a different kind: Joan Maragall (1860-1911), who was better suited than he to lead the mainland school to the heights attained by the Majorcan poets.

Although Barcelona had become the literary capital to which all writers looked for guidance, Maragall was the first important poet of the Renaixença to be born there. He was city-bred, feeble in body, nervously feverish in mind, and died just as he seemed to be nearing the fullest illumination of his world. He was inevitably associated with a reaction against Verdaguer, because he led Catalan poetry away from the countryside by submitting it to its first modern intellectualisation. The first noteworthy distinction between them lay in Maragall's insistence on a poet's need to rationalise experience in terms of an aesthetic system. His own was complicated and self-contradictory; although he attacked all cults of form he was so deeply moved, through Goethe, by the Greeks, that his inspiration was tinged from the start with a classicism which necessarily affected the pattern of his verse as well. In his early days he introduced the works of many of the great German Romantics into Catalonia; later he turned to Homer, Hesiod and Pindar, and then to men like Schlegel and Amiel, who are in strange contrast with his early mood. Maragall was to maintain this strange capacity for harbouring contradictions throughout his life — in life itself as well as in aesthetics. Yet he was never insincere, vacillatory though he was in all his attitudes.

The intensification of his natural sensitivity led him into conflict with society, but there was never any direct clash such as has often given rise to the greatest work of other poets. He was married to an Englishwoman with some Andalusian blood, Clara Noble, and her care maintained the feminine ascendancy to which he had become accustomed as a child; wife, family, surroundings, and his journalistic work, combined to make him fit quite happily into the society against which he protested. The lack of forcefulness in his character, which his sheltered upbringing had exaggerated, allowed a simple transposition of his rebellion onto a purely intellectual level. He read Nietzsche, wrote violent articles, and poems on the dramatic qualities of Barcelona, but in his active life as a citizen he exercised a definite and wholesome influence on his contemporaries.

His faith in his lyrical purpose, was unopposed, and it made no great demands on him except for some attention and a few hours' work each day. Believing devoutly in his own poetry, Maragall feared that attention to form might kill its soul and wisdom stifle his dreams. He was conscious of an innate magic which he wished to keep unsullied by artistry, and his greatness as a lyric poet sprang from this belief in his own genius. He rejected high-flown rhetoric and destroyed established formulae by sheer neglect, demanding that the poet should wager his life on every line he wrote. That was how he composed his own poems; some were successful, others were not, but those which were, prove him as great a lyric poet as any which Catalonia has produced up to the present day. His use of language is inferior to that of Verdaguer; his learned vocabulary has a townsman's emphasis upon ideas, lacking the richness of his predecessor's country idiom. Maragall discovered Catalonia in another way, finding the subtler places within a smaller radius: the Empordà, the plain of Olot, and the valleys of the Pyrenean foothills. This was the Catalonia with which later poets have dealt and which became the centre of a political, as well as a poetic, vision. Lleida, the Ebro and Valencia were half-forgotten.

As a love poet, Maragall was simple and so sincere that he went far beyond Romanticism, appealing to the reader in an intimate, direct and unselfconscious manner which he was the first Catalan poet to achieve. The contrast which he perceived between the eternity of nature and the transience of human life killed the joy of contemplating the love which he sought to perpetuate, and the landscape which he sought to understand. By concentrating upon the resurrection of the flesh, he reduced death to a mere interruption of the things he loved, and that dogma became the third great theme of his work. He was struck by the same preoccupation with sin, redemption and salvation in the folklore of his people. As he grew older, an increasing interaction between his Christian conscience and his humanistic wisdom intensified this concern for the after-life in such masterly pieces as *La fi d'En Serrallonga* and *El comte Arnau*. Homer and Goethe were the major influences behind his tragic poem *Nausica*, a spiritual handling of the fable which found redemption through poetry. The shorter *Cant espiritual* is one of the most complete statements of himself which any poet has attempted; it was written towards the close of his life, when he had been led to focus his attention on his Mediterranean heritage by the Germanic admiration for this sea. This interest had given him an even greater love for life itself and had let him find a joy in the formal beauties of his verse, which thus reached classicism at the last. It inspired a fervent longing to trascend his melancholy by a reconciliation of this Christian faith with the fervour of his sensual perception. Apostrophizing God, he reached what seemed to him a clear and logical solution by the last line of the poem: God was all around him, and to meet Him face to face in death would be to regain an even nobler life within His world for all eternity. As in the case of Ausiàs March, Joan Maragall owes much of his fame to a final *Cant espiritual.*

By the time of his death, his influence was assured. No poet adopted his aesthetic theories in their original form, but later writers took them to their logical conclusion, which was more stable and more useful. They saw, for instance, that his violent reaction against the insincerities of rhetoric could only perform a useful function if it led to a regard for formal dignity, not just to contempt for structure in itself. Those who failed to see this, and tried to follow him too closely, were unsuccessful. Catalan poetry has not been troubled by formal problems since the true conclusion was established; this fact is enough to prove that it is now mature. Maragall came at the most dangerous time, and only survived it by the miracle of his lyrical genius, but his inchoate work led straight to the classicism which still obtains today. Another feature became the common property of almost all the moderns: that curious lack of personal conflict. Poets have tended to ignore their own subjective problems in order to reflect the collective feelings of the Catalans, analysing the conflicts which have been their country's destiny in preference to those of their own fate. The majority of poets since his day have all been intellectual townsmen like himself, with leanings towards scholarship, and each in turn has found his own means of evading a personal clash with society. One ardent disciple of Maragall's, Salvat-Papasseit, was an exception to this rule, but he died comparatively young. Maragall's own early death did not leave Catalonia devoid of poets, for Costa i Llobera, Alcover, and the other Majorcans were then still in their prime.

The writings of Maragall's immediate followers were rich and varied, complex in their elements and aims. One can do no more than list the major figures, such as Magí Morera i Galicia (1853-1927), the Trans-Pyrenean Catalan Josep-Sebastià Pons (b. 1886) —who brought the Roussillon back into literary Catalonia— and Salvador Albert (b. 1868). The last was one of the few truly successful disciples of Maragall, thanks to a greater emphasis upon the personal element in his deftly gentle lyrics. Another Josep Lleonart (1880-1951), was prompted by the influence of Maragall to become the most Germanic of the Catalans. He expresses a decadent and precious romanticism in poems which seem written with half-concealed regret, achieving a high degree of craftsmanship without his verse becoming stiff. Ventura Gassol (b. 1894) wrote rhetorical verse admirably suited to the ingenuous but impassioned patriotism of the twenties. The Majorcan School gave us one of its most restrained and contemplative poets in Miquel Ferrà (1885-1947). Llorenç Riber (b. 1882), in contrast, has devised an excessively erudite rhetoric of his own. But the simple and unpretentious clarity of poets like Alexandre Plana (1889-1940) and Joan Maria Guasch (b. 1878) is the normal mood for a poetry by now assured of its own standing and importance.

The Early Twentieth Century

Josep Carner (b. 1884) was the undisputed leader of the generation which succeeded Maragall. Carner took the language which Verdaguer had enriched, and which Maragall poeticised, to mould it into style. Maragall had admired Homer, but Carner followed the Greek poets of the Alexandrine School, reviving the cult of artifice with masterly facility and concentrating more and more on perfection of form in his copious writings. His long poem *Nabí* is perhaps his best effort to record the substance of poetry, concentrating on the graveness of his mood. On such ocasions personal sorrow has been the catalyst which true poetry requires. "Guerau de Licst" (Jaume Bofill i Mates, 1878-1933), has gained a universal appeal through the word-magic of his humanised vision of nature; his was a creative genius. He was the best poet of the Catalan countryside after Verdaguer; love, death, and the future life are the other themes on which his lasting poetry was written. Satires were a by-product of his human interests, but his love survived all disillusions unimpaired. Josep Maria López-Picó (b. 1880) is a writer whose intellectual brilliance has had a considerable influence in certain spheres, but he can only be called a true poet in those few moments when the clearness of his vision has produced a poem which gives a glimpse into the nature of things. His rationalised Franciscan attitude and the world he sees and describes are often interesting, but most of his poems lack real appeal because of the aridity to which his intellectual refinement tends. This emphasis upon the tangible essentials of poetic matter had, however, an extremely good effect on others when his early works appeared.

Among subsequent writers are Joaquim Folguera (1894-1919), Joan Salvat-Papasseit (1894-1924), Agustí Esclasans (b. 1895), J. V. Foix (b. 1894), Clementina Arderiu (b. 1893), Josep Maria de Sagarra (b. 1894), Marià Manent (b. 1898), and Carles Riba (b. 1893), perhaps the most noteworthy of them all. Most of these had published poems during the first decade after Maragall's death, and Catalan poetry entered upon one of its richest phases with their appearance. Their number and variety attest to Catalonia's intellectual autonomy. Joaquim Folguera was a fecund writer, but he died at twenty-five; in spite of a dangerous gift for versification, his writings contained the promise of good work. Agustí Esclasans embarked upon the project of compiling no less than a thousand *Ritmes*. As might have been expected, their rich but monotonously majestic cadence only rarely rises to real poetry. Whilst they contain splendid lines, these are drowned in the particular poem or volume or in the vastness of a life's incessant productivity. Josep Maria de Sagarra is likewise a copious writer, but his poems are very different in tone. He appears to have an unlimited capacity for expressing himself in verse, and this has proved prejudicial to his art. Drama provided an outlet for this gift, and he has been perhaps more successful as a dramatist than as a lyric poet. Even his longer poems are essentially theatrical in plot and character. His best lyrics, all written in his youth, reflect the influence of Leopardi and Maragall as refined by the formal classicism of the Majorcan poets. This synthesis enriched Catalan poetry by a number of works presenting the strength and savour of the people in a typically Catalan form. Visions of nature, new versions of traditional themes and songs, created by the intellectual elaboration of very simple material, attest to his power. Sagarra is a considerable figure in modern Catalan poetry because of the colourful aspect with which he has endowed it, and his lead in returning to popular sources.

The poems of Joan Salvat-Papasseit, few in number, are of great lyric merit. He distilled a certain magic from the mood of Maragall and formulated it in revolutionary ways which he borrowed from abroad. These technical innovations, for which he was chiefly indebted to the French, are of small importance beside the violence of his presentation. This forcefulness was responsible for the influence which he has had on later poets, for whom his tortured yet joyous life, and his early death at thirty, summed up the essence of Romanticism. His love poems move in a world of passionate purity, whilst his poems of loneliness and city life are full of a charity which led him to face the major problems of his day in a fashion which none had attempted, in the emotional field, since Verdaguer.

J. V. Foix did the same thing on the intellectual plane. His work belongs to no school and responds to nothing except his own creative impulse, which has harmonised his mind with his senses and his body. His lyrical message has become explicit since he reached intellectual maturity. Its verbal forcefulness recalls the Mediaeval poets of Provence, Italy and Catalonia. There is exultant power and restraint about the way in which he deals with man beset by passionately transcendental dreams in a Mediterranean landscape.

In recent years, the man with the most significant message is Carles Riba, a hellenist, a humanist, and a poet of exceptional lyric power. He has made the greatest advance since Maragall, and he did so in his earliest writings. Thanks to his critical faculty and knowledge of classical tradition, Riba has avoided both the dangers of Maragall's contempt for formal polish, and those of the appeal to alien aesthetic doctrines which had been made by others. Their failure had only resulted in disillusioned scepticism towards all aesthetic theory. Passionate yet reflective, Carles Riba has an inflexible creative impulse which has driven him to write in a climate of constant lyrical intensity. Neither wholly intellectual nor wholly emotive, his poetry seems to give direct access to himself. Mature from the start, its tone has hardly changed at all, although one can distinguish subtle shifts of emphasis. These mark an internal evolution which only posterity will be able to see in true perspective. Like Yeats or Valéry or Rilke, Riba is a lyric poet whose piercing vision seems amazed at the mere fact of being alive.

Subsequent Catalan poets have explored the possibilities revealed by all the modern schools abroad with a kaleidoscopic zeal. Under the guidance of the Majorcan classicists and the stimulus of Maragall, they have escaped from both the tardy and ingenuous romanticism of the early *Renaixença*, which employed a vocabulary full of borrowed words, and the disorderly magnificence of Verdaguer. Today, Carles Riba and his generation have brought Catalan poetry into line with that of Europe as a whole, just as though neither tongue nor literature had ever undergone three centuries of decadence and missed the greatest splendours of the Renaissance.

Poets like Marià Manent, Tomàs Garcés (b. 1901), Clementina Arderiu, "Pere Quart" (Joan Oliver: b. 1899) and Joan Llacuna (b. 1905) have shown in how many different ways this experience can be assimilated. Marià Manent succeeds in conveying that mysterious magic which is the substance of true poetry, in a direct and unmysterious fashion, most notably in his more recent work. Influenced by Carner and, like Carner, by the English poets, Manent has discovered an alchemy whereby all that he lives and sees can become poetry. The lyrics of Clementina Arderiu embody a serene passion, as grave in her songs as in her elegies; their sincerity is profoundly femenine. Lyrical power is also the most notable quality of Tomàs Garcés; in his case it has led to writing the kind of poem which has to be read aloud and needs to be set to music before it can convey the fullness of its meaning. The dreamlike nature of his vision has enveloped words and images in an ever subtler way. "Pere Quart" has carried on the satirical tradition which has always formed part of Catalan literature, although its medium has as often been prose as verse. His satire, however, never loses all touch with lyrical exaltation and the ardour of creative intellectual effort. Joan Llacuna has produced a single slender volume, matured for some years, and which has yet survived the dangers of a virtuosity which might have proved banal had it not been for his intense sincerity and innate charm.

Since the Spanish Civil War

Events since the Civil War, which began in 1936, are still too close for one to be able to analyse the literary panorama with detachment. The work of most living poets has continued to develop. One who has died, B. Rosselló-Pòrcel (1913-1938), was the most recent of the Majorcans, and his few surviving poems should perpetuate his name. By virtue of Carles Riba's example he was able to blend his unrest with the restrained traditions of the island school. He would be a vital figure for any study of the most recent Catalan poetry, for this if for no other reason. He is also important because his approach seems typical of the young poets who have succeeded him: it is marked by a characteristically precocious dominion over very varied formulae. His works include such dissimilar pieces as classical elegies and experiments in the manner of the French surrealists. Everything he had to say was conveyed with a vigour which completely dominated the pattern of his poems. He died young, as those whom the Gods love are always supposed to die, but his poetic life had already been a full one before the world he knew began to disintegrate around him in the year before his death. Salvador Espriu (b. 1913) and Joan Vinyoli (b. 1914) stand out amongst those of his generation as having fulfilled the promise of their earliest work in the poems which they have written since the Civil War. Poems by these and other post-war poets, such as Josep Palau Fabre (b. 1917), appear in an appendix to this anthology; sympathetic reading is the best form of criticism we can as yet accord them.

Catalans have not stopped writing poetry, Catalonia is not dead. This is an affirmation which has had to be made more than once. It is borne out by the productivity of those who were writing when the Civil War began and of the poets who have started to write in Catalan since that war ceased, in Catalonia itself, in Mallorca, Valencia, and abroad. Many are still at the university, young men who have lived more than half their lives in the difficult atmosphere of the past decade. During this time their language has again been banished from education and from public life. They have been denied the opportunity of making contacts and of forming schools — even the possibility of publication. Their very existence is thus a valid reason for faith in Catalonia's destiny.

J. T.

University of Liverpool, 1949.

(*Translated by R. D. F. Pring-Mill, Senior Demy of Magdalen College, Oxford.*)

ACKNOWLEDGMENTS

I am indebted to Senyor Jordi Sarsanedas, formerly lecturer in Catalan at the University of Glasgow, for his valuable help in the initial stages of the compilation of this Anthology.

The publishers and I gratefully acknowledge the kindness of authors, or their heirs, in giving permission to print poems. I also owe my thanks to Senyors J. M.ª de Casacuberta, Pere Bohigas, Ferran Soldevila, and to Josep Romeu, for his help in fixing the text and dates of anonymous ballads.

Three of my own poems have been included at the request of the editor.

J. T.

RAMON LLULL

1233?-1315?

A vós, Dona Verge Santa Maria

A vós, Dona Verge Santa Maria,
dó mon voler qui es vol enamorar
de vós tan fort, que sens vós no volria
en nulla re desirar ni amar;
car tot voler ha melloria
sobre tot altre qui no sia
volent en vós, qui és maire d'amor,
qui vós no vol no ha d'on s'enamor.

Pus mon voler vol vostra senyoria,
lo meu membrar e el saber vos vull dar;
car sens voler, Dona, jo què els faria?
E vós, Dona, si us plai, façats membrar,
entendre, amar, a clerecia,
per ço que vagen en Suria
los infeels convertir, preïcar,
e els crestians facen pacificar.

Mant home se vana que morria
pel vostre Fill, si lloc venia;
mas paucs són cells qui el vagen preïcar
als infeels, car mort los fai dubtar.

Cant de Ramon

Són creat e ésser m'és dat
a servir Déu que fos honrat,
e són caüt en mant pecat

e en ira de Déu fui pausat.
Jesús me venc crucificat,
volc que Déus fos per mi amat.
Matí ané querre perdó
a Déu, e pris confessió
ab dolor e contrició.
De caritat, oració,
esperança, devoció,
Déus me fé conservació.

Lo monestir de Miramar
fiu a frares Menors donar
per sarraïns a preïcar.
Enfre la vinya e el fenollar
amor me pres, fé'm Déus amar,
enfre sospirs e plors estar.

Déus Paire, Fill, Déus espirat
de qui és Santa Trinitat
tracté com fossen demonstrat.
Déus Fill, del cel és devallat,
de una Verge està nat,
Déu e home, Crist apellat.

Lo món era en damnació;
morí per dar salvació
Jesús, per qui el món creat fo.
Jesús pujà al cel sobre el tro,
venrà a jutjar li mal e el bo:
no valran plors querre perdó.

Novell saber hai atrobat,
pot-n'hom conèixer veritat
e destruir la falsetat:
sarraïns seran batejat,
tartres, jueus e mant orat,
per lo saber que Déus m'ha dat.

RAMON LLULL

Pres hai la crots, tramet amors
a la Dona de pecadors
que d'ella m'aport gran socors.
Mon cor està casa d'amors
e mos ulls fontanes de plors.
Entre gauig estaig e dolors.

Som hom vell, paubre, menyspreat,
no hai ajuda d'home nat
e hai trop gran fait emperat.
Gran res hai del món cercat,
mant bon eximpli hai donat:
poc són conegut e amat.

Vull morir en pèlag d'amor.
Per ésser gran no n'hai paor
de mal príncep ne mal pastor.
Tots jorns consir la deshonor
que fan a Déu li gran senyor
qui meten lo món en error.

Prec Déus trameta missatgés
devots, scients e verdaders
a conèixer que Déus home és.
La Verge on Déu hom se fes
e tots los sants d'ella sotsmès
prec que en infern no sia mès.

Llaus, honor al major Senyor
al qual tramet la mia amor
que d'ell reeba resplandor.
No són digne de far honor
a Déu, tan fort són pecador,
e són de llibres trobador.

On que vage cuit gran bé far,
e a la fi res no hi puc far,
per què n'hai ira e pesar.

RAMON LLULL

Ab contrició e plorar
vull tant a Déu mercè clamar
que mos llibres vulla exalçar.

Santedat, vida, sanitat,
gauig, me do Déus e llibertat,
a guard-me de mal e pecat.
A Déu me són tot comanat:
mal esperit ne hom irat
no hagen en mi potestat.

Man Déus als cels e als elements,
plantes e totes res vivents
que no em facen mal ni turments.
Do'm Déus companyons coneixents,
devots, lleials, humils, tements,
a procurar sos honraments.

Laus et honor essentiae Dei et divinis personis et dignitatibus earum. Et recordemur Iesum Nazarenum et Mariam Virginem matrem eius.

Medicina de Pecat

De temor

Temor d'amor fina, lleial,
  contrició en vostre hostal
és medicina de dolor
  qui fa plorar li pecador
per la paor qui ser no val,
  e tots los sens gita a mal:
e car vas vós fa tant d'engan
  no em tenc per seu d'aquí avant,
e maldic lo jorn que l'ha'm pres
  car li Senyor de tot quant és
no hai tant temut com lo món

qui de null bé no ha aon.
Ah temor d'hom enamorat,
qui tem e plora son pecat!
A vós deman contrició
ab qui pusca trobar perdó
e qui em faça sovent plorar
los meus pecats, e Déus amar;
e qui vós no ha, res no val
ni fa d'amor son cor hostal.

D'esperança

Quan par l'estela en l'albor
e s'aparellon tuit li flor
que el sol montiplic llur color
d'esperança,
mi vest alegrança
d'una douçor, confiança
que hai en la Dona d'amor;
e adoncs deman confessor,
e tuit m'acús per pecador,
e que ell me man
que reta tot lo dan
que hai donat gran, en pecant,
a cells qui estan servidors
de la Regina de valors,
per ço que n'esper tal secors
que a null pecat
no sia obligat,
pus que en sia bé confessat.

D'oració de temps

Aor vós, Déus, on temps no és,
car eternal sots per jamés.
Ah sènyer Déus! ¿e quan serà
aquell temps que hom vos veurà

en glòria perpetuat
  veent la vostra Trenitat
ab vista d'enteniment,
  veent lo sant engerament
que el Paire fa de son Fill car
  ni veser lo sant espirar
del Sant Esperit gloriós?
  Car aquell veser és joiós
e és veser esperital
  qui veu infinit, eternal
produiment e iximent:
  que hom veurà manifestament
sens tot mijà, e la bontat,
  infinitat, eternitat,
poder, saviea, amor,
  virtut, veritat e valor,
glòria e tot compliment.
  Hom veirà manifestament
veent vostre bonificar,
  vostre entendre, eternar,
e de cascuna dignitat
  hom veurà s'obra per vertat.
Aquell veser tam bell serà,
  tan gloriós, e tant valrà
que boca no poria dir.
  Ah sènyer Déus! e tant desir
aquell temps, que eu pogués veser
  vostra essència, vostre esser! ;
car no pot haver marriment
  qui ella veu, car compliment
ha hom en ella tan gran
  que tot quant vol ha a son talant.
Perquè l'aor, e l'am e el cre,
  desir la veser mais que re.
Ah Jesucrist! quan vos veurai
  en paradís on joi estai
tan gran, que dóna compliment
  a seny e imaginament

e a sentiment corporal
tan gran, que null bé temporal
no pot donar tant de plaer,
con hom ha en vostre veser!
Perquè vos aor e us reclam,
e per mercè, pus que tant am
vostre veser, sia'm donat;
e car grans dons donats de grat,
hai en lo do gran esperança
e d'ell tots jorns n'hai remembrança.

Jesucrist, Sènyer, ah, si fos
en aquell temps que nasqués vós
e vos vesés infant petit,
vostres carns nues e poc llit,
pobre de draps, ple de bontat!
Ah, con fóra enamorat
en vos veser, tenir, tocar
e contra ergull contrastar,
veent lo rei del cel e el tro
jaer en paubre lliteló!
Ah, qui fos en cell temps nuirit
que Jesús fo infant petit,
a com tots jorns ab ell anàs,
ab ell estés, ab ell jugàs!
Ah, con fóra gauig de plaer!
Ah, qui volgra als mais haver!
E quan Jesús hac sa etat,
que hom lo servís a son grat!
E quan fo lliat e pres,
que hom son companyó estés
en tota la greu passió
e en la greu mort! Anc gauig no fo
major que cell que hom pogra haver!

Ah Jesús, per vostre plaer,
Faits-me vos veser en lo cel
on vos adora Gabriel,

Micael, Serafín, Rafael!
  E eu en est món vos aor,
vos desir, que en sospir e plor.
  Ah sènyer Jesús, quan serà
aquell temps que hom mais amarà
  vos amar, honrar e servir
a per vós treballs sostenir,
  per exempli de bon pastor,
que per si mateix e sa honor,
  per son parent, per son castell,
per ben menjar e bell mantell!
  Ah sènyer Déus, e tan mal és
aquest temps en què m'havets mès,
  car no el despèn en vós servir,
e veig-me a la mort venir,
  e no en sé lo temps que morré
ni si de mi haurets mercè!
  Ah sènyer Déus, tan gran esglai
hai, que temps no em defalla çai!
  Car si eu muir sen vos amar,
sens penedir, sens reclamar,
  e que no em sia confessat
de mon falliment e pecat,
  irai en temps on foc no mor
en què hom està tant en plor
  que mil vets porà mais plorar
d'aigua que no han fonts ni mar,
  e que el compte renovellàs
de llàgremes, e retornàs
  lo compte infinidament
porà ésser lo nombrament
  de cascuna gota de mar.
Ah sènyer Déus, quan vull pensar
  lo temps en què estan pecador
en infern, e pens la dolor
  que hauran, del pensar són las!
E quan pens quant estan li llaç
  ab què el demoni llaça e pren

per ço que vagen al turment,
no em pusc abstenir de plorar!

Per què eu us volria demanar
tal temps en est món, on estés
així fermat per tot quant és
trastot mon ésser corporal
e mon ésser espiritual;
que per tot ço que en lo món és
no feés falliment en res,
e que amàs mais oració
que honrament ni l'aur qui fo
ni que és, ni jamés serà.
Ah sènyer Déus, e quan veirà
aquell jorn lo vostre sotsmès
que am mais orar que nulla res!

A honor del Sant Esperit
Ramon ha fenit son escrit,
en Mallorca, dins la ciutat,
el nombre que Déus fo encarnat
mil e trescents, el mes de jullol.
Qui és en pecat e eixir en vol,
ab est escrit ha son poder,
car ab ell porà mantener
la fi a la qual és creat
e en sabrà eixir de pecat.
El tractat sia corrigit
si en res eu hi hai fallit.
Sia a Santa Maria dat,
e per sa amor sia amat.
Amén.

Plant de Nostra Dona Santa Maria

Despullat

Despullat és mon Fill e tot quant ha li par;
cell qui és tal Senyor de terra e de mar

no ha un petit drap d'on se pusca abrigar.
Ah lassa!, car lo veig en així nuu estar
e per los fals judeus tan fort vituperar,
ab pauc no perd lo sen, e el cor vol esclatar!
Senyors, aquest vel meu plaça-us en ell pausar!
E ells com a enics no em volgren escoltar.
Ah Fill gloriós!, pus vos lleixats despullar,
de vostra innocència vos vullats adossar,
car trop hai gran ira dels escarns qui vos veig far,
ni car eu, lasseta, no vos pusc abraçar!

Lo Desconhort

Déus amorós, ab ta virtut comença
aquest desconhort de Ramon Llull.

I

Déus, ab vostra vertut començ est desconhort,
lo qual faç en xantant, per ço que me'n conhort,
e que ab ell reconte lo falliment e el tort
que hom fa envers vós qui ens jutjats en la mort.
E on mais mi conhort, e menys hai lo cors fort,
car d'ira e dolor fa mon coratge port,
per què el conhort retorna en molt greu desconhort
e per açò estaig en treball e en deport,
e no hai null amic qui negú gauig m'aport,
mas tan solament vós, per què eu lo faix en port
en caent e en llevant e són çai en tal sort
que res no veig ni auig d'on me venga confort.

II

Can fui gran e sentí del món sa vanitat
comencé a far mal e entré en pecat,
oblidant Déus gloriós, siguent carnalitat;
mas plac a Jesucrist per sa gran pietat
que es presentà a mi cinc vets crucifigat

per ço que el remembràs e en fos enamorat
tan for que eu tractàs com ell fos preïcat
per tot lo món, e que fos dita veritat
de la sua Trinitat, e com fo encarnat:
per què eu fui espirat en tan gran volentat
que res als no amé mas que ell fos honrat,
e adoncs comencé com lo servís de grat.

III

Can pris a consirar del món son estament,
com paucs són cristians e molt li descreent,
adoncs en mon coratge hac tal concebiment
que anàs a prelats e a reis eixament,
e a religioses, per tal ordenament,
que se'n seguís passatge, e tal preïcament
que ab ferre e fust e ab ver argument
se donàs de nostra fe tan gran exalçament
que els infeels venguessen a convertiment.
Ez eu aiçò tractant trenta anys ha verament
no ho hai pogut obtenir, per què n'estai dolent,
tant que en plore sovent e en són en llanguiment.

IV

Dementre que en així estava en tristor
e consirava sovent la gran deshonor
que Déus pren en lo món per sofratxa d'amor,
com a home irat qui fuig a mal senyor
me n'ané en un boscatge on estava en plor
tan fort desconhortat, que el cor n'era en dolor;
mas per ço car plorava hi sentia dolçor
e car a Déu parlava feent a ell clamor,
car tan pauc exoeix li just e el pecador,
adoncs can lo requeren en tractar sa honor,
car si mais los donava d'ajuda e favor
tost convertirien lo món a sa valor.

V

En així eu estant en malencolia
esgardé e vi un hom qui venia,
un bastó en sa mà, e gran barba havia,
e en son dos cilici, e qui pauc vestia:
segons son captener eremità paria.
E can fo pres de mi dix-me què havia
ni lo dol que eu menava, e d'on me venia
ni si ell en res ajudar-me podia;
ez eu respos-li que tal ira sentia
que per ell ni per altre no em consolaria,
car segons que hom perd creix la fellonia:
—Ço que eu hai perdut e dir-ho qui ho poria?—

VI

—Ramon! —dix l'ermità—, vós què havets perdut?
Per què no us consolats en lo rei de salut
qui abasta a tot ço qui per ell és esdevengut?
Mas aquell qui el perd no pot haver vertut
en ésser consolat, car trop és abatut.
E si vós no havets null amic qui us ajut,
digats-me vostre cor, e què havets haüt;
car si havets flac cor e si sots decebut,
bé poria ésser que us fos acorregut
per la mia doctrina, tant que si sots vençut
que us mostrarà a vençre vostre cor combatut
ab ira e dolor ab què Déu vos ajut.—

VII

—N'ermità, s'eu pogués aportar a compliment
la honor que per Déu tracté tan llongament,
no hagra repperdut ni en fera clamament,
ans guasanyara tant que a convertiment
ne vengron li errat, e lo sant moniment
hagren los crestians; mas per defalliment

d'aquells a qui Déus ha donat mais d'honrament
qui no em volen ausir e tenen a nient
mi e mes paraules, com hom qui follament
parla e res no fa, segons enteniment,
per què eu per ells perd tot lo procurament
que faç en honrar Déu e d'hòmens salvament.

VIII

Encara us dic que port una Art general
que novament és dada por do espirital
per qui hom pot saber tota re natural,
segons que enteniment ateny lo sensual.
A dret e a medicina e a tot saber val
e a teologia, la qual m'és mais coral,
e a soure qüestions nulla art tant no val,
e a destruir errors per raó natural,
e tenc-la per perduda car quaix a hom no en cal;
per què eu en planc e en plor e n'hai ira mortal
car null hom qui perdés tan preciós cabal
no poria haver mais gauig de re eternal.—

IX

—Ramon, so vós faits ço que a vos se cové
en procurar honor a Déu e a faire gran bé
e no sots escoltat ni ajuda no us ve
d'aquells qui n'han poder, per tot ço no es cové
que siats despagats, car Déus qui tot ho ve
vos n'ha aitant de grat com si es complís de se
tot ço que demanats, car hom qui bé es capté
en tractar sa honor, aconsegueix en se
mèrit, esmende e do, pietat e mercè;
per què fa gran pecat qui en son cor reté
ira ni desconhort faent Déus a ell bé
qui es concorda ab gauig, esperança e fe.

X

Ramon, de vostre Art no siats consirós,
ans en siats alegre e n'estiats joiós,
car pus Déus la us ha dada, justícia e valors
la multiplicaran en lleials amadós.
E si vós en est temps n'havets un pauc d'amargós,
en altre temps mellor haurets ajudadós
tals qui l'apendran e en venceran les errors
d'aquest món, e en faran molts bons faits cabalós;
per què us prec, mon amic, que conhort sia ab vós,
e hui mai no plorets contra fait virtuós
enans vos alegrats contra fait viciós,
e de Déu esperats gràcia e secors.

XI

Ramon, per què plorats e no faits bell semblant
e que vos conhortets de vostre mal talant?
E car no ho faits mi faits ésser dubtant
que siats en pecat mortal tam mal estant,
per què siats indigne a far res ben estant,
car Déus no es vol servir per mull home en pecant.
E si no ve a fi ço que desirats tant
no és culpa d'aquells d'on vos anats clamant,
car Déus no vol que vostre fait vaja en avant
si estats en pecat, car de bé tant ni quant
no pot hom pecador d'ell ésser començant,
car bé e pecat en res no són semblant.

XII

—N'ermità, no m'escús que no haja pecat
mortalment mantes vets, d'on me són confessat;
mas depús que Jesucrist a mi es fo revelat
en la crots, segons que d'amont vos he contat,
e en la sua amor mon voler confermat,
no pequé a scient en null mortal pecat;

mas poria ésser que per ço qui és passat
can era ser del món, amant sa vanitat
no sia per Jesús en far bé ajudat;
emperò si no ho era, tort faria e pecat
si no m'ajudava depús que l'hac amat
e per la sua amor lo món desemparat.—

XIII

—Ramon, hom negligent no sap bé procurar
e està negligent, car molt no vol membrar
ço que entén acabar, per què mi fas dubtar
que lo públic negoci que tu vols acabar
ab los molt grans senyors qui no et volen ajudar,
no es perda per ço car molt no ho vols amar,
car ab pauca amor gran fait no es pot menar;
e si és pereós de tu et deus rancurar,
ni de ton falliment no deus altre encolpar,
ni tu estant ociós no et deus desconhortar
per altre, mas per tu, qui no et vols esforçar
en far tot ton poder con Déus pusques honrar.—

XIV

—N'ermità, vós vejats si eu són ociós
en tractar públic bé de justs e pecadós,
car muller n'hai lleixada, fills e possessiós
e trenta anys n'hai estat en treball e llangors,
e cinc vets a la Cort ab mes messiós
n'hai estat, e encara a los Preïcadors
a tres capítols generals, e a los Menors
altres tres generals capítols; e si vós
sabíets què n'hai dit a reis e a senyors
ni con hai treballat, no seríets dubtós
en mi que sia estat en est fait pereós,
ans n'hauríets pietat si sots hom piadós.—

XV

—Ramon, tot hom qui vol adur a compliment
negú fait que sia de molt gran estament
covć que el sàpia tractar discretament;
mas si vós no sots home discret ni entenent
segons lo fait, si en faits rancurament
rancurat-vos a tort, e sots-ne reprendent
d'aquells qui són discrets e qui fan sàviament
ço qui a bo fait se cové e a l'exausament
de la fe cristiana; per què us consell breument
que estiats consolats en vostre defalliment
consirant que no sots a lo fait convinent,
e estats emfre vós humil e pacient.—

XVI

—N'ermità, eu no só de tal discreció
que a fait tan cabalós abastàs ma raó;
e si eu ignorant vas ell faç fallió
per sofraita d'entendre, e car discret no só,
segons que el fait és gran per ço vull companyó
qui el m'ajut a complir, mas no em val pauc ni pro
requerir companyia, ans són sol abandó,
e can los guard en la cara e els vull dir ma rasó
no em volen escoltar, ans dien que fat só
los de més, per ço car los dic aital sermó;
emperò al Judici pairà qui ha discreció
e qui de sos pecats atrobarà perdó.—

XVII

—Ramon, home avar can vol negú fait far
ço que volria no ho sap acabar,
on si vós sots avar e no volets donar
del vostre, per ço que Déus poguéssets honrar,
de vostre cobeetat vos deuríets clamar,
car ella vos empatxat el bo fait procurar.

O si dar no podets, paupertat pot estar
contra vostre negoci, e deuríets pensar
que els senyors mais se clinen per donar que pregar
a los precs que hom los fa; per què us vull consellar
que, si donar podets, pensats tost de l'anar,
car per donar porets tota res acabar.

XVIII

—N'ermità, certs siats que anc mais cobeitat
de deners ni d'honors a mon coratge plac,
e en aquest negoci de mon patrimonat
hai tota hora despès e n'hai tan llarguejat
que li meu infant n'estant en paupertat;
per què d'avarícia no em tem ésser reptat
ni donar eu no pusc a los hòmens, de grat,
car no só home ric ni senyor de ciutat,
per què de ço d'on m'encolpats m'hajats excusat;
ans si eu fos senyor d'emperi o regnat
tant del meu hi donara tro que fos acabat,
mas home qui pauc dóna no és bé escoltat.—

XIX

—Ramon, vana glòria si fa a hom amar
per ço que hom faça de si les gents parlar
dients de hom llausor per ço que els sia car
e que l'amen e l'honren en sovint nomenar;
on si vós treballats per vós mateix llausar,
ergull e vana glòria vos fan tant menysprear
a cells ab qui volets vostre fait acabar,
que no us denyon veer ni us volen escoltar,
car null fait tan honrat, vil hom no deu menar,
e tot hom és vil qui estia en pecar,
e qui mais qui no es tany se vulla far honrar;
per què de vostre tort no vullats altre encolpar.

XX

—N'ermità, eu no sai per qual entenció
havets de mi tanta mala cogitació,
car ans deu hom haver bona presumpció
de hom que no coneix, que mala opinió,
¿e com no vos pensats que a fait que és tam bo
se pusca tot donar home qui pauc ni pro
no valla en lo fait? Car si en tot mal só,
segons que ho requer natura e rasó,
tractaria lo contrari. E, si Déus me perdó,
anc mais en mon coratge entenció no fo
que per haver llausor parlàs d'aital sermó,
car en hom pecador null llaus pot ésser bo.—

XXI

—Ramon, per aventura vós no sots conegut
e per açò podets ésser en lo fait decebut,
car null tresor qui sia en terra escondut
no es cové que sia desirat ni volgut;
on si vostre saber no és apercebut
co'us pensats, que per ço ne siats creegut,
mas mostrats ço que sabets per ço que vos ajut
vostra Art e saber, car hom desconegut
no ha, per ignorància, honrament ni vertut.
E si vós, mon amic, amats d'hòmens salut
e de Déu honrament, e que no sia perdut
vostre saber, faits tant que sia conegut.—

XXII

—N'ermità, ¿co'us pensats que eu tal saber celàs
ab lo qual home nostra fe en provàs
a los hòmens errats, per ço que los salvàs
Déus, lo qual tant desir que tot home l'amàs?
Ans siats segur que de mostrar en són las;
mas si hom en mos llibres fortment estudiàs

e que per altre saber en res no los oblidàs
jo en fóra conegut; mas com gat que passàs
tost per brases, los lligen, per què a ells no faç
quaix res de mon negoci. Mas si fos qui els remembràs
e qui los entesés e que en ells no dubtàs,
hom pogra per mos llibres posar lo món en bon cas.—

XXIII

—Ramon, tot ço que dic faç per vós conhortar,
mas pus no us volets abstenir de plorar
poria ésser que me'n vulla enujar;
emperò escoltats e vejats si es pot far
ço que vós demanats al Papa, car no par
que sia possíbol la nostra fe provar
ni que home pusca tals hòmens atrobar
ni que si mateix se donen a marturiar
a los mals sarraïns, per ells a preïcar.
On per ço vós, amic, no us devets meravellar
si el Papa e els cardenals no us volen atorgar
ço que les demanats, pus que no es pusca far.

XXIV

—N'ermità, si la fe hom no pogués provar,
los cristians Déus no pogra encolpar
si a los infeels no la volon mostrar,
e els infeels se pogren per dret de Déu clamar,
car major veritat no lleix argumentar
per ço que l'enteniment ajut a nostre amar,
com mais am Trinitat e de Déu encarnar
e a la falsetat mais pusca contrastar.
Escrit hai lo passatge on hai mostrat tot clar
com lo sant Sepulcre se pusca recobrar
e com hom atrob hòmens qui vajen preïcar
la fe sens paor de mort, e qui ho sabion far.—

XXV

—Ramon, si hom pogués demostrar nostra fe
hom ne perdria mèrit, e per ço no es cové
que es pusca demostrar, pus que se'n perdés bé;
car en perdre lo bé fóra lo mal, de se,
causa al demostrar qui contra el mèrit ve
lo qual hom ha per creure veritat que no es ve
per força d'argument, mas solament per fe,
encara que l'entendre humà gens no conté
tota la veritat de Déu que infinida es manté
tant, que causa finida tota ella no té;
per què vostra rasó no par que valla re;
e, car no us consolats, faits ço que descové.—

XXVI

—N'ermità, si hom fos a si mateix creat,
ço que entenets provar contengra veritat,
mas car Déus creà home per ço que en sia honrat
qui és pus noble fi e ha mais d'altetat
que la fi que hom ha en ésser gloriejat,
no val vostra raó, e és ja damunt provat
que la fe es pot provar, si bé n'havets membrat;
e si bé es pot provar, no es segueix que creat
contenga e comprena tot lo éns increat,
mas que n'entén aitant com a ell se n'és dat,
per ço que hom haja plena de Déu sa volentat,
son membrar e entendre, poder e bontat.—

XXVII

—Ramon, com vos pensats que hom per preïcar
pusca los sarraïns adur a batejar?
Car segons que Mafumet ha volgut ordenar
que aquell qui en diu mal no pusca escapar
e que ses raons hom no vulla escoltar,
per què a mi no par utilitat l'anar;

encara que home qui no sabria parlar
llenguatge arabesc, mas per enterpretar
no pot per res ab ells molt enansar,
e si el llenguatge aprèn porà-hi trop trigar;
per què vos consell que anets Déu pregar
en una alta muntanya ab mi Déu contemplar.—

XXVIII

—N'ermità, els sarraïns són en tal estament
que aquells qui són savis, per força d'argument
no creen en Mafumet, ans tenen a nient
l'Alcorà, per ço car no visc honestament;
per què aquells venrien tost a convertiment
si hom ab ells estava en gran disputament
e la Fe los mostrava per força d'argument;
e aquells convertits convertirien la gent.
En apendre llur llenguatge hom no està llongament,
ni no cal que hom blastom Mafument el començament:
e qui fa ço que pot, lo Sant Expirament
fa ço que a ell cov47 donant lo compliment.—

XXIX

—Ramon, can Déus volrà que el món sia convertit,
adoncs darà los llenguatges per lo Sant Esperit
e convertirà lo món, segons que havets ausit
de Crist e dels Apòstols, d'on és fait mant escrit,
e aquell convertiment serà per tot lo món sentit
tant, que en un ovili seran li hom unit,
lo qual mais no serà en est món despartit.
E aquell serà nostre e per Déu estabilit
e jamais null pecat no serà consentit.
E car en aquest temps cascú hom ha fallit
tam fortment que no vol que sia eribit
Déus ha a far en ell miracles pus que tant l'han aunit.—

XXX

—N'ermità, en tots temps ama Déus veritat
e vol ésser per home conegut e amat,
e per ço en tots temps ha home llibertat
en far bé e no mal, e seria forçat
si en aquest temps en qui son no havia potestat
en tractar honrament a Déu, e caritat
a son proixme a veer; per què eu no són pagat
de ço que dit havets, e havets gran pecat
en ço que afermats, que tot hom és lligat
en est temps, on no pot convertir li errat,
ni per Déu no pot ésser a sa honor ajudat;
per què en lo vostre parlar estaig desconsolat.—

XXXI

—Ramon, molt mellor seny és qui sap retenir
ço que ha guanyat, que anar convertir
los sarraïns malvats con no volen ausir;
per què a los crestians deu hom tant de bé dir
de Déu en preïcant, que els faça Déu servir.
Encara que hom no sap si bé se pot seguir
d'anar als sarraïns, car poria-hi fallir
en tant que hom volguessen destruir;
e ço que mais és que no porien esdevenir
null temps bons cristians, car no es poden partir
de ço que han acostumat. Per què us plaça jaquir
vostra ira e mudats alor vostre desir.—

XXXII

—N'ermità, si fossen pauc li Preïcador
e li clergue seglar e li frare Menor,
encara li monge que han abat e prior,
ço que vós en deïts fóra consell mellor;
mas car en nostra fe ha mant hom de valor
qui desiren morir per far a Déu honor

e qui poden abastar e a nòs e a llor,
per ço hai desplaer, car cells qui són major
no fan ço que deuen en dar de Déus llausor.
E si els paires convertits no han a la fe amor
hauran-ho llurs infants, e deïts gran follor
car null hom no perd si mor per son Creador.—

XXXIII

—Ramon, segons que auig dir, mant hom és anat
preïcar als tartres e pauc han enansat,
e encara als sarraïns, d'on són meravellat
can així estats forts en vostra volentat,
car de tot fait on hom se sia fadigat,
e majorment con tantes vets l'haja assajat,
se deu tot hom partir, pus que sia senat,
e si no se'n parteix fa-se'n tenir per fat;
per què us consell, germà, que hajats pietat
de vostre cors mateix que tant havets hujat,
e estats en un lloc on sia reposat,
e de vostres damnatges estiats consolat.—

XXXIV

—N'ermità, cell qui vo molt servir e honrar
son bon senyor no se'n deu per nulla re lleixar
ni d'ell a servir no es deuria enujar;
e car en vostre cor ha fretura d'amar,
no sabets vós mateix ni altre consellar,
car si hom en un temps no pot son fait acabar
porà l'acabar en altre, si ho sap bé menar;
e qui bon fait comença no l'ha a començar,
e si els primers fan pauc los altres poran molt far;
per què us prec, per mercè, que em lleixàssets estar,
car no em par que ab vós pogués res guasanyar,
ans on mais me diets mais me faits entristar.—

XXXV

Ramon s'enfelloní, e no volia ausir
l'ermità qui el pregava con se degués jaquir
del dol que menava, e començà a dir:
—Senyor Déus gloriós! ¿ha el món tal martir
com aquest que sostenc con tu no pusc servir
car no hai qui m'ajut com pusca romanir
esta Art que m'has dada d'on tant de bé es pot seguir,
la qual tem que sia perduda aprés lo meu fenir?
Car null hom no la sap bé segons mon albir,
ni eu no pusc forçar null hom d'ella ausir.
Ah las! si ella es perd, ¿a tu què porai dir,
qui la m'has donada per ella enantir?—

XXXVI

—Ramon, li filosof qui foren antigament,
d'esta Art que tu has no hagren coneiximent,
per què par que no sia de gran profitament;
e si ella fos vera, fóra en lo començament
per los filosofs atrobada, car llur enteniment
fo pus alt que lo teu; emperò si eu ment
e que l'hajes haüda de Déu, fas falliment
con tems que aprés ta mort ella vinga a nient,
car tot açò que Déus dóna ve a bo compliment,
encara que els antics dementre eren vivent
les Arts que faïen no eren en gran exalçament
enans són exalçades per li altre conseqüent.—

XXXVII

Consolar se volc Ramon, emperò felló fo
can ausí que l'ermità havia opinió
que li filosof antic, en los quals Fe no fo,
sien estats començament de tot ço qui és bo
a conèixer Déu, Trinitat e Encarnació;
car null filosof antic no hac opinió

que en Déus fos Trinitat ni ab hom unió,
ni l'obra que Déus ha en si per producció
no amà ni conec; e doncs, ¿per qual rasó
li filosof antic hagren menys de visió
en llur enteniment que aquells que aprés són
qui han llig e creença e esperen resurrecció?

XXXVIII

—Ramon, no pusc far res com sies consolat.
Entín esta rasó e no sies irat:
en què no és Déus si lo món no és en bo estat?
Car no lleva ni baixa a ell quant és creat
con sia en si complit e no haja necessitat
de nulla creatura. D'on deus ésser pagat
del compliment que Déus ha en si per sa bontat;
e tu, foll, estàs trist quaix si Déus fos mirvat
per lo mal estament en què el món has trobat.
Foll! com no t'alegres en plena deïtat,
e que gits a no cura tot ço qui és creat,
per ço que a ton cor abast Déus no mermat?

XXXIX

—N'ermità, mal me fa lo vostre consolar,
per què aquell punt fo fort on vos pusc atrobar!
e si no fos que eu tem vergonya e mal estar,
de hui mais en avant ab vós no volgra parlar.
E ¿com podets dir que em pusca consolar
en veer Déus aunir, no servir ni membrar
ni conèixer ni amar? E si bé pot bastar
Déu per si mateix, a mon cor per amar
no m'abasta, car no vei molt fortment honrar;
e car per tan vils causes lo veig tant menysprear
estaig en desconhort e no em pusc alegrar,
mas en ço que Déus és estaig en confortar.—

XL

—Ramon, Déus tot quant fa tot ho fa justament,
e si met en infern li malvat discreent,
no devets per tot ço haver desconsolament;
e car vós sots irat car Déus fa jutjament,
és vostra ira pecat, e fallits malament
contra Déu, e amats aquells qui falsament
creon contra Déu e estan desobedient;
e si en vós fos bo e lleial amament
vós fórets molt pagat, car Déus dóna turment
a cells qui tot dia fan ves ell falliment,
car home qui bé am no fa rancurament
de ço que fa l'amant, pus que fa dretament.—

XLI

—N'ermità, eu no dull per ço que fa el Senyor,
ans en tot ço que fa lo llou e l'aor;
mas per ço car volria que hom li fes honor
e que sobre quant és hom li hagués amor,
me dull e mi complanc e estaig en tristor;
e car vós no sabets d'on ve ma greu dolor
no em sabets conhortar ni donar null secor;
per què és bo que em lleixets estar en ira e plor
e aprenets com siats millor consolador,
car molt pauc en sabets, e ja li pecador
per vós mais no valran, car no havets vas llor
caritat, com Déus sia d'ells perdonador.—

XLII

—Ramon, per ço car am que en gauig estiats
e que ira ni dolor e nulla re hajats,
vos vull consolar, e prec-vos que aujats:
Déus sofer que lo món sia així malvats
per ço que mills pusca perdonar a tots llats,
car on mais Ell perdona, mais ha de pietats

e mais li en covć grat; per què segur siats
que Déus ha a son poble tan gran caritats
que quaix tots los hòmens del món seran salvats,
car si mais no n'eron los salvats que els damnats
la sua mercè seria sens grans caritats:
per què en la gran mercè de Déu siats consolats.—

XLIII

—N'ermità, tot dia em tenits en parlament
e no em lleixats membrar en mon angoixós turment,
e faits-ho per ço que git a oblidament,
l'ira e el desconhort d'o me ve llanguiment,
mas res no acabats e faits avocament
mais de gran pietat que de gran jutjament;
per què en això errats car en Déu egalment
estan jutjar e perdonar, segons ordenament
de les sues vertuts, car nulla no consent
que en la sua justícia sia null minvament;
per què en deu pecador haver gran espavent,
per què eu no plor mas car no ha Déu honrament.—

XLIV

—Ramon, aquells hòmens qui són predestinat
covć per fina força que ells sien salvat,
car, si no ho eren, poria ésser mudat
lo saber que Déus ha en contrarietat,
lo qual mudament no està en possibilitat;
car si estar hi poria no seria acabat
lo saber que Déus ha, ans seria mermat;
e car està complit, siats, doncs, consolat
en lo seu compliment, contra el qual faits pecat
en quant no us conhortats en ço que sia jutjat
e per la volentat de Déu, en així autrejat,
com ho sap son saber e en fa ver veritat.—

XLV

—N'ermità, si vós fóssets home qui fos lletrat
mills sabríets parlar d'home predestinat
e no hàgrets en oblit de Déu sa llibertat
la qual ha en si mateix e en quant ha creat,
per la qual a home ha dada llibertat
con lo vulla molt servir sens que no sia forçat
con Déus sia tan bo que es deu servir de grat;
lo qual servir no pot ésser, si de necessitat
per hom predestinat fos servit e amat,
e fóra hom salvat sens què no fóra jutjat;
car judici no pot ésser senes llibertat
ni llibertat no costreny precís ni predestinat.—

XLVI

—Ramon, si en vós fos molt gran esperança,
si tot lo món està en molt greu balança,
del seu mal estament no hàgrets malenança,
car Déus, qui és tot ple de gran pietança,
aportarà lo món en breu en benanança
tan gran, que cascú home n'haurà alegrança:
e que això sia ver hajats-hi fiança
per ço car Déus dóna a hom començança,
ab mercè e bondat qui ha en sa semblança;
e si vos per això no lleixats tristança
no haurets en bontat ni mercè, confiança,
e serets contra Déu e la sua amistança.—

XLVII

—N'ermità, ans que el món sia en bo estament
serà fait a Déu molt vituperament
encara que no veig far null cadenament
con lo temps sia prop, car ço que en Cort present
al Papa e als cardenals no ho prenon mantinent
ans ho van allongant, per què n'hai marriment

tant, que no pusc haver negú consolament,
car ço que eu los present mostra tan clarament
l'ordenament del mọn qui es pot far en breument,
e no ho tenen a re, ans se'n fan gabament
com si ho fes home fat qui parlàs follament:
per què d'aitals hòmens hai desperament.—

XLVIII

Consirà l'ermità si per res poria
aconhortar Ramon qui tan fort planyia,
e dix a Ramon que Santa Maria
e que ab ella cascuna gerarquia
dels àngels pregavon e de nuit e de dia
a Jesucrist son Fill que per mercè li sia
que en breu donàs al món ordenament e via
en ell honrar, servir: —Per què açò us deuria
consolar, Ramon, car Crist tota via
fa ço d'on és pregat per sa maire pia,
per los àngels e els sants; per què en aiçò sia
trastot vostre conhort, e gauig en vós estia.—

XLIX

—N'ermità, can consir que la Dona d'amor,
Dona de valor, de just e pecador
e cascú dels sants pregon Nostre Senyor
con tot lo món faça a Jesucrist honor,
e veig que lo món li fa tan gran deshonor,
adoncs cuit morir d'ira e dolor,
car tant són indigne li malvat pecador
que Déus no es sosté que quaix negú prec per llor
e en així lo món roman en sa error,
e quaix no ès qui de Déu vulla donar llausor,
ans llausa si mateix, son fill e son austor:
e doncs, qui deuria haver gauig mas tristor?—

L

—Ramon, a mi no par siats home pacient
per ço car per re no volets haver consolament;
e ¿com no membrats Job que hac tan perdiment
e qui en sa persona sofrí tant de turment
e esdevenc si paubre que no hac nient?
Emperò consolà's, e vós per re vivent
no us volets consolar, e estats sanament,
e havets heretat, deners e vestiment,
infants e d'altres causes d'on hom ha pagament;
e cor a Déu no plau home impacient
no sosté que per vós venga a compliment
lo seu fait que menats, ni haja honrament.—

LI

—N'ermità, no és molt si hom és desconsolat
en perdre infants, diners e heretat
e en estar malaute pus que a Déus ve de grat;
mais ¿qui es pot consolar que Déu sia oblidat
menyspreat, blastomat e tam fort ignorat
com de tot ço sia Déus fortment despagat?
Encara ¿que no sabets com eu soi menyspreat
per Déu, tantes vets maldit e blastomat,
e en perill de mort e per barba tirat,
e per vertut de Déu pacient són estar?
mas que Déus en lo món sia tam pauc amat
no és hom en lo món qui me'n feés conhortat.—

LII

—Ramon, segons que em par, tu fas tot ton poder
con Déus per tot lo món honor pogués haver,
per què Déus te'n deu aitant de grat haver
con si el fait se complia, per què et deurà valer
aiçò a consolar e ton dol remaner,
car mèrit n'has molt gran e pots n'haver esper

de molt gran guasardó, e gita en noixaler
lo falliment dels altres que a Déus fan desplaer,
e alegra't en tu e en ton captener,
e no sies trop forts en ço que vols haver
ni per ço car los altres no fan a ton voler;
e a tu abast Déus per amar e temer.—

LIII

—N'ermità, no és hom creat principalment
per ço que haja gran gloriejament,
ans ho és per tal que Déus haja gran honrament
en lo món, per son poble; per què eu no són jausent
si hai gran guasardó, ni no estaig dolent
si n'hai pauc, car no és d'aiçò mon començament,
ans és tota ma ira, mon dol, mon marriment,
car no és en lo món fait un tal ordenament
con Déus fos honrat, amat per tota gent
e que tot hom fos en via de salvament;
e car vós me volets dar consolament
de ço d'on no es pot dar parlats-me per nient.—

LIV

—Ramon, qual és lo fait que vós tant desirats
per lo qual en lo món fos Déus tan fort honrats?
Car poria ésser que en lo fait no siats
e que altre sia lo fait que vós no procurats,
per lo qual lo món sia a bona fi menats;
car si altre és lo fait, per nient treballats,
e poríets treballar si mil ans viviats
que ja vós no venríets a ço que volriats,
car hom no pot complir fait on és desviats.
Per què us prec que lo fait clarament me digats
e que amdós vejam si el fait on vós estats
és aquell per què Déus pot ésser mais amats.—

LV

—N'ermità, la manera con Déus fos mais amat
ja la vos hai contada, si bé ho havets membrat,
ço és que el Papa hagués mant home lletrat
qui desiràs per Jesús ésser marturiat
per ço que per tot lo món fos entès e honrat,
e que cascú llenguatge fos mostrat,
segons que a Miramar ha estat ordenat
—e haja'n conciència qui ho ha afollat!—.
Encara que al passatge fos lo deé donat
de tot quant posseeixen li clergue e el prelat;
e que açò tant duràs tro que fos conquistat
lo Sepulcre; e d'aiçò llibre n'hai ordenat.

LVI

N'ermità, encara és altre ordenament
lo qual seria al passatge gran avantament
e a destruir la error de la gent:
que lo Papa feés que a reüniment
venguesson los cismàtics per desputament,
del qual desputar havem fait tractament;
e els cismàtics cobrats, qui són tants hòmens vivent,
no és qui pogués contrastar malament,
a l'Esgleia, per ferre ni per null argument;
e que del Temple e l'Espital fos fait un uniment
e que llur major fos rei del sant muniment:
per què a honrar Déus no sai pus alt tractament.—

LVII

Consirà l'ermità si Ramon deia veritat,
e emfre si mateix estec molt apensat
e no poc atrobar pus profitós tractat
que cell que diu Ramon, d'on li pres pietat
e penedís molt fort con tant l'hac treballat,
e volc ésser ab Ramon trist e desconsolat,

e pregava Ramon que li fos perdonat
en plorant, suspirant, e dix: —Ah, veritat,
devoció, caritat! Evvas on és anat
lo grat que a Déu deuria ésser donat?—
Can Ramon viu l'ermità que ab ell s'era acordat,
adoncs lo va baisar: ensems han molt plorat.

LVIII

—Ramon—dix l'ermità—, com poríem mover
lo Papa e los cardenals e lo fait obtener?
Car en tan noble fait vull tots temps remaner
e a ell a tractar vull far tot mon poder,
car fait és on lo món porà molts mais valer;
e car eu ans no el vi hai-ne gran desplaer,
car si eu ans lo vis, res no em pogra tener
que eu no apresés arabesc e lo vostre saber,
per anar als sarraïns e la fe mantener
senes paor de mort, e gran plaer haver
en morir, per Jesús honrar e car tener,
car mais val per ell morir que per si vida haver.—

LIX

—N'ermità, eu són las d'aquest fait amenar
en la Cort, pus no hi puis nulla re acabar;
e si vos volíets en la Cort procurar
aquest fait de Jesús e vostre poder far
en la Cort llongament, bé poria estar
que el fait vengués a fi, si us volien escoltar
lo Papa e els cardenals, sinó que quaix joglar
vos feiéssets en la Cort e los Cent Noms cantar,
los quals hai faits de Déu, e posats en rimar,
per ço que els hi cantàs e parlàs sens dubtar;
mas no n'hai de consell per ço que menysprear
no faça los meus llibres que Déus m'ha faits trobar.

LX

—Ramon, si eu en la Cort estaig, vós on irets?
ni per què ab mi en la Cort no procurarets
lo fait de Jesucrist pus que mogut l'havets!
Ni si hom vos escarneix, e vós en què en serets?
Vós manats a mi far ço que far no volets!
Per què em par que en est fait ni en altre no valets.
Mas anem a la Cort e en res no dubtets,
e no siats d'aquells qui dion: Senyors, fets
ço que ells no farien; per què d'açò devets
ésser envergonyit, e escusa no havets,
ans faits hipocresia de qui pecat havets,
e el bé que havets fait per vergonya perdets.—

LXI

—N'ermità eu prepòs als sarraïns tornar
per ço que a la Fe los pusca aportar;
on vaig sens paor de mort, que fa pus greu portar
que vergonya sofrir per Jesucrist honrar,
lo qual en res no tem, ans la deu hom amar.
Mas per ço que ma Art no faça menysprear
en tenir la manera que tenon li joglar,
encara que en altre lloc creu mais de bé far;
per què no prepòs ara a Cort retornar;
e car vós tan fortment me volets encolpar,
pot ésser que ho façats per vós a excusar
a venir a la Cort, per què ho lleixem estar.—

LXII

Penedís l'ermità car hac Ramon reprès
e dix-li que per ço que ab ell en Cort estegués
l'havia tan fortment en així escomès.
—Ramon —dix l'ermità—, dos ans prepòs o tres
a estar en la Cort sotsposat, que no res
hi faça, mas aprés prepòs que eu tengués

per lo món ça e lla, a prelats e marquès,
religioses e reis, e fer ço que pogués
en menar aquest fait que m'havets escomès,
mas volria que en mon lloc altre en Cort estegués
e que en així un tal cercle se'n feés
tro que aquest fait en la Cort se presés.—

LXIII

—N'ermità —dix Ramon—, bé havets consirat,
car per aital cercle pot ésser acabat
lo fait qui és tam bo a crestianitat;
e digats ça e lla, a rei e a prelat
que si el fait tost no es pren que ja és ordenat
per sarraïns que els tartres a el sion girat,
e ja n'han convertits una gran quantitat;
e els tartres convertits en sarraïnitat
lleu poran destruir quaix tota cristianitat
en tant que no serà cristià qui haja regnat
ni negú prelat haurà cavall sejornat.
Vejats, doncs, n'ermità, lo món a què és tornat.—

LXIV

—Ramon —dix l'ermità—, fort volria saber
per qual raó Déus se pot en així captener
del món, qui és seu, e el gita en nonxaler,
ni la sua bontat com ho pot sostener
que tans pecadors vagen en infern mal haver.
Per què us prec, Ramon, que me'n digats vostre saber,
car on mais me'n direts mais en sabrai retrer,
e lo fait qui em lliurats mills porai mantener.
Car pus que lo mon fo fait tro ara a mon parer,
si és un home salvat mil ne són en doler
en infern, per tots temps, ¿e açò, co es pot fer
que l'Esgleia ni hom no hi fa son poder?—

LXV

—N'ermità, ja us hai dit, si bé vos pot membrar,
que Déus mais creà hom per si servir e honrar
que per ço que hom hagués gloriejar;
e car hom no està en la de fi crear
en quant mais desira a si mateix procurar
salvació, que a Déu honor, e bé estar,
per açò aital home no pot en gràcia estar,
ans està en pecat, e assí és l'abissar,
per què lo món se perd e no es vol despertar,
e gens no em meravell si Déus no el vol amar
ni si lleixa el demoni en lo món tant mal far,
per ço que del tort que pren se pusca fort venjar.—

LXVI

L'ermità e Ramon preseren comiat
e amdós en plorant se són baisat e abraçat,
e cascú dix a l'altre que a Déu fos comanat
e en oració l'u per l'autre membrat.
Al partir s'esguardaren ab molt gran caritat,
pietat e dolor, cascú agenollat,
e cascú senyà l'altre e hac agraciat.
La un se partí de l'altre ab mant suspir gitat
car mais no preposaven que fossen asemblat
en est món, mas en l'altre, si a Déus ve de grat.
E can cascú de l'altre se fo un petit llunyat
tantost fo l'un per l'altre molt fortment desirat.

LXVII

L'ermità remembrà lo treball e l'afan
en què Ramon havia estat en mant an,
e encara que es metia en perill qui és molt gran.
Al cel llevà sos ulls, mans juntes agenollant,
ab pietat e amor a Déu dix en plorant:
—O Déus humil, piadós, per mercè vos deman

que ab vós sia Ramon, tant que el gardets de dan!
A vós, Déus, poderós, mon amic Ramon coman,
e al món trametets hòmens que hagen talant
a morir per vostra amor, e qui vagen mostrant
veritat de la fe, per lo món preïcant,
segons que Ramon ho va ara començant.—

LXVIII

Can Ramon remembrà la molt gran tempestat
en la qual llongament ha estat tabuixat
e membrà l'ermità que a ella s'era dat,
adoncs plorà molt fort e hac d'ell pietat,
e dix a Jesucrist, mans juntes agenollat:
—O vós, ver Déus e hom, per què eu hai treballat
com per tot lo món fòssets conegut e amat?
Si a dretura plau que vós me n'hajats grat,
plàcia'us que l'ermità ne sia remunerat,
pus que s'és mès tam fort en ma societat,
e faits per ell complir ço on hai pauc enançat,
e a mi ajudats enançar cristianitat.—

LXIX

Fenit es lo Desconhort que Ramon ha escrit,
en lo qual l'ordenament del món ha dit,
e en rimes posat, per ço que no s'oblit,
car poria ésser que molt home ardit
se meta en lo fait, tro que sia complit
ço que ha Ramon al Papa requerit.
Car si per lo Papa lo fait és estabilit
e que los cardenals hi hagen consentit,
poran ésser del món tot li mal departit,
e tot lo món serà a Déu tan abellit
que a la fe romana no serà contradit.
Aquest Desconhort coman al Sant Espirit.—

Amén.

Lo Concili

XI

Senyor Déus, pluja,
perquè el mal fuja,
car pecat puja!
Senyor, tal pluja donats
que en amor, Papa, prelats,
el Sepulcre sia cobrats
e lo gran nom vostre honrats.
Senyor Déus, pluja,
perquè el mal fuja,
car pecat puja!
Quan el concili er justats,
ver Déus, justícia donats
per conseller e los prelats,
car no hi serà null barats.
Al concili, ver Déus, aydats.
Senyor Déus, pluja,
perquè el mal fuja,
car pecat puja!
Prudència sia conseller,
que consella fait verdader;
a lo concili és mester;
sens ella no valrà diner.
Senyor Déus, pluja,
perquè el mal fuja,
car pecat puja!
Fortitudo de gran confort
de lo concili sia port,
si no ho és, ja me'n desconhort,
car lo bé hi perdrà son sort.
Senyor Déus, pluja,
perquè el mal fuja,
car pecat puja!
Si lo concili ha son for,

temprança gran serà el tresor
car tot serà vestit d'or
e de virtuts e de bon cor.
  Senyor Déus, pluja,
  perquè el mal fuja,
  car pecat puja!
Si la fe grans amics no ha
a lo concili, què farà?
Lo concili es clamarà
a Déu, car la fe no hi valrà.
  Senyor Déus, pluja,
  perquè el mal fuja,
  car pecat puja!
Qui el concili volrà honrar
esperança vulla menar,
car ab ella es porà acabar;
fals hom no hi porà contrastar.
  Senyor Déus, pluja,
  perquè el mal fuja,
  car pecat puja!
Caritat, venits aidar
al concili per lo bé far
e el Papa enamorar
e cardenals aconsellar.
  Senyor Déus, pluja,
  perquè el mal fuja,
  car pecat puja!
Avarícia és camí
per qui hom va a mala fi,
si és ella al concilí
ell no valrà un peitaví.
  Senyor Déus, pluja,
  perquè el mal fuja,
  car pecat puja!
Glotonia es destral
ab colp mortal,
si al concili ha hostal
lo concili en res no val.

Senyor Déus, pluja,
perquè el mal fuja,
car pecat puja!
Luxúria és pecat
per tot lo món escampat;
del concili sia gitat
e tot hom d'ella enamorat.
Senyor Déus, pluja,
perquè el mal fuja,
car pecat puja!
Si al concili va ergull
ab null hom, ne en ell l'acull
tot hi serà de mal escull:
no hi cal anar Ramon Llull!
Senyor Déus, pluja,
perquè el mal fuja,
car pecat puja!
Accídia e neclijar
de far bé e destorbar
si al concili pot entrar
no hi cal null hom bo anar.
Senyor Déus, pluja,
perquè el mal fuja,
car pecat puja!
Enveja és desijament
de fembra, castell e argent;
si lo concili és son parent
tot serà vestit de nient.
Senyor Déus, pluja,
perquè el mal fuja,
car pecat puja!
Ira és trista passió,
d'ella no ve consell bo;
si al concili ha maisó
lo concili no serà bo.
Senyor Déus, pluja,
que Ramon s'huja,
car lo mal puja!

Llibre d'amic e amat

2. Les carreres per les quals l'amic encerca son amat són llongues, perilloses, poblades de consideracions, de sospirs e de plors, e enluminades d'amors.

17. Qüestió fo enfre los ulls e la memòria de l'amic, car los ulls deien que mellor cosa és veer l'amat que membrar-lo, e la memòria dix que per lo remembrament puja l'aigua als ulls e el cor s'enflama d'amor.

22. Malalte fo l'amic, e pensava'n l'amat: de mèrit lo peixia, e ab amor l'abeurava, en paciència lo colgava, d'humiliat lo vestia, e ab veritat lo metjava.

25. Cantaven los aucells l'alba, e despertà's l'amic, qui és l'alba; e los aucells feniren llur cant, e l'amic morí per l'amat, en l'alba.

35. Consirós anava l'amic en les carreres de son amat, e ensepegà e caec enfre espines, les quals li foren semblants que fossen flors, e que son llit fos d'amors.

37. Cantava e plorava l'amic cants de son amat, e deia que pus ivaçosa cosa és amor en coratge d'amador, que llamp en resplandor, ni tro en oïment; e pus viva és aigua en plor que en ondes de mar; e pus prop és sospir a amor que neu a blancor.

46. Estava l'amic tot sol, sots la ombra de un bell arbre. Passaren hòmens per aquell lloc, e demanaren-li per què estava sol. E l'amic respòs que sol fo quan los hac vists e oïts, e que d'abans era en companyia de son amat.

57. Cantava l'aucell en un ram de fulles e de flors, e lo vent menava les fulles e aportava odors de les flors. Demanava l'amic a l'aucell què significava lo moviment de les fulles ni la odor de les flors. Respòs: —Les fulles signifiquen, en llur moviment, obediència; e la odor, sofrir e malanança.

58. Anava l'amic desirant son amat, e encontrà's ab dos amics qui ab amor e ab plors se saludaren, e s'abraçaren e es

besaren. E esmortí's l'amic: tan fortament li remembraren los dos amics son amat.

69. Les vies d'amor són llongues e breus per ço cor amor és clara, pura, nédea, e vera, subtil, simple, forts, diligent, llugorosa, abundosa de novells pensaments e de antics remembraments.

151. Vedà la paraula l'amat a son amic, e aconsolava's l'amic en l'esguardament de son amat.

234. Amor és mar tribulada de ondes e de vents, qui no ha port ni ribatge. Pereix l'amic en la mar, e en son perill pereixen sos turments e neixen sos compliments.

329. Ixen amors d'amors, e pensaments de llanguiments, e plors de llanguiments; e entren amors en amors, e pensaments en plors, e llanguiments en sospirs. E l'amat esguarda's son amic, qui ha per sa amor totes aquestes tribulacions.

332. Comprà l'amic un dia de plors per un altre de pensaments, e vené un dia d'amors per altre de tribulacions; e muntiplicaren ses amors e sos pensaments.

333. Era l'amic en terra estranya, e oblidà son amat, e enyorà's de son senyor, e sa muller, e sos infants, e de sos amics. Mas retornà remembrar son amat, per ço que fos consolat e que la sua estranyedat no li donàs enyorament ni marriment.

341. Cogità l'amic en la mort e hac paor tro que remembrà la ciutat de son amat, de la qual mort e amor són portals e entrament.

363. Embriagava's l'amic de vi, qui membrava, entenia e amava l'amat. Aquell vi amarava l'amat ab sos plors e ab les llàgremes de son amic.

JORDI DE SANT JORDI

1395?-1430?

Estramps

Sus lo front port vostra bella semblança
De que mon cors nit e jorn fa gran festa,
Que remirant vostra bella figura
De vostra faç m'és romasa l'empremta
Que ja per mort no se'n partrà la forma;
Ans quant serai del tot fores d'est segle
Cels qui lo cors portaran al sepulcre
Sobre ma faç veuran lo vostre signe.

Si com l'infants quan mira lo retaule
E contemplant la pintura ab imatges,
Ab son net cor no lo'n poden gens partre,
Tant ha plaser de l'aur qui l'environa;
Atressí'm pren davant l'amorós cercle
De vostre cors, que de tants bens s'enrama,
Que mentre'l vei mas que Déu lo contemple,
Tant hai de joi per amor qui'm penetre!

Axí'm té pres e liatz en son carçre,
Amors ardents, com si'stés en un coffre
Tancat jus claus, e tot mon cors fos dintre,
On no pusqués mover per null encontre.
Car tant és gran l'amor que us hai e ferme
Que lo meu cor no's part punt per angoixa,
Bella, de vós, ans estai ferm com torres
En sol amar a vós, blanxa colomba.

Bella sens par ab la presensa noble,
Vostre bel cors, bell fec Déu sobre totes,
Gais e donós lluu pus que fina pedra,
Amorós, bels, plus penetrants que estella;

D'on quant vos vei ab les autres en flota
Les justaments si com fai lo carvoncles
Que de virtuts les fines pedres passa,
Vós etz sus lei, com l'estors sus l'esmirle.

L'amor que us hai en totes les part mascle
Quan no n'amec pus coralment nuls hòmens,
Tan fort amor, com sesta que'l cor m'obre,
No foncs jamais en nul cors d'hom ne arme.
Mas sui torbats que no fonc Aristòtills
D'amor qui m'art e mos cinc senys desfer-me,
Col monjos bos que no's part de la setla
No's part mon cors da vós tant com dits d'ungla.

Ho, cors d'honors, net de frau e delicte,
Prenets de me pietats, bela dona,
E no suffratz que-z amant vos peresca,
Pus que eu vos am mai que nulls homs afferme;
Per que us supplei a vós que etz le bells arbres
De tots los fruits on valor grans pren sombra,
Que'm retenyats en vostra valent cambra
Pus vostre sui e serai tant com visque.

Tornada

Mos rics balais, cert vos portats lo timbre
Sus quantes són el mundanal registre,
Car tots jorns naix en vós cors e revida
Bondats, virtuts, més que en Pantasilea.

L'Aimia

D'HAVER lo nom e lo dret tall d'aimia
Cert paucas són que'l pusquen bé mostrar,
Si com vós faits, dona, per triunfar,
Bella ab cors bell, linda sens maestria.
Ben haja Dieu qui mandec a natura
Que us formàs tal que a vós degués servir

E dar lausor, duptar e cartenir,
Perquè bendic mon Dieu e ma ventura.

Que'l vostra gest mostra tan gran valia
Que tot lo món devets senyorejar,
E pren-lin mal a la que vol estar
Apprés de vós per far-vos companyia,
E més que més la de xiqua estatura;
E als amadors eu los vull desmentir
Que no's tan ço d'aimia ne's deu dir,
Si com faits vós, per compas o dretura.

Alguns diran que eu hai dit gran follia
Per ço com vull lo cor d'altra jutgar,
Car cascun met son poder en amar
Femna desaut quina que's vol que sia.
Eu dic que bé, mas que fan oradura
Dir nom de rei al vassall que no u mir,
Car vos mostrats que us devon obeir
Li grane'l pauc, mirant vostra figura.

Si com l'estors ha dreta senyoria
Dessús lo poc semirle sens comptar,
Havets dret vós de tot cor subjugar
De leis, que eu dic cent tant per milloria;
Perquè defall per conexença pura
Aicell qui dits al jaspi clar saffir,
Ne la del camp rosella flor de lir,
Car Dieu no'ns fec a tots d'una factura.

Enquer diran, dones, per quina via
Hai heu volgut de tal raisó parlar,
E que perdent, me'n pert un bon callar,
Que sui petits e curt d'alfizomia.
Eu los atorc, mala dona procura
Perquè de tots se deu ensenyorir:
Vos ests senyor, eu servents, tal no quir
Perquè-s a me l'àvol tall no fa cura.

Tornada

Reina d'honor, tots homs qui bé figura
Vostre bell cors, porà ben presomir
Que havets los gets d'aimia sens mantir
E que de cert lo prets en vós s'atura.

Endreça

A, dones prous! que hajats bona ventura!
Per ço que hai dit no'm vullats maleir.
Car molts de bens fan un fait enrequir,
Aisí per vós, lei que eu am sens malura.

Dansa e Scondit

TANT són li mals que'm faits sofrir...
Com no'm cresets, dona valent
Que de cert vos am leialment
Que'l cor del cors me vol sortir?

Lo jorn que eu vi vostre cors gai
Al punt que'm mis en vós amar
Mon cor no's pot certes lunyar
De vós un punt per autra mai.
Doncs cresets me que als no desir
No tenc null autre pensament
Mas sol que eu pusca finament
A vós amar e cartenir.

Si no us dic ver que prec a Déu
Que de tal crim sia acusats
D'on prenga mort apedregats
Per mans d'un malestruc jueu;
Si que planguts d'aicest martir
No sia pas de nulla gent
Aus me maldiguen cruselment
E ma fas vengan escopir.

Si no'n dic ver, que ans de ma fi
Ab ira fort me desesper,
Que l'arma e'l cors ab Lucifer
Dimonis mil porten prop si,
E no'm puixen mai sabollir
Ans per tostemps haja turment
E no trop amic ne parent
Que'm vulla bé si no maldir.

Tornada

Castells d'honor, prec Déu m'asir
Ab tots los Sants, si coralment
No us só fis e leial servent
Que us vulh amar sens defallir.

Comiat de Mossèn Jordi, Cavaller

Sovint sospir, dona, per vós, de luny,
E sospirant va crexent ma follia
De vostre amor que en aisí fort me puny
Que'm gira gauig en gran malenconia.
Cant me record del vostre departir
Cassar me ve de vostra bella vista
E del comiat que pendrai al partir,
Tant que tristor m'assauta e'm conquista.

Certes bé sai que'm valgre més morir,
Com fec Sent Peire o sent Johan Babtista,
A cruzel mort, que en aicest punt venir
De veure tal cerimònia trista
Que del pensar ne pert sauber e seny
E vau com folls, parlant en oradura,
Ab mi me senys e si algú diu que'm seny
Eu li respon rasó fora mesura.

Mas fin amor ara ten fort mestreny,
Ans del partir no vull en tal pressura

Metre mos ulls, car no'm valdria seny,
Arts ne saber; mas pus que es ma ventura
Que així forçat m'ai de vós alunyar,
Lo comiat prenc eu per tota vegada
Del vostre cors bell e linde sens par
E lais mon cor en la vostra posada.

O Déu! e com porai de mort campar
Quant me veurai sols, ab pença torbada,
En un vexell de fust llai en la mar,
Absens de vós, lunyats d'esta encontrada.
Si recordau que'm serai tant lunyats
Del país dolç on vostre cors habita,
Ladoncs morís si com desesperatz
Malcint mi, fortuna i maladita.

A Déu, coman, bella, vostres beutats,
Vostre capteny que tots mals foragita,
A Déu coman a vós que'l nom honrats,
Que al mig del cor portats honor scrita;
A Déu coman vostre amorós esguard
Ab que'm tresqués lo cor d'on se devisa,
A Déu vos don ara, puix que eu m'apart
De la millor qui mai vestís camisa.

Tornada

Reina d'honor, heu sui en tota part,
O vius o morts vostres en tota guisa,
E prec a Déu que ja de mal no'm guard
Si eu part l'amor que ai jus mon cor assisa.

Enyorament

Enyorament, enuig, dol e desir
M'han dat assalt des que'm partí de vós
Tant fort que ja res no'm pot abellir
E tot quan veig plasent, m'és enujós.

JORDI DE SANT JORDI

Tant m'ha fet mal lo vostre departir
Que m'entrenyor com no us veig com solia
E per greu dol sovint lanç mant sospir
Si que he pahor que desir no m'aucia.

A, cors gentil! quant de vós me partí
E us viu sus alt al vostre mirador,
Morir cuidí, tant greu dolor sentí:
Axí'm destreny de son poder amor!
Mas, com forçat, jo forcí mon voler,
E pris comiat de vós, goig de ma vida,
Planyent, plorant e ab greu desesper
Maldint lo jorn de ma trista partida.

Si bé dellà visc eu ab desplaser
Per los gelos que us n'havien lunyat,
Mas sols quant eu vos podia vaher
Encontinent tot l'als m'era oblidat.
Mas ara'm veig de tot plaher absent,
Cargat d'amor e pobre de ventura
No vahent vos, que us am tan finament
E per açò morré si gaire'm dura.

Quant me record en lo departiment
E pens en vós, me semble que us veig clar;
En aquell punt me corre un sentiment
Per tot lo cors que'm fa los ulls plorar:
Puis vaig al cor e fas-li dir plorant
Ab agres veus «Ai! on és ma senyora?
On est, mon bé? per que'm muir desirant
Pel no veher», tant fortment vos anyora!

Enquer vos veig la nuit en somiant,
De que'l meu cors pren un poc de repòs,
E'l jorn aprés vau tot joiós pensant
Con són estat ab vostre donós cors.
Per que us suplic vos vaja'l cor ab me
Una hora'l jorn, per bona conaxença,

Car com més va més vos am, per ma fe,
E més m'entenc en vostra benvolença.

Tornada

Na Isabel, tant havets sobre me
Que quant no us veig visc en fort penitença,
Mas al pus tost e pus breu que poré
Iré veher la vostra continença.

Altra tornada

Car lo meu cors es tant irat ab me
E tant felló per vostra departença,
Que'm vol aucir e diu que, par sa fe,
Tro us haja vist no m'haurà benvolença.

Presoner

DESERT d'amics, de béns e de senyor,
En strany loc, en estranya encontrada,
Luny de tot bé, fart d'ennuig e tristor,
Ma voluntat e pensa cativada;
Me trob del tot en mal poder sotmès,
No veig negú que de mi s'haja cura;
Be sui guardats, enclòs, ferrats e pres
De que'n fau grat a ma trista ventura.

Eu hai vist temps que no'm plasia res,
Ara'm content de ço qui'm fa tristura,
E los grillons leugers ara preu més
Que en temps passat la bella brodadura.
Fortuna vei que ha mostrat son poder
Sus me volent que en tal punt vengut sia,
Però no cur, car hai fait mon dever
Ab tots los bons que'm trob en companyia.

Car prenc conhort de com sui presoner
Per mon senyor servir tant com podia,

D'armes sobrat e per major poder
No per deffaut gens de cavalleria.
E prenc conhort e hom no pot conquerir
Honor en res sens que treball no senta,
Mas d'altra part cuit de tristor morir
Com vei que'l món del revers se contenta.

Tots aquests mals no'm són res de soffrir
En sguard d'hu qui al cor me destenta
E'm fa tot jorn d'esperança pertir:
Com no vei res que'ns avanç d'uns espenta
En acunçar nostre desliurament;
E més com vei, ço que'ns demana sforça,
Qui no soffer algun rahonament,
De que langueix ma virtut e ma força.

Perquè no sai ne vei res al present
Que'm puixa dar en valor d'una scorça
Mas Déu tot sol, del qui prenc fundament,
E de qui fiu e ab qui mon cor s'esforça;
E d'altra part, del bon Rei liberal
Qui'm socorrà per gentilesa grande,
Cells qui'ns ha més del tot en aquest mal
Que ell me'n traurà, car sui jus sa comanda.

Tornada

Rei virtuós, mon senyor natural,
Tots al present no us fem altra demanda
Mas que us record que vostra sang real
Mai defallí a qui fos de sa banda.

Cançó d'opòsits

Tots jorns aprenc e desaprenc ensems,
E visc e muir, e fau d'enuig plaser,
Axí mateix fau de l'àvol ben temps,
E veig sens ulls, e sai menys de saber.

E no strenc res e tot lo món abraç;
Vol sobre'l cel e sol no'm moc de terra;
Açò que'm fuig incessantment acàs
E'm fuig açò que'm segueix e m'afferra.

Lo mal no'm plau e sovint lo percàs,
Am sens amor, e no crec ço que sé,
Par que somiï tot quant veig pres ma faç;
Oi he de mi e vull a altre gran bé,
E parlant call e auig menys del oir;
De l'hoc cuit no, lo ver me par falsia,
E mengs sens fam, e grat me sens pruhir,
E sens mans palp, e fau de seny follia.

Com vull muntar devall sens que no'm gir
E devallant puig corrent en alt loc,
E rient plor, e'l vetllar m'és dormir,
E quant só fret pus calt me sent que foc.
E a dret seny jo fas ço que no vull,
E perdent guany, e'l temps cuitat me tarda
E sens dolor mantes voltes me dull,
E'l simple anyell tinc per falsa guinarda.

Colgant me leu e vestint me despull,
E trop leuger tot fexuc e gran carc,
E quant me bany me pens que no'm remull,
E sucre dolç me sembla fel amarc.
Lo jorn m'és nuit e fau clar del escur,
Lo temps passat m'és present cascun hora,
E'l fort m'és flac, e'l blanc tenc molt per dur,
E sens fallir me fall ço que'm demora.

No'm part d'un loc e jamés no m'atur,
Ço que no cerc ivarçosament trob,
Del qui no'm fiu me tenc molt per segur,
E'l baix m'és alt, e'l luny me sembla prop.
E vaig cercant ço que no's pot trobar,
E ferma veig la cosa somoguda

E lo fons gorc aigua sus prat me par
E ma virtut no'm té pro ne m'ajuda.

Quant cant me par de que'm prenc udolar
E lo molt bell me sembla fer e leig,
Abans m'entorn que en loc no vull anar,
E no he pau e no tinc qui'm guerreig.
Açò'm ve tot per tal com veig entès,
De revers fets aicest món e natura
E jo qui so en lurs fets tant empès
Que m'és forçat de viure sens mesura.

Tornada

Prenga cascú ço que millor li és
De mon dit vers reversat d'escriptura,
E si'l mirau al dret e al revers
Traure poreu de l'àvol cars dretura.

AUSIÀS MARCH

1397-1459

Cants d'amor

Cant I

Així com cell qui'n lo somni's delita
e son delit de foll pensament ve,
ne pren a mi, que'l temps passat me té
l'imaginar, qu'altre bé no hi habita.
Sentint estar en aguait ma dolor,
sabent de cert qu'en ses mans he de jaure,
temps d'avenir en negun bé'm pot caure:
ço qu'és no res a mi és lo millor.

Del temps passat me trob en gran amor,
amant no res, puis és ja tot finit.

D'aquest pensar me sojorn e'm delit,
mas, quan lo perd, s'esforça ma dolor:
sí com aquell qui és jutjat a mort
e de llong temps la sap e s'aconhorta
e creure'l fan que li serà estorta
e'l fan morir sens un punt de record.

Plagués a Déu que mon pensar fos mort
e que passàs ma vida en dorment!
Malament viu qui té son pensament
per enemic, fent-li d'enuigs report,
e, con lo vol d'algun plaer servir,
li'n pren així com don' ab son infant,
que, si verí li demana plorant,
ha tan poc seny que no'l sap contradir.

Fóra millor ma dolor soferir
que no mesclar poca part de plaer
entr' aquells mals qui'm giten de saber
com del passat plaer me cov' eixir.
Llas mon delit dolor se converteix,
dobl' és l'afany aprés d'un poc repòs,
sí col malalt que per un plasentmos
tot son menjar en dolor se nodreix.

Com l'ermità qu'enyorament no'l creix
d'aquells amics qu'havia en lo món,
essent llong temps qu'en lloc poblat no fon,
fortuït cas, un d'ells li apareix
qui los passats plaers li renovella,
sí que'l passat present li fa tornar;
mas, com se'n part, l'és forçat congoixar:
lo bé, com fuig, ab grans crits mal apella.

Plena de seny, quan amor és molt vella,
absença és lo verme que la gasta,
si fermetat durament no contrasta
e creure poc si l'envejós consella.

Cant II

Pren-me'n així com al patró qu'en plaja
té sa gran nau e pens' haver castell.
Veent lo cel ésser molt clar e bell,
creu fermament d'un' àncor' assats haja.
E sent venir sobtós un temporal
de tempestat e temps incomportable:
lleva son juí que, si molt és durable,
cercar los ports, més qu'aturar, li val.

Moltes veus és que'l vent és fortunal,
tant, que no pot sortir sens lo contrari;
e cella clau, qui'ns tanca dins l'armari,
no pot obrir aquell mateix portal.
Així m'ha pres, trobant-m' enamorat,
per sobresalt qui'm ve de vós, m'aimia:
del no amar desalt ne té la via,
mas un sol pas meu no hi ser' atrobat.

Menys que lo peix és en lo bosc trobat
e los lleons dins l'aigu' han llur sojorn,
la mi' amor per null temps pendrà torn,
sol coneixent que de mi us doneu grat;
e fiu de vós que'm sabreu bé conèixer
e, conegut, no'm serà mal graïda,
tota dolor havent per vós sentida:
lladoncs veureu les flames d'amor créixer.

Si mon voler he dat mal aparèixer,
creeu de cert que Ver' Amor no'm lluny.
Pus que lo sol és cald al mes de juny,
ard mon cor flac, sens algun grat merèixer.
Altre sens mi d'açò mereix la colpa;
vullau-li mal, com tan humil servent
vos té secret, per son defalliment:
cest és Amor que mi amant encolpa!

Ma Volentat ab la Raó s'envolpa
e fan acord, la qualitat seguint,
tals actes fent que'l cos és defallint,
en poc de temps, una gran part de polpa.
Lo poc dormir magres' al cos m'acosta,
dobla'm l'enginy per contemplar Amor.
Lo cos molt gras, trobant-se dormidor,
no pot dar pas en aquest' aspra costa.

Plena de seny, donau-me una crosta
del vostre pa qui'm lleve l'amargor:
de tot menjar m'ha pres gran dessabor,
sinó d'aquell qui molt' amor me costa.

Cant IV

Així com cell qui desija vianda
per apagar sa perillosa fam
e veu dos poms de fruit en un bell ram
e son desig egualment los demanda;
no'l complirà fins part haja 'legida,
sí que'l desig vers l'un fruit se decant:
així m'ha pres dues dones amant,
mas elegesc per haver d'Amor vida.

Sí com la mar se plany greument e crida,
com dos forts vents la baten egualment,
u de llevant e altre de ponent,
e dura tant fins l'un vent l'ha jaquida
sa força gran per lo més poderós:
dos grans desigs han combatut ma pensa,
mas lo voler vers u seguir dispensa:
jo'l vos public, amar dretament vós.

E no cuideu que tan innocent fos,
que no veés vostr' avantatge gran!
Mon Cos no cast estava congoixant

de perdre lloc qui l'era delitós.
Una raó fon ab ell de sa part,
dient «qu'en ell se pren aquest' amor,
sentint lo mal e lo delit major
sí qu', ell content, cascú pot ésser fart».

L'Enteniment a parlar no venc tard
e planament desféu esta raó,
dient «que'l Cos, ab sa complexió,
ha tal amor com un llop o renard,
que llur poder d'amar és limitat,
car no és pus que apetit brutal;
e, si l'amat veen dins la fornal,
no serà plant e molt menys defensat.

»Ell és qui venç la Sensualitat:
si bé no és en ell prim moviment,
en ell està del tot lo jutjament:
cert guiador és de la Voluntat.
Qui és aquell qui en contra d'ell reny?
Que Voluntat, per qui'l fet s'executa,
l'atorg senyor, e, si ab ell disputa,
e la perfí se guia per son Seny».

Diu més avant al Cos, ab gran endeny:
«Vanament vols e vans són tos desigs,
car, dins un punt, tos delits són fastigs:
romans-ne llas, tots jorns ne prens enseny.
Ab tu mateix delit no pots haver.
Tant est grosser, qu'Amor no n'és servit.
Volenterós acte de bé és dit,
e d'aquest bé tu no saps lo carrer.

»Si bé complit lo món pot retener,
per mi és l'hom en tan sobiran bé;
e, qui sens mi esperança'l reté,
és foll o pec e terrible grosser.»
Aitant com és l'Enteniment pus clar,

és gran delit lo que per ell se pren;
e subtil art és subtil pensament
qui de fins pasts no'l jaqueix endurar.

Plena de seny, no pot Déu a mi dar
fora de vós que descontent no camp;
tots mos desigs sobre vós los escamp:
tot és dins vós lo que'm fa desijar.

Cant VII

Sí com rictat no porta béns ab si,
mas val aitant com cell qui n'és senyor,
Amor no val mas tant com l'amador:
manxa bufant orgue fals no ret fi.
Amor val poc, com tot enamorat
ha Falsedat en son pits fals enclosa
o és ajunt ab una tal esposa:
Peguea és son dret nom apellat.

Amor no pot haver desordenat
ço que Déus fa, Natura mitjançant,
car home pec no pot ser fin amant
ne lo subtil contra sa qualitat.
Mal pendrà pint' en l'aigua sa figura,
molt menys Amor pendrà lo no dispost;
ne pot estar l'aigua dins un lloc rost:
així Amor en cap d'hom foll atura.

Per ben amar, ab angoixosa cura,
en temps passat eren lladoncs volguts.
Ovidi'l prous dix qu'amor és crescuts
per altr' amor demostrant sa factura.
Verdader fon son dit e sos presics,
tant quant Amor fon prop de Coneixença;
mas, en est cas, entr' ells ha malvolença
tal, que no creu null temps sien amics.

Si fóssem nats, vós e jo, 'ntre'ls antics,
lai quan Amor amant se conqueria,
sens practicar alguna maestria,
lo vostre cor no fóra tan inics.
En vós conec gran disposició
de fer tot ço que Gentilea mana;
mas criament veig que natura 'ngana,
car viur' ab mals és d'hom perdició.

Per mal grair ne per mala saó
mon cor no pot Amor desemparar.
Devotament los me plau remembrar,
aquells passats, a qui don Déus perdó;
e, com seré traspassat d'aquest món,
lletres diran sobre la mia tomba:
Plena de seny, no tingau a gran bomba,
car per vós muir e vaig no sabent on.

Enveja 's tal que tot primer confon
a tots aquells qui ab si la s'ajusten;
los envejats un poc ne molt no gusten
aquell mal tast que'ls envejosos fon.
Tal és Amor, car jo, qui la m'ajust,
sent grans dolors dant-me folls moviments;
e vós haveu d'açò tals sentiments,
com fort destral ha de tallar molt fust.

Sí com Adam pres mal del vedat gust,
com sa muller li mostrà mal camí,
dient: «Adam, mengem d'aquest bocí
e semblarem a Déu qui és tot just»,
ne pren a mi, car mon Seny ha cregut
la Voluntat fent-li promissió,
que, bé 'nservint, aconsegria do
que per null temps tal no fon conegut.

Per mal servir no crec l'haja perdut,
car, si'ls treballs hagués soferts per Déu,

cos gloriós fóra 'n lo Regne seu;
e ja plorant sovint me trobe mut.
Si'm fos donat aquest temps en entendre
los grans secrets enclosos en Natura,
no fóra'l món cosa que'm fos escura;
dels fets divins gran part ne pogr' atendre.

Plena de seny, tot mon seny vull despendre
amant a vós, sens algun grat consegre;
e durarà fins que del riu de Segre
l'aigua corrent amunt se puga 'stendre.

Cant X

Sí com un rei, senyor de tres ciutats,
qui tot son temps l'ha plagut guerrejar
ab l'enemic, qui d'ell no's pot vantar
mai lo vencés, menys d'ésser-ne sobrats,
ans si'l matí l'enemic lo vencia,
ans del sol post pel rei era vençut;
fins qu'en les hosts contra'l rei fon vengut
un soldader qui lo rei desconfia.

Lladoncs lo rei perdé la senyoria
de les ciutats sens ulla posseir;
mas l'enemic dues li'n volc jaquir,
dant fe lo rei que bon compte'n retria
com a vassall, la renda despenent
a voluntat del desposseïdor:
de l'altra vol que no'n sia senyor
ne sia vist que li vinga 'n esment.

Llong temps Amor per enemic lo sent,
mas jamés fon que'm donàs un mal jorn
qu'en poc instant no li fes pendre torn,
foragitant son aspre pensament.
Tot m'ha vençut ab sol esforç d'un cos
ne l'ha calgut mostrar sa potent força;

los tres poders qu'en l'arma són me força:
dos me'n jaqueix, de l'altr' usar no gos.

E no cuideu que'm sia plasent mos
aquest vedat, ans n'endure de grat;
si bé no puc remembrar lo passat,
molt és plasent la càrreg' a mon dos.
Jamés vençó fon plaer del vençut,
sinó de mi, que'm plau qu'Amor me vença
e'm tinga pres ab sa 'nvisible llença
mas paren bé sos colps en mon escut!

De fet que fui a sa mercè vengut,
l'Enteniment per son conseller pres
e mon Voler per alguzir lo mès,
dant fe cascú que mai serà rebut
en sa mercè lo companyó membrar,
servint cascú llealment son ofici,
sí que algú d'ells no serà tan nici
qu'en res contrast que sia de amar.

Plena de seny, vullau-vos acordar
com per Amor vénen grans sentiments
e per Amor pot ser hom innocents;
e mostre-u jo, qui n'he perdut parlar.

Cant XI

Quins tan segurs consells vas encercant,
Cor malastruc, enfastijat de viure,
amic de plor e desamic de riure?
Com soferràs los mals qui't són davant?
Acuita't, doncs, a la Mort qui t'espera;
e per tos mals te allongues los jorns,
aitant és lluny ton delitós sojorns.
Com vols fugir a la Mort falaguera?

Braços oberts és eixid' a carrera,
plorant sos ulls per sobres de gran goig.

Melodiós cantar de sa veu oig,
dient: «Amic, ix de casa 'strangera!
En delit prenc donar-te ma favor,
que per null temps home nat l'ha sentida;
car jo defuig a tot home que'm crida,
prenent aquell qui fuig de ma rigor.»

Ab ulls plorants e cara de terror,
cabells rompent ab grans udolaments,
la vida'm vol donar heretaments
e d'aquests dons vol que sia senyor,
cridant ab veu horrible i dolorosa,
tal com la Mort crida'l benauirat,
car, si l'hom és a mals aparellat,
la veu de Mort li és melodiosa.

Bé'm meravell com és tan ergullosa
la voluntat de cascun amador.
No demanant a mi qui és Amor,
en mi sabran sa força poderosa.
Tots, maldient, sagramentejaran
que mai Amor los tendrà 'n son poder,
e, si'ls recont l'acolorat plaer,
lo temps perdut, sospirant, maldiran.

Null hom conec o don', a mon semblant,
que, dolorit per Amor, faça plànyer.
Jo són aquell de qui's deu hom complànyer,
car de mon cor la sang se'n va llunyant
per gran tristor que li és acostada;
seca's tot jorn l'humit qui'm sosté vida,
e la tristor contra mi és ardida:
en mon socors mà no s'hi trob' armada.

Llir entre cards, l'hora sent acostada
que civilment és ma vida finida.
Puis que del tot ma 'sperança 's fugida,
m'arma roman en aquest món damnada.

Cant XII

Colguen les gents ab alegria festes,
lloant a Déu, entremesclant deports;
places, carrers e delitables horts
sien cercats ab recont de grans gestes,
e vaja jo los sepulcres cercant,
interrogant ànimes infernades,
e respondran, car no són companyades
d'altre que mi en son continu plant.

Cascú requer e vol a son semblant;
per ço no'm plau la pràtica dels vius:
d'imaginar mon estat són esquius,
sí com d'hom mort de mi prenen espant.
Lo rei Xipré, presoner d'un heretge,
en mon esguard no és malauirat,
car ço que vull no serà mai finat;
de mon desig no'm porà guarir metge.

Cell Texion qui'l buitre'l menja'l fetge,
e per tots temps brota la carn de nou
—en son menjar aquell ocell mai clou:
pus fort dolor d'aquesta'm té lo setge,
car és un verm qui romp la mia pensa,
altre lo cor, qui mai cessen de rompre,
e llur treball no's porà enterrompre
sinó ab ço que d'haver se defensa.

E si la Mort no'm dugués tal ofensa:
fer mi absent d'una tan plasent vista,
no li graesc que de terra no vista
lo meu cos nu, qui de plaer no pensa
de perdre pus que lo imaginar
los meus desigs no poder-se complir,
e, si'm cové mon darrer jorn finir,
seran donats térmens a ben amar.

E si 'n lo cel Déu me vol allojar,
part veur' a Ell; per complir mon delit,
serà mester que'm sia dellai dit
que d'esta mort vos ha plagut plorar,
penedint-vos com per poca mercè
mor l'innocent e per amar-vos martre:
cell qui lo cos de l'arma vol departre,
si ferm cregués que us dolríeu de se.

Llir entre cards, vós sabeu e jo sé
que's pot bé fer hom morir per amor;
creure de mi que só en tal dolor,
no fareu molt que hi doneu plena fe.

Cant XXIII

Sobresdolor m'ha tolt l'Imaginar;
l'Enteniment no's dol ni's pot esbatre:
aitant esdolc, que l'ha calgut abatre
e mon afany, plorant, no's pot mostrar.
No trob remei, car ma dolor és tanta,
que mon Voler en parts ne tinc partit
n'en sol un lloc lo'm trobe aünit,
sinó 'n morir e viure que's decanta.

Sí com l'hom flac, qui l'és forçat triar
ab qual de dos hòmens forts s'ha combatre,
no sap pensar ab qual deja debatre;
espaordit, sos comptes no pot far:
ne pren a me, que lo viure m'espanta
e lo morir me serà gran despit;
com viure vull, la mort prenc en delit;
com vull morir, la vida tinc per santa.

Sí com aquell qui és verí donant
al mestre seu e, quan veu sa dolor,
ha pietat del mal de son senyor
e sobr' aquell vol ésser ajudant:

vós, Pensament, per qui mon seny s'absenta,
per los treballs dant-li alterament,
a son afany donau acorriment,
puis que sos mals per mitjà vostre'ls senta.

Jo contrafaç nau en golf perillant,
l'arbre perdent e son governador,
e, per contrast de dos vents, no discor;
los mariners embadalits estan,
e cascú d'ells la sua carta tempta
e són discords en llur acordament:
u volgra ser prop terra passos cent,
l'altre tan lluny com vent pot dar empenta.

Ma Voluntat, ab qu'en la mar fui mes,
fallida és, e pogra'm fer ajuda!
Ja ma Raó de son lloc és caiguda;
mos pensaments contraris m'han atès.
Ja mos desigs no saben elegir
vida ne mort, qual és la millor tria.
Natura 'n mi usa de maestria
e pren la mort, per major dan fugir.

Plena de seny, no's pot ben soferir
vida i dolor, sens pendr' algun espai.
Lo meu desig se converteix en glai,
quan me record que res vos haj' a dir.

Cant XXXIX

Sí com aquell qui per sa 'nfinitat
no pot ésser de res finit content,
sí que res fet ab algun element
en son delit no l'haurà contentat;
per imperfet lo delit mundà posa
e, si no 'n Déu, sa pensa no s'atura:
així Amor, vos amant, m'assegura;
tot lo restant del món li fa gran nosa.

En vós pensant ma Pensa és enclosa:
domda's per vós; ma Voluntat no's farta,
car ma Raó la té cativ' ab carta,
que res no vol e demanar no gosa.
No'm meravell si jo ame vós tant,
coneixent vós, veent vós e sentint.
Al meu voler lo saber lo desmint;
lo meu saber al voler va davant.

Jo'm meravell com no muir desijant,
creent en vós ésser un Paradís,
e no sé hom qu'en vós aitant sentís
que no's mostràs de vós ésser amant.
No'm llou de tant qu'en saber tots los pas,
mas per Amor he sentit més en vós:
Amor ha fet, dels seus bons servidors,
del pec sabent e franc del pus escàs.

A desijar mon desig no és llas,
mas la valor vostra més ne mereix:
en estimar hom bé no la compleix;
no us am' assats qui amant no 'sclatàs.
Ja per Amor amadors morts ne són,
e jo só viu: en fet no rest egual;
la causa d'on los venc aitant de mal
no és tan gran com la que mi confon.

E puis semblant de vós jamés no fon,
jo degra ser sus tots avantajat;
nou pensament Déu me pogr' haver dat
que no servís a pus afer al món,
sinó en vós per tots temps contemplar,
car jo'm conec que meriu vaga pensa,
e pas dolor com no'm trob tal defensa
que no'm jaquís altra pens' acostar.

Llir entre cards, ço que'm fa vos amar
no m'entra pas solament per la vista:

vostr' esperit és aquell qui'm conquista,
e com de mi no us mostrau desaltar.

Cant XLII

Ab tal dolor com l'esperit s'arranca
e dins lo cos començ' a fer camí
e roman fred lo lloc d'on parteix si,
la viva carn s'altera 'n groga i blanca:
molt e pus fort dolor mon desig sent
com ha partir de la mia 'sperança.
No és del tot, mas en lo camí's llança;
ja mon esper demostr' alterament.

No'm pens que Déu me done tal turment
que'm veja'l món, si perd lo meu desig;
no'm restarà sinó que mude llig,
car de tot l'als mon esforç és potent.
Tots los assaigs que amadors han fets,
tots me són pocs, sinó mort acordada:
si'm fall amor, no'm fall pensa irada
per castigar mos passats malifets.

Tan gran amor hauria 'n desherets,
que tal afer menys de senyal passàs!
De bé o mal se'n deu mostrar gran cas:
Amor li plau que's mostren sos secrets.
Tant mon voler Amor ha obeït,
que no'm dolrà sa perillosa plaga,
si per null temps la fama no s'apaga
com Sent Francesc de la sua jaquit.

Cant XLVI

Sí com l'hom ric qui per son fill treballa
e sol per ell vol que l'haver servesca,
e, quan la Mort vol que'l fill jorns fenesca,
dóna sos béns e tot goig de si talla,

ne pren a mi, qui llanç tot mon delit,
perdent a vós, lo goig de mon entendre,
car mon voler en als no pot empendre,
ans tota res m'és enuig e despit.

Amor a mi vostre cos ha 'bellit,
tant, que lo blanc d'altres cos negre par,
e la negror qu'en l'ull belles' apar
sembla'm vermell, mostrant cor enfortit.
A la valor la fama 's enganosa.
Aitant valeu, que no sé deïdor
que us lloàs prou, sinó vostr' amador:
aquest parlar no us faça ergullosa!

Ma vida és amarga e plorosa,
si perd a vós e per vós perd lo món.
Tots los camins d'aquests tancats me són,
si fall a mi la 'sperança dubtosa.
Lo malfactor, qui a sa 'sgleia cuita,
torbat, no's mou, si d'ella perd camí:
ne pus ne menys de cert ne pren a mi:
torbat me sent, perdent compte de fuita.

Ma voluntat ab la raó no lluita:
cascuna fa lo més de son poder.
Ma voluntat pus d'amar no pot fer;
son poder fa, e ma raó l'ha 'n cuita.
D'un ventre trist eixir m'ha fet Natura!
Per vos amar fon lo meu naiximent;
no sé als Fats com no'ls fon de present
en fer que vós d'amar haguésseu cura.

Sobresamor dos extrems me procura
e lo mig d'ells no pusc haver trobat:
d'un poc esper no puc ésser llançat
per gran desig qui li dóna mesura;
e, d'altra part, lo desig és tan gran,
que no consent ab si ferma creença

que per null temps me hajau benvolença:
de u en als vaig així redolant.

Llir entre cards, delits d'amor estan
partits segons d'on surt la voluntat;
algú d'ells mor ab lo desig finat,
altre delit perdurable roman.

(*Altra versió de la tornada*)

Llir entre cards, quan lo desig és gran,
vol compliment per fugir a dolor,
e, ja complit, ensems mor ab amor:
en mi tot sol tal ús és ja errant.

Cant XLVII

Sí col malalt que'l metge lo fa cert
que no's pot fer que de la mort escap,
si doncs no beu de verí un anap;
e lo perill no li està cobert:
ne pren a mi, qui vull experiment
molt perillós, e sens ell no pusc viure:
lo dilatar per mort se pot escriure
e tem l'assaig ab la mort egualment.

Qui és aquell estimant lo turment
e lo perill en què m'arma està,
veent-se prop d'on veu que tots perdrà
ço per què fon vengud' al món present?
En dubt' estic; la mia mà tremola,
que no consent que mate mi mateix;
e, d'altra part, mort certa no'm jaqueix:
jo'm desesper de ma 'sperança sola.

En lo meu coll veig penjar una mola
e lo gran fons on seré trabucat,
si doncs Mercè no vol haver tallat

la corda fort; mas coltell no esmola.
Mercè deman ab veu espaordida,
mostrant negar al qui per mi 's request.
Vós no guardeu que mostra pauruc gest,
mas pietat sia en vós complida.

Puis que per vós pot ésser ben sentida
la part d'amor que jo no puc mostrar,
vullau un poc la pensa empatxar
en quin fil prim penja la mia vida.
Jo són aquell qui del carçre l'han tret
i ab torbat pas va pendre cruel mort,
que no he pus remei n'altre conhort,
sinó mercè del qui'l juí ha fet.

Jamés d'amor fon un cas tan estret
com és aquell del qual no puc fugir:
per u són cert de la vida finir,
l'altr' és verí per apagar ma set.
O vós, qui sou causa de mon perill,
e fins ací no mereixeu gran culpa,
Poca Mercè per avant vos enculpa,
si per defalt d'aquella prenc eixill.

Llir entre cards, no veu degun perill
fin amador e, si'l veu, punt no'l tem:
tot cas és poc, essent lo pus extrem;
la torre gran li sembla gra de mill.

Cant LI

Qui'm tornarà lo temps de ma dolor
e'm furtarà la mia llibertat?
Catiu me trob, llicenciat d'Amor,
e, d'ell partit, tot delit m'és llunyat.
Sí col senyor avorreix lo servent,
que null càstic ne càrrec li vol dar,
així Amor me dan bandonament,
que son poder en mi no'l plau mostrar.

En ira 'stà de Déu lo pecador,
com en est món treball no li és dat;
dels béns de Déu no sia 'sperador:
no ha lloguer qui no ha treballat.
Així d'Amor qui no sent lo turment
en sos delits no's cure delitar.
Tot amador prenga 'n açò esment,
que sens tristor no's pot molt alegrar.

Dolor és gran de tot fin amador,
com desesper li és davant posat;
mas per mercè Amor l'és donador,
que d'esperar delit no és llançat.
Goig e tristor li estan de present;
esper e por lluny li volen mostrar
son mal o bé, dels quals u tostemps sent;
e lo que perd aprés torna cobrar.

Aprés lo mal, qui sent de bé sabor
no pot ser dit de tot malauirat:
lo past d'amor no ha tant' amargor
que sus tot dolç no sia estimat.
De tal sabor no'm conec sentiment
e pus amarg que fel he de gustar,
car jo sofir dolor d'enyorament
ne veig camí per algun bé 'sperar.

Qui d'Amor fuig d'ell és encontrador,
e jo qui'l cerc dins mi no l'he trobat:
en llocs lo veig difamat per traidor
e fuig de mi, qui l'he més qu'altr' honrat.
Jo no'l deman dona 'n lo món vivent,
mas que dins mi ell vulla reposar.
Sembla la Mort, qu'encalça lo fugent
e fuig d'aquell qui la vol encontrar.

Cremat vull ser d'Amor per sa calor,
car dins son foc jo'm trobe refrescat,

si com lo sant havent en Déu ardor
en son turment se troba consolat.
Tant quant Amor és fort i en mi potent,
lo seu delit prop mi sent acostar;
si'l trob escàs, altre m'ha fer content:
fora de mi mon delit he trobar.

Aitant pot fer d'Amor sa gran favor,
que bastarà fer que l'enamorat
no'l tocarà esperança ne por:
tant estarà en goig present torbat.
Jo'm só 'blidat havent tal sentiment:
propri 's a mi tal estat desijar;
a l'ignorant desig no'l ve 'n esment:
enemic és de Amor ignorar.

L'home no pot ser al món vividor,
si de humor mal serà netejat;
lo bo i el mal conserven la calor
d'hom radical, que sens ell' és gastat:
així d'Amor qui lo seu mal no sent,
no pot en ell sa passió durar;
desig lo té, qui 's de bé falliment,
i, ell bé atès, tal desig ha cessar.

Amor, Amor, jo só ver penident
com de ingrat vos he volgut reptar,
per no trobar lloc a mi convinent:
és lo defalt com jo no pusc amar.

Cant LIII

No só gosat en demanar mercè
a ma dolor que del tot m'abandon:
un poc espai la prec de temps que'm don
a poder dir lo mal que d'ella'm ve;
e, si mon cor en sa força retorn
i el torbament de l'enteniment perd,

porà saber qui d'amor no és cert
Ira i Amor com dins mi han contorn.

Sí com l'hom cec no coneix nit ne jorn,
si dels veents ell no és avisat,
d'Ira i Amor no sé qual m'ha sobrat:
haja'n avís dels qui m'estan entorn!
Jo desig molt qu'Amor m'abandonàs,
car sola és la causa de mon mal;
mas de poder Ira no té cabal
qu'en contr' Amor jo tant me rebel·làs.

E si remei a ma dolor trobàs,
fóra content, car jo'n desig eixir:
los vostres fets me fan vos avorrir,
e no's pot fer que ab vós praticàs.
Mon partiment no pusc ben acabar:
en vós pensant, estrany turment n'atenc
e, quan l'estat de mi saber m'estrenc,
lladoncs jo caic en mi pus ignorar.

No sé remei potent mi consolar,
si altr' amor nova no conseguesc.
O tu, Amor, colp vell guareix ab fresc
o de aquest me vulles bandonar;
veges mon cor en quina dolor jau:
en ton hostal no mereix tan dur llit.
Qui és l'hom viu d'on sies mills servit?
Tant és humil, qu'esforç no'l pot fer brau.

Plagués a Déu qu'ab mi mateix fes pau,
mi acordant ab cor ferm a la mort!
Jo mir e pens si'l món ha cas tan fort,
com de Amor e d'Ira 'sser esclau.
Afany té sats l'hom dos senyors sirvent
e quant més, doncs, essent ells enemics;
quan u complac, l'altr' és vers mi inics:
no sé com bast complaure'ls egualment.

O Foll' Amor, si és ver que'l jovent
és ocasió de tu a mi forçar,
si bé lo món res tant no pot prear,
vellea'm plau, qui de mals és sement.

Cant LXI

Als fats coman tot quant serà de mi,
puis só estolt de ma elecció:
mon seny és mort, a qui Déu no perdó,
puis al començ del tot me derenclí.
Ja no és temps tenir frens al voler:
malalta és ma bona voluntat
e vaig en lloc on no vull ser portat;
só descontent de tot quant pusca fer.

Sí com a l'hom no li basta poder,
paralític quan és en peus llevat,
anar al lloc on vol ésser anat,
ans cau o tort va contra son mester,
ne pren a mi, que faç lo que no'm plau
i aquell voler de la raó 's vençut
e, si'l complac, mon delit és perdut,
perquè sens cor faç quant de mi vejau.

Sí com als vents és donada la nau,
mentr' és debat als mariners vengut;
lladoncs la nau son camí ha tengut
per senya tal qual ans del contrast jau,
ne pren a mi, car mon enteniment
ha gran debat ab lo voler del cos;
determenar llur debat clar no gos:
proejant lo temps, l'apetit vaig siguent.

Passà lo temps que fui d'Amor content,
si bé tostemps sentí ses grans dolors,
mescladament, dolçors ab amargors:
creia rei ser, veent-me d'ell sirvent.

Jo fui content de sos mals sens los béns,
per bé que'l mal sens bé no pot venir;
mas jo emprenc per ell més que morir:
malament viu qui 'n mal fer no té frens.

O tu, Amor, qui ton poder m'estens
així fortment que no't pusc resistir,
ix fora mi, puis en plaer no gir
ma voluntat a fer tos manaments.
Vulles haver en contra mi ergull:
lleixa vassall qui no't vol per senyor.
Quin moviment venç aquesta dolor,
fent-me jaquir ben fer, de qui'm despull?

Aquest meu fet, bona fi no l'acull,
e lo present és ple de gran tristor;
aquesta ve del dan avenidor,
que de present li tinc davant mon ull.
Jo'l soferré si, ab cor molt ardit,
la que jo am per mi passa lo mal.
Sens penedir, qui 's penit grat no val;
lladoncs la mort no'm serà sens delit.

Llir entre cards, gran és lo meu delit,
mentre no pens lo que poríeu fer.
Tot act' és prop de lla on és poder,
si al voler governa l'apetit.

Cant LXIII

On és lo lloc on ma pensa repose?
On serà, on, que mon voler contente?
Ab escandall jo cerc tot fons, e tempte,
e port no trob on aturar-me gose.
Lo que d'abans de tot vent me guardava
és envers mi cruel plaja deserta;
vagabund vaig la casa qui m'és certa;
treball és gran en part on jo vagava.

On és aquell delit, quan jo pensava
ésser amat de la qui m'entenia?
Tot mon voler i el seu no'm defenia
d'amar, en tant com son poder bastava.
Tots los senyals qu'amor donen entendre
en ella viu, no tolent-ne la obra.
Qui és aquell qu'en amor tant descobra,
que no'm pogués d'ella sentiment pendre?

Ja res del món dolor no'm pot defendre:
perdut és ja tot lo goig de mon viure;
a mos amics de tristor puc escriure;
no'm basta temps a poder-me'n rependre.
Tant la tristor ha falagat ma pensa,
que tot m'és trist quant puc oir ne veure,
tant, que m'és greu que jo vinga en creure
que a tristor jo pusc' haver defensa.

Puis que Amor ab lo cor ferm dispensa
que sos delits follament los espere,
e per açò del món me desespere,
car sens amor tot delit m'és ofensa,
l'arma coman a Déu, lo qui l'ha feta:
lleixant lo cos desastruc per mal astre,
ja no li plau de sos volers lo rastre,
puis ab dolor viu per ell, no discreta.

Sí com l'hom vell, qui 'n son temps vid' ha feta
sats plaentment en algun' art apresa
e per fort cas aquella l'és defesa,
no sap en què son giny de viure meta,
ne pren a mi, que no sé com me visca,
perquè d'Amor me veig tancada porta
ne sé pus fer ne'l voler me comporta
que d'aquest ús per altre jo'm desisca.

O Foll' Amor, malament se arrisca
qui per virtuts vol amar nulla dona;

sa qualitat i el lloc la fan ser bona;
car, en raó, qual serà la que ·i visca?

Cant LXVII

Tant he amat que vinc en desamar,
sí com aquell qui amics ha tengut
per llur defalt havent-lo decebut,
a tot lo món se gira 'n aïrar.
La gran amor port' ab si càrrec gran:
viure no pot sens gran sosteniment;
lo seu semblant voler l'és sostinent
i, aquell no ferm, amor va tremolant.

Qui ama poc no deu ser desijant
que son amant li sia 'xtrem volent,
car poc voler no és delit sintent
del gran voler que li porta l'amant.
Sol per amor se desij' altr' amor:
per si mateix no port' altre delit;
e dóna cels dant congoixós despit
si lo delit d'ésser amat no 'ncor.

Ja en amor no seré durador,
car son afany sobrepuja'l delit.
Al temps antic jo degra 'sser eixit,
que innocent era tot amador
e l'home vell solia 'sser fadrí;
i en temps present és vell qui barba met;
cascun' amor vol temps sens cald ne fred:
jo crem d'hivern e d'estiu tremolí.

Lo meu voler en amor no fartí
d'ésser entès e molt menys satisfet;
Déu, mi e'l món a tot oblit tramet:
és molt escàs lo grat que jo'm sentí.
Per aquell preu qu'Amor deu ser venut,
jo, dant aquell, no viu que l'atengués.

Aquell voler, que sens dir és entès,
per mal sentir no fon bé conegut.

Ab gran voler de parlar, jo fui mut
per no trobar raó qui'm satisfés,
e ma dolor que bastament digués;
e per ço fui hom sens amor tengut.
Mon cor sostrac la paraula de se,
ma boca tenc aquella no passàs;
vergonya i por guardaren aquest pas
e no fon vist com d'amor tal cas ve.

Menys mal d'aquest, qual fort cor lo sosté?
Qui és aquell qui sobtós no 'sclatàs,
que sa dolor a mostrar no bastàs
e fos cregut hom sens amor e fe
e son voler vengués ésser jutjat
per saber gros e voler deslleal,
l'entendre seu, veent-lo cominal,
que fos entès d'enteniment tapat?

Si ans de temps só vist blanc e ruat
e lo meu cos mostr' haver passat mal,
serà per ço com Amor ja no val
a 'quell a qui Natur' ha 'namorat.
Per Déu, a mi solament jo no planc,
mas a cascú qui 'n tal cas se verà!
Bé són jo cert qu'en tot no'm semblarà,
car per honor jo'm sec en pus alt banc.

Amor, Amor, vostre poder és manc
o de sensgrat ésser podeu reptat:
qual d'aquests noms voleu en vós posat,
de qualsevol costat jaeu en fang.

Cant de mort

Cant IV

La gran dolor, que llengua no pot dir,
del qui's veu mort e no sap on irà!
No sap son Déu si per a si'l volrà
o si 'n l'Infern lo volrà sebollir.
Semblant dolor lo meu esperit sent,
no sabent què de vós Déus ha ordenat,
car vostre bé o mal a mi és dat:
del que haureu, jo'n seré sofirent.

Tu, Esperit, qui has fet partiment
ab aquell Cos qual he jo tant amat,
veges a mi qui só passionat:
dubtant estic fer-te raonament.
Lo lloc on est me farà canviar
d'enteniment de ço que't volré dir.
Goig o tristor per tu he jo complir:
en tu està quant Déu me volrà dar.

Pregant a Déu les mans no'm cal plegar,
car fet és tot quant li pot avenir.
Si és al Cel, no's pot lo bé 'spremir;
si en Infern, enfoll és mon pregar.
Si és així, anul·la'm l'esperit;
sia tornat mon ésser a no-res;
e majorment, si 'n lloc tal per mi és,
no sia jo de tan adolorit!

No sé què dir que'm fartàs d'haver dit;
si crit o call, no trob qui'm satisfés;
si vaig o pens, he temps en va despès;
de tot quant faç, ans de fer, me penit.
No planc lo dan de mon delit perdut,
tanta 's la por que'm ve de son gran mal:

tot mal és poc, si no 's perpetual,
e tem aquest no l'haja merescut.

Lo dan mortal és molt més que temut,
e tol-ne part ésser a tots egual.
O tu, Dolor, sies-me cominal;
encontr' oblit vulles-me ser escut.
Fir-me lo cor e tots los senys me pren:
farta't en mi, car no'm defens de tu;
dóna'm tant mal que me'n planga cascú;
tant com tu pots, lo teu poder m'estén.

Tu, Esperit, si res no te'n defèn,
romp lo costum que dels morts és comú:
torna 'n lo món e mostra qu'és de tu!
Lo teu esguard no'm donarà 'spavent.

Cant Espiritual

PUIS que sens tu algú a tu no basta,
dóna'm la mà o pels cabells me lleva;
si no estenc la mia 'nvers la tua,
quasi forçat a tu mateix me tira.
Jo vull anar envers tu a l'encontre.
No sé per què no faç lo que volria,
puis jo són cert haver voluntat franca
e no sé què aquest voler m'empatxa.

Llevar mi vull e prou no m'hi esforce;
ço fa lo pes de mes terribles colpes.
Ans que la Mort lo procés a mi cloga,
plàcia't, Déu, puis teu vull ser, que ·u vulles,
fes que ta sang mon cor amollesca:
de semblant mal guarí ella molts altres.
Ja lo tardar ta ira'm denuncia;
ta pietat no troba 'n mi que obre.

Tan clarament en l'entendre no peque
com lo voler he carregat de colpa.

Ajuda'm, Déu, mas follament te pregue,
car tu no vals sinó al qui s'ajuda
e tots aquells qui a tu se apleguen
no'ls pots fallir, e mostren-ho tos braços.
Què faré jo que no meresc m'ajudes,
car tant com puc conec que no m'esforce?

Perdona mi, si follament te parle;
de passió parteixen mes paraules.
Jo sent paor d'Infern, al qual faç via;
girar-la vull e no hi disponc mos passos.
Mas jo'm record que meritist lo Lladre:
tant quant hom veu, no hi bastaven ses obres.
Ton esperit lla on li plau espira:
com ne per què no sap qui en carn visca.

Ab tot que só mal crestià per obra,
ira no't tinc ne de res no te'n colpe.
Jo són tot cert que per tostemps bé obres
e fas tant bé donant mort com la vida.
Tot és egual quan surt de ta potença;
d'on tinc per foll qui vers tu's vol irèixer.
Amor de mal e de bé ignorança
és la raó que'ls hòmens no't coneixen.

A tu deman que lo cor m'enfortesques
sí que'l voler ab tu voluntat lligue,
e, puis que sé que lo món no'm profita,
dóna'm esforç que del tot l'abandone;
e, lo delit que'l bon hom de tu gusta,
fes-me'n sentir una poca centilla,
perquè ma carn, qui m'està molt rebel·le,
haj' afalac; que del tot no'm contraste.

Ajuda'm, Déu, que sens tu no'm puc moure,
perquè el meu cos és més que paralític.
Tant són en mi envellits los mals hàbits,
que la virtut al gustar m'és amarga.

O Déu, mercè! Revolta'm ma natura,
que mala és per la mia gran colpa;
e, si per mort jo puc rembre ma falta,
esta serà ma dolça penitença.

Jo tem a tu més que no't só amable
e davant tu confés la colp' aquesta.
Torbada és la mia esperança
e, dintre mi, sent terrible baralla.
Jo veig a tu just e misericorde;
veig ton voler qui sens mèrits gracia;
dónes e tolls de grat lo do sens mèrits.
Qual és tan just, quant més jo, que no tema?

Si Job lo just por de Déu lo premia,
què faré jo, que dins les colpes nade?
Com pens d'Infern, que temps no s'hi esmenta,
lla és mostrat tot quant sentiments temen.
L'arma, qui és contemplar Déu eleta,
en contr' aquell blasfemant se rebel·la.
No és en hom de tan gran mal estima.
Doncs, com està qui vers tal part camina?

Prec-te, Senyor, que la vida m'abreuges
ans que pejors casos a mi'n seguesquen.
En dolor visc, faent vida perversa,
e tem dellà la mort per tostemps llonga;
doncs, mal deçà e dellà mal sens terme.
Pren-me al punt que millor en mi trobes;
lo detardar no sé a què'm servesca:
no té repòs lo qui té fer viatge.

Jo'm dolc perquè tant com vull no'm puc doldre
de l'infinit damnatge lo qual dubte,
e tal dolor no la recull natura,
ne's pot asmar e menys sentir pot l'home.
E doncs açò sembl' a mi flaca 'xcusa
com de mon dan tant com és no m'espante.

Si'l Cel deman, no li do basta 'stima;
fretura pas de por e d'esperança.

Per bé que tu irascible t'amostres,
ço és defalt de nostra ignorança;
lo teu voler tostemps guarda clemença.
Ton semblant mal és bé inestimable.
Perdona'm, Déu, si t'he donada colpa,
car jo confés ésser aquell colpable.
Ab ull de carn he fets los teus judicis:
vulles dar llum a la vista de l'arma.

Lo meu voler al teu és molt contrari
e'm só 'nemic pensant-me amic ésser.
Ajuda'm, Déu, puis me veus en tal pressa.
Jo'm desesper, si los mèrits meus guardes;
jo m'enuig molt la vida com allongue
e dubte molt que aquella fenesca.
En dolor visc, car mon desig no's ferma
e ja en mi alterat és l'arbitre.

Tu est la fi on totes fins termenen
e no és fi, si en tu no termena.
Tu est lo bé on tot altre's mesura
e no és bo qui a tu, Déu, no sembla.
Al qui't complau tu aquell Déu nomenes:
per tu semblar major grau d'home'l muntes;
d'on és gran dret del qui plau al diable
prenga lo nom d'aquell ab qui's conforma.

Alguna fi en aquest món se troba,
n'és vera fi, puis que no fa l'hom fèlix.
És lo començ per on l'altra s'acaba,
segons lo cors qu'entendre pot un home.
Los filòsofs, qui aquella posaren,
en si mateixs són ésser vists discordes.
Senyal és cert qu'en veritat no's funda:
per consegüent, a l'home no contenta.

Bona per si no fon la Llei judaica;
en Paradís per ella no s'entrava,
mas tant com fon començ d'aquesta nostra:
de què's pot dir d'aquestes dues una.
Així la fi de tot en tot humana
no da repòs a l'apetit o terme,
mas tampoc l'hom sens ella no ha l'altra:
Sent Joan fon senyalant lo Messias.

No té repòs qui null' altra fi guarda,
car en res als lo voler no reposa;
ço sent cascú e no hi cal subtilesa,
que fora tu lo voler no s'atura.
Sí com los rius a la mar tots acorren,
així les fins totes en tu se n'entren.
Puis te conec, esforça'm que jo t'ame:
vença l'amor a la por que jo't porte!

E, si amor tanta com vull no m'entra,
creix-me la por, sí que tement no peque,
car, no pecant, jo perdré aquells hàbits
que són estats perquè no t'am la causa.
Muiren aquells qui de tu m'apartaren,
puis m'han mig mort e'm tolen que no visca!
O senyor Déu, fes que la vid' allargue,
puis me apar qu'envers tu jo m'acoste.

Qui'm mostrarà davant tu fer excusa,
quan hauré dar mon mal ordenat compte?
Tu m'has donat disposició recta
e jo he fet del regle falç molt corba.
Dreçar-la vull, mas he mester t'ajuda.
Ajuda'm, Déu, car ma força és flaca.
Desig saber què de mi predestines:
a tu 's present i a mi causa venible.

No't prec que'm dons sanitat de persona
ne béns alguns de Natura i Fortuna,

mas solament que a tu, Déu, sols ame,
car jo só cert que'l major bé s'hi causa.
Per conseqüent, delectació alta,
jo no la sent per no dispost sentir-la;
mas, per saber, un home grosser jutja
que'l major bé sus tots és Delitable.

Qual serà'l jorn que la mort jo no tema?
E serà quan de t'amor jo m'inflame
e no's pot fer sens menyspreu de la vida
e que per tu aquella jo menyspree.
Lladoncs seran jus mi totes les coses
que de present me veig sobre los muscles.
Lo qui no tem del fort lleó les ungles
molt menys tembrà lo fibló de la vespa.

Prec-te, Senyor, que'm faces insensible
e qu'en null temps alguns delits jo senta,
no solament los lleigs qui't vénen contra,
mas tots aquells qu'indiferents se troben.
Açò desig perquè sol en tu pense
e pusc' haver la via qu'en tu's dreça.
Fes-ho, Senyor, e si per temps me'n torne,
haja per cert trobar t'orella sorda.

Tol-me dolor com me veig perdre'l segle,
car, mentre'm dolc, tant com vull jo no t'ame
e vull-ho fer, mas l'hàbit me contrasta:
en temps passat me carreguí la colpa.
Tant te cost jo com molts qui no't serviren
e tu'ls has fet no menys que jo't demane;
per què, 't suplic que dins lo cor tu m'entres,
puis est entrat en pus abominable.

Catòlic só, mas la Fe no m'escalfa
que la fredor lenta dels senys apague,
car jo lleix ço que mos sentiments senten
e Paradís crec per Fe i raó jutge.

Aquella part de l'esperit és prompta,
mas la dels senys, rossegant-la, m'acoste.
Doncs, tu, Senyor, al foc de Fe m'acorre,
tant que la part, que'm porta fred, abrase.

Tu creïst me perquè l'ànima salve
e pot-se fer de mi saps lo contrari.
Si és així, per què, doncs, me creaves,
puis fon en tu lo saber infal·lible?
Torn' a no res, jo·t suplic, lo meu ésser,
car més me val que tostemps l'escur càrcer!
Jo crec a tu, com volguist dir de Judes
«que'l fora bo no fos nat al món home».

Per mi, segur, havent rebut batisme,
no fos tornat als braços de la vida,
mas a la mort hagués retut lo deute,
e de present jo no viuria 'n dubte.
Major dolor d'Infern los hòmens senten
que los delits de Paradís no jutgen.
Lo mal sentit és d'aquell altr' exemple
e Paradís sens lo sentir se jutja.

Dóna'm esforç que prenga de mi venja:
jo'm trob ofès contra tu ab gran colpa
e, si no·i bast, tu de ma carn te farta,
ab que no'm tocs l'esperit, qu'a tu sembla.
E, sobretot, ma Fe que no vacil·le
e no tremol la mia Esperança!
No'm fallirà Caritat, elles fermes,
e, de la carn si't suplic, no me n'oges.

O quan serà que regaré les galtes
d'aigua de plor ab les llàgremes dolces?
Contrició és la font d'on emanen;
aquesta 's clau que'l Cel tancat nos obre.
D'atrició parteixen les amargues,
perqu' en temor, més qu'en amor, se funden;

mas tals quals són d'aquestes me abunda,
puis són camí e via per les altres.

JOAN BERENGUER DE MASDOVELLES

14...—1467?

Un jorn, mirant, així com far solia

(*Complants per departiments*)

Un jorn, mirant, així com far solia,
mos ulls malvats me feren abellir
ço qui em fonc mal, e volguí'ls abstenir,
mas cascun d'ells fortment hi reestia;
d'on me covenc, en breu, fer departença,
per traure a mi d'enuig, càrrec e dan,
mas, en partint, sentí dolor molt gran,
e diguí baix: «Soberg mal me comença.»

De tristor ple, ab ferma malvolença,
Amor blasmí e mos ulls, tot ensems,
e fort blasmant, vaent-me en tals extrems,
emprí lo cor, pregant-lo em fes valença.
Mas ell, ja pres, sens gens perdre acordança
me respost prest: «En va és ton treballar.
Segueix los ulls, lleixa't de follejar,
car, seguint ells, hauràs gran benaurança.»

E jo, sentint lo mal qui en mi s'avança
pels ulls e el cor, vinguí deslliberat
que el pensament fos molt per mi pregat
que no es metés en los altres en dansa.
Mas, en pregant, sentí que era sa cura
tostemps pensar com se poguera fer
que em fes venir, com vingués al darrer,
en complir ço d'on tinc tanta tristura.

Vent-me en tal cas, per ma desaventura,
en aquest fet esmaginar volguí,
creent trobar alguna bona fi
en mon enuig e passió tan dura;
mas no fonc tal la fi com trobar creia,
ans sentí bé l'esmaginar me'n pres
en voler ço d'on seria reprès
si, per ma sort, tal deshonestat feia.

Si tot el món, ensems justat, me deia
que dec fer ço en què el voler consent,
pus Amor vol sia del tot servent
de la qui sé mon enuig li despleia,
de mon parer gens no em poria moure;
ab tot, conec que prest seré vençut,
car sol me trob, e per tants combatut
que, defensant, molt poc los poré noure.

Aquest procés molt no es trigarà a cloure,
pus que portat en tant fort punt m'han ja
que el seny, saber me fal e em fallirà,
car de mi prest crec serà'n a descloure.
Malhaja Amor, ma Sort e ma Fortuna,
mon pensament, voler, mos ulls e el cor
pels quals morré, e em morré per vil for,
abans que es gir una volta la lluna!

Jo us prec, Amor, me deixeu amar una
a qui sabeu dien Elienor,
car sens càrrec pusc haver son tresor.
Bé ho sabeu vós e persona cascuna.

HUG BERNAT DE ROCABERTÍ

Segle xv

Cant de la segona comèdia de la glòria d'amor

Amor qui ve d'un natural sospir
—Del lac del cor parteix son nodriment—
Mort m'ha sens mort, e morint puc guarir.
De nov' amor nova dolor sentia,
D'estrany turment remei estrany cercava;
Vers ne dictat d'amor fer no podia
La voluntat aquesta dolor mena.
Gran és lo dan quan lo remei no troba
Res no m'és cert sinó de major pena
Semblant dolor me fa viure en turment;
De sos afanys, enuigs e pensaments
Pense jo parlar entre la demés gent.
Dalent se alguns de dolor que no senten,
Altres, sentint l'ésser, dolre no es poden;
Molts són qui tot ho senten e no menten.
L'ànima sent dins lo cors és perduda,
Cridant la mort amb veu tan dolorosa
Com fa la mar per dos vents combatuda.
Trist, esperant lo bé que desig veure,
Lo foc m'encén amb grans flames la pensa.
Qui tal no sent ma dolor no pot creure.

JOAN ROIÇ DE CORELLA

147...?-15...?

La Balada de la Garça i la Smerla

Ab los peus verds, los ulls e celles negres,
pennatge blanc, he vista una garça,
sola, sens par, de les altres esparça
que del mirar mos ulls resten alegres;
i, al seu costat, estava una smerla,
ab un tal gest, les plomes i lo llustre,
que no és al món poeta tan illustre,
que pogués dir les llaors de tal perla;
i, ab dolça veu, per art ben acordada,
cant e tenor, cantaven tal balada:

«Del mal que pas no puc guarir,
si no em mirau
ab los ulls tals, que puga dir
que ja no us plau
que jo per vós haja morir.

»Si muir per vós, llavors creureu
l'amor que us port,
e no es pot fer que no ploreu
la trista mort
d'aquell que ara no voleu;
que el mal que pas no em pot jaquir
si no girau
los vostres ulls, que em vullen dir
que ja no us plau
que jo per vós haja morir.»

JOAN ROIÇ DE CORELLA

Oració a Nostra Senyora tenint son Fill Jesús a la falda davallat de la Creu

Ab plor tan gran que nostres pits abeura,
e greu dolor que el nostre cor esquinça,
venim a vós, Filla de Déu e Mare,
que nostra carn dels ossos se arranca
i l'esperit desija l'ésser perdre,
pensant que, mort per nostres greus delictes,
ver Déu e hom, lo Fill de Déu e vostre
jau tot estès en vostres castes faldes.

Ab fonts de sang rega lo verge estrado
on xic infant lo bolcàs ab rialles:
i els vostres ulls estil·len tan gran aigua,
que pot lavar les sues cruels nafres,
fent ab la sang un engüent e coliri
d'infinit preu, per llevar-nos les taques
que el primer hom, com a vassall rebel·le
nos ha causat ensems ab nostra culpa.

Lo vostre cor, partit ab forta escarpra,
de gran dolor nos mostrà tan greu plànyer,
que els serafins ensems ab tots los àngels,
mirant a vós, planyent, aprenen dolre.
Plany-se lo món, cobert d'aspre celici:
crida lo sol, plorant, ab cabells negres,
e tots los cels, vestits ab negra sarja,
porten acords al plant de vostra llengua.

«O Fill, tot meu, oïu a mi que us parle,
que en lo dur pal haveu oït lo lladre!
Puix no voleu que de present jo muira,
estiga ab vós tancada en lo sepulcre!
Jo us acollí en lo meu verge ventre:
ara vós, Fill, rebeu-me dins la tomba,
que no es pot fer entre els vius jo converse,
puix que, vós mort, és ja ma vida morta.

»En major lloc no penseu jo m'estenga
del que vós, Fill, pendreu dins en la pedra:
giteu a mi primera en lo marbre,
que no us és nou dormir en los meus braços!
Cobrir-vos ha lo mantell que a mi encobra;
e si no us par vos baste tal mortalla,
la mia carn que, viu, haveu vestida
no us sia greu que, mort, encara us cobra.»

Mare de Déu, humil tostemps e verge,
llum d'aquest món, del cel lluent carboncle!
mirra portam de nostra vida amarga,
dolent-nos fort com havem fet ofensa
al vostre Fill, Déu e Senyor benigne;
encens tenim que nostre cor perfuma,
que som contents se faça el sacrifici
de nostra carn, si vostre Fill ho mana.

E no gosam les nostres mans estendre
per a untar del vostre Fill insigne
lo cos sagrat, mas preneu aquest bàlsem,
que sens temor nostra llengua el confessa
Redemptor Déu, a Déu plaent oferta,
qui al terç jorn traent del fondo carçre
los sants catius, lo veureu dins la cambra
més clarejat que el sol alt en lo cercle.

Tragèdia de Caldesa

Mouràs corrent — la tremuntana ferma,
e tots ensems — los cels cauran en trossos;
tornarà fred — lo foc alt en la spera,
i, en lo més fons, — del món veuran lo centre;
tinta de sang — se mostrarà la lluna,
e tot escur — lo sol perdrà la forma,
ans que jamés — de mi siau servida;
e lo meu cos, — del prim cabell fins l'ungla,

e, tornat pols, — no prenga sepoltura,
ni reba·l món — tan celerada cendra;
ni·s puga fer — algú gire la llengua
a dir: «Bon pos» — a l'ànima maleita,
si Déu permet — mos ulls vos puguen veure.
E, si és ver — vos digui mai Senyora,
nos trobe en l'any — lo jorn de ma naxença,
mas lo meu nom, — a tots abominable,
no sia al món — persona que l'esmente;
ans, del tot ras — de les penses humanes,
sia passat — com un vent lo meu ésser;
tinguen per fals — lo que fon de mon viure,
e res de mi — en lo món no hi romangue;
e, si per cas, — del meu cos gens ne resta,
sia menjar — als animals salvatges:
prenga'n cascú — la part d'una centilla,
perquè en tants locs — sia lo meu sepulcre,
que'l món finit, — nos trobe la carn mia,
ni·s puga fer — que mai jo ressucite.

Desengany

Los qui amau, — preneu aquesta cendra
sobre lo cap, — que no perdau l'arbitre:
Amor és tal, — que si us obre la porta,
tart s'esdevé — que pels altres la tanque.
La part del mur — que'l fort enemic trenca,
mostra camí — per on se puga vençre;
e som tan folls — los ferits d'esta fleixa,
que tots pensam — tenir un esmaradge
ab tal virtut, — que'ns fa trobar la senda,
vedant aprés — algun altre no hi passe.

Ama Narcís — a si mateix, en l'aigua;
Pigmaleon — volc bé una imatge
qu'ell, amb ses mans, — esculpi en lo marbre;
aquests dos sols — no els calia gens tembre

de lurs amants — altri n'hagués triunfo.
Però jo viu — mon luminós carboncle,
ab gran repòs, — en mans del qui amava,
fer-li present — de festa tan ben colta,
que no hi romàs — d'amor una centilla
no s'acabàs, — venint al darrer terme.

Fi

E no us penseu — que parle gens en somnis;
que no és tan clar — lo sol alt en lo cercle,
com jo viu clar — aquest tan gran oprobi;
e, del recort, — tan gran dolor m'assombra,
que'l meu cor trist — en quatre parts vol rompre.

Requesta d'amor

Una sou vós — lo remei de ma vida,
sola en lo món — que mon voler adora,
on mos desigs — speren fi complida.
La gran amor, — me força i em convida
a vos servir, — i pendre per senyora.
Del que volent vos servir no reposa,
ço és, sens ventura, espera la fi;
lo que es prest a vós servir,
lo nom no us fretura a dir,
cors de que vós sou la vida.
A dos departir, units d'un voler,
no hi baste poder, sinó lo morir;
lo que podeu entendre
sens paraules comprendre.
Ma libertat — ves vostres peus se lança,
l'enteniment del qual
jamai de vós se parteix.
O cor, i bé em vols mal,
que em fas pessar pena mortal!
Pena pas, no menys — del que vós sabeu!
Feu-me socors e no us anugeu,

que, ans del temps, vós e jo serem
ensems, e parlarem
del que are dir no gose;
com serem en loc — que ningú no no·ns oge.

PERE TORROELLA

1430?-1501?

No sent ne veig...

No sent ne veig ni oic ne conec res,
ans m'és semblant que en aquest món no sia,
volent fer juí ab la raó demès,
que com més pens més mon seny se desvia.
E io no só o no es pot fer que sia
res del passat semblant del que és present;
ans só estrany, mir tot quant fa la gent
e mon semblant representa follia.
Per sentiment he perdut lo sentir,
que el pler no em val ne em mou malenconia
mes noves són variant de partir,
mostrant que fon d'aquest meu dan la guia.
Entre lo bé e mal mon juí detria
sol me regesc pel sentit de natura;
apoderat de dolor perdí cura
e mon semblant representa follia.
Sol bast sentir que he mon desig perdut
per desijar lleixant la fantasia,
car acte tal que em fa devenir mut
mirant aquell al record que solia.
Llavors somnií despert, e que dormia
ab dret sentir, plorant, conec que só,
e despertat retorn sense passió,
que mon semblant representa follia.
Los ulls, lo cor, lo seny e lo voler,
e el pensament, que amor dins ell nodria,

van esperduts, abstrets de llur poder
seguint amor no sabent per qual via.
E si per cas negú d'ells se canvia,
volent mostrar de mon estat l'encontre,
tots los restants ensems venien contra,
e mon semblant representa follia.

Tornada

Bé de mos mals que per veure tenia
los béns quals sent han mon seny desviat,
dels dans preniu, no de mi, pietat,
pus mon semblant representa follia.

PERE SERAFÍ

Segle XVI

Cançó

Si em lleví de bon matí
i aní-me'n tota soleta
i entrí-me'n dins mon jardí
de matinet,
l'aire dolcet, la fa rira riret
per collir la violeta:
ai lasseta, què faré
ni què diré?
Valga'm Déu que estic dolenta,
l'Amor és que m'aturmenta.

A mon dolç amat trobí
adormit sobre l'herbeta,
despertà's dient així,
de matinet,
l'aire dolcet, la fa rira riret,
si vull ésser sa 'mieta:
ai lasseta, què faré
ni què diré?

CANÇONER ANÒNIM

Valga'm Déu que estic dolenta,
l'Amor és que m'aturmenta.

Jo li en responguí que sí,
mas que no fos sentideta,
ai que tant pler mai prenguí,
de matinet,
l'aire dolcet, la fa rira riret,
que restí consoladeta:
ai lasseta, què faré
ni què diré?
Valga'm Déu que estic dolenta,
l'Amor és que m'aturmenta.

CANÇONER ANÒNIM

Els estudiants de Tolosa

Mitjans del segle XIV

A la vila de Tolosa n'hi ha tres estudiants
que segueixen els estudis per a ser-ne capellans.
Ja n'encontren tres donzelles que els van conversejant,
comencen a dî'ls-hi mofes, mofes els hi van tornant.
Les ninetes en són sardes, el Batlle van a trovâ'n:
—Vingui, vingui, senyor Batlle, a agafar tres estudiants.
—Com los agafarem, senyores, si no tenen culpa gran?
—Que els agafin i els-e lliguin que ja ne tenen bastant.—
Ja els agafen, ja els-e lliguen i a la presó els van menant.
El més petit sempre plora, el mitjancer ja no tant.
El més gran los aconsola: —No en ploreu los meus germans,
que en tenim un germà a França, servidor del rei d'Orlan,
que quan ell ho arribi a sebre aquí vindrà a deslliurâ'ns.—
No passa l'espai d'una hora que els hi donen paper blanc,
no passa l'espai d'una hora que a la forca els van penjant,
no passa l'espai d'una hora que el seu germà va arribant:
—No em diria, l'hostalera, allà tanta gent què fan?
—Allà pengen i despengen tres pobrets estudiants

que en seguien els estudis per a ser-ne capellans.
Ja en baixa d'un cavall negre, ja en puja en un cavall blanc;
de tan de pressa que anava les pedres van foguejant.
Encontra el Batlle i el Jutge que venien de penjâ'ls:
—No em diria el senyor Jutge, què s'han fet los estudiants?
—Els estudiants són a la forca que no en pateixen cap dany.
—No em diria el senyor Jutge què n'han fet dels meus ger-
[mans?
—Ment pel coll, el cavallero, que aquells no te són germans.
—Ment pel coll, el senyor Jutge, que tots tres me són germans.
A la vila de Tolosa de mi se recordaran.—
Se desenvaina l'espasa i venta cop al dogal,
els hi fa un petó a les galtes: —Déu vos perdó, els meus ger-
[mans!
A la vila de Tolosa de mi se recordaran,
que de la sang de les dones los carrers se rentaran
i dels caps de los seus homes muralles s'en formaran.

El guerrer mal ferit

Finals del segle XVI

Don Ramon s'ha mort al camp, don Joan ve de batalla.
La mare l'en veu venir per un camp que verdejava:
—¿D'a on veniu, el meu fillet, d'a on veniu, el meu fill, ara?
—Mare, vinc de cal barber que una sangria m'ha dada.
—Malhaja lo tal barber, quina sangria t'ha dada!
—Mare, no digueu això, vós mateixa me'n sou causa.
No teníeu sinó un fill i aqueix feu anar en batalla,
a la batalla del rei, n'hi van molts, no en tornen gaires.
Trist de mi, si en só tornat amb cinquanta-nou llançades:
el xivall porta les nou, trist de mi, porto les altres.
Mare, aneu-me'n a fer el llit, allà on solia jaure,
no me'l fàsseu gaire bé que no hi dormiré pas gaire,
moriré a la mitja nit, mon xivall a punta d'alba.
En a mi m'enterrareu a l'altar de Santiague,
el xivall l'enterrareu a la porta dels claustres;
a desobre del xivall posareu les meves armes.
La gent que iran i vinran: —«¿De qui són aquestes armes?»
I vós, mare, responreu: —«Del meu fill, mort en batalla.»—

Escrivaneta

Segle XVI

TAN petita l'han casada la filla del Mallorquí,
tan petita l'han casada, no se sap calçar i vestir.
Adéu, Escrivaneta, valenciana gentil,
son marit la n'ha deixada perquè no l'en sap servir;
se n'és anat a la guerra, de set anys no vol venir.
Al cap d'aquesta setena el cavaller fou aquí;
se posa a trucar la porta: —Escrivana, baixa a obrir.—
La seva mare fou prompta, promptament lo baixa a obrir.
—Com ne baixarà l'Escriva si no n'és en tot per 'quí?
El rei moro se l'ha enduda, el rei moro Xalandrí.
—M'aniré de porta en porta tot vestit de pelegrí,
m'aniré de porta en porta tot captant del pa i del vi.—
El primer castell que troba és del moro Xalandrí;
allí veu l'Escrivaneta, la veu que es pentina allí,
la pinteta n'és de plata, l'escarpidor n'és d'or fi.
—Feu-ne caritat, senyora, a un pobre pelegrí.
—Com voleu que jo us en faci, si tan sols no en tinc per mi?—
El rei moro és a la cambra que tot això va sentir:
—Fes-li caritat, Escriva, a aquest pobre pelegrí.—
Mentre baixava de l'aigua, ella llança un gran sospir.
—Per què en sospireu, Escriva? Que em coneixeu en a mi?—
—En la cara moreneta pareixeu el meu marit.—
Mentre li dóna de l'aigua l'anell li salta del dit:
—Què n'és això, Escrivaneta, que vos ha saltat del dit?
—És l'anell que me posàreu del vostre en al meu dit.—
—Voldríeu venir, Escrivana, voldríeu venir amb mi?
—Si pot ésser, volgués Déu que ja fóssim pel camí.—
Ja n'entren a l'escriptori, or i plata s'emportí.
A les dues de la tarda, el rei moro es despertí,
surt el cap a la finestra, els veu per la mar lluir:
—Calla, calla, Escrivaneta, ai traïdor del pelegrí!

La presó de Lleida

Segle XVII

A la presó de Lleida tots los presos hi són,
cent i cinquanta presos,
petita bonica,
canten una cançó,
lireta liró.
Dama se'ls escoltava detràs d'un finestró;
los presos se n'adonen, en paren la cançó:
—Per què no en canteu, presos, per què no en canteu, no?
—Com cantarem, Senyora, si estem en greu presó,
sense menjar ni beure sinó una volta al jorn,
i encara aquesta volta ens en donessin prou?
—Canteu, canteu, los presos, que ja us en trauré jo;
aniré en el meu pare a demanar-li un do.
—Ai pare, lo meu pare, me'n voleu donar un do?
—Ai filla Margarida, quin do vols que jo et do?
—Ai pare, lo meu pare, les claus de la presó.
—Ai filla Margarida, això no ho faré jo;
demà serà dissabte, els penjarem a tots.
—Ai pare, lo meu pare, no pengeu l'aimador.
—Ai filla Margarida, qui és lo teu aimador?
—Ai pare, lo meu pare, és el més alt i ros.
—Ai filla Margarida, serà el primer de tots.
—Ai pare, lo meu pare, pengeu-me a mi i tot.
—Ai filla Margarida, això no ho faré jo.
Les forques són de plata, els dogals ne són d'or,
a cada cap de forca poseu-hi un ram de flors;
la gent quan passaran sentiran gran olor,
diran un parenostre per lo pobre aimador.—

El testament d'Amèlia

Segle XVII

MALALTA n'està l'Amèlia, la filla del rei francès.
Ja la van a veure comtes, comtes i barons i reis.

Ai, que el meu cor se'm nua
com un ram de clavells!

També hi va la seva mare, hi va en companyia d'ells:
—Què és estat això, ma filla, que vós malalta n'esteu?
—Ai! el mal que jo tinc, mare, estona ha que me'l sabeu.
Metzines me n'haveu dades; mare, morta me veureu.
—Confesseu, la meva filla, i després combregareu;
acabat de combregar-ne, vós testament ne fareu:
—Tres castells ne tinc a França, tots tres penso que són meus.
Lo primer lo deixo als pobres, als pobres i als romeus;
lo segon deixo a los frares que enterraran lo cos meu;
lo terç lo deixo a Don Carlos, a Don Carlos, germà meu.
La creu i les arrecades us deixo, Mare de Déu;
tot l'or i tota la plata us deixo, Senyor Déu meu.
—I a mi, la meva filla, i a mi què em deixareu?
—Vos deixaré prou i massa, que us deixaré l'espòs meu,
que el tingau tancat en cambra, governant-lo com soleu.

El comte Arnau

Segle XVII

—TOTA sola feu la vetlla, muller lleial?
Tota sola feu la vetlla, viudeta igual?
—No la faig jo tota sola, comte l'Arnau;
no la faig jo tota sola, valga'm Déu, val!
—Qui teniu per companyia, muller lleial?
Qui teniu per companyia, viudeta igual?

—Déu i la Verge Maria, comte l'Arnau;
Déu i la Verge Maria, valga'm Déu, val!
—A on ne teniu les filles, muller lleial?
a on ne teniu les filles, viudeta igual?
—A la cambra són que broden, comte l'Arnau;
a la cambra són que broden, valga'm Déu, val!
—Me les deixaríeu veure, muller lleial?
me les deixaríeu veure, viudeta igual?
—Massa les espantaríeu, comte l'Arnau;
massa les espantaríeu, valga'm Déu, val!
—A on teniu les criades, muller lleial?
a on teniu les criades, viudeta igual?
—A la cuina són que renten, comte l'Arnau;
a la cuina són que renten, valga'm Déu, val!
—A on ne teniu els mossos, muller lleial?
a on ne teniu els mossos, viudeta igual?
—En el llit són que reposen, comte l'Arnau;
en el llit són que reposen, valga'm Déu, val!
—Pagueu-los bé la soldada, muller lleial,
pagueu-los bé la soldada, viudeta igual.
—Tant prest com l'hauran guanyada, comte l'Arnau;
tant prest com l'hauran guanyada, valga'm Déu, val!
—Per on heu entrat vós ara, comte l'Arnau?
Per on heu entrat vós ara, valga'm Déu, val?
—Per la finestra enreixada, muller lleial;
per la finestra enreixada, viudeta igual.
—Ai que me l'haureu cremada, comte l'Arnau!
ai que me l'haureu cremada, valga'm Déu, val!
—Solament no l'he tocada, muller lleial;
solament no l'he tocada, viudeta igual.
—Què és això que us ix per la boca, comte l'Arnau?
Què és això que us ix per la boca, valga'm Déu, val?
—Males paraules que he dites, muller lleial;
males paraules que he dites, viudeta igual.
—Què és això que us ix pels ulls, comte l'Arnau?
—Què és això que us ix pels ulls, valga'm Déu, val?
—Males mirades que he dades, muller lleial;
males mirades que he dades, viudeta igual.

—Què és això que us ix per les orelles, comte l'Arnau?
Què és això que us ix per les orelles, valga'm Déu, val?
—Són flames de foc que em cremen, muller lleial;
són flames de foc que em cremen, viudeta igual.
—Què és això que us surt per les mans, comte l'Arnau?
Què és això que us surt per les mans, valga'm Déu, val?
—Les coses mal manejades, muller lleial;
les coses mal manejades, viudeta igual.
—Què és això que us surt pels peus, comte l'Arnau?
Què és això que us surt pels peus, valga'm Déu, val?
—Els mals passos que donava, muller lleial;
els mals passos que donava, viudeta igual.
—Què és això que hi ha a l'entrada, comte l'Arnau?
què és això que hi ha a l'entrada, valga'm Déu, val?
—És el cavall que m'espera, muller lleial;
és el cavall que m'espera, viudeta igual.
—Baixeu-li grana i civada, comte l'Arnau;
baixeu-li grana i civada, valga'm Déu, val!
—No menja gra ni civada, muller lleial;
sinó ànimes condemnades, viudeta igual.
—Quina hora és que el gall ja canta, muller lleial?
Quina hora és que el gall ja canta, viudeta igual?
—Les dotze hores són tocades, comte l'Arnau;
les dotze hores són tocades, valga'm Déu, val!
—Vos dic que no em feu l'oferta, muller lleial;
que com més me feu l'oferta més pena em dau.
—Per què sou condemnat ara, comte l'Arnau?
Per què sou condemnat ara, valga'm Déu, val?
—Per soldades mal pagades, muller lleial;
per soldades mal pagades, viudeta igual.
—Ara per la despedida, muller lleial,
ara per la despedida dem-nos les mans.
—Massa me les cremaríeu, comte l'Arnau;
massa me les cremaríeu, valga'm Déu, val!

El rei mariner

Segle XVII

A la vora de la mar hi ha una donzella
que broda d'un mocador la flor més bella;
com ne fou a mig brodar li faltà seda.
En veu venir un mariner que el mar navega:
—Mariner, bon mariner, si'n porteu seda?
—De quin color la voleu, blanca o vermella?
—Vermelleta la vull jo, que és millor seda:
vermelleta la vull jo, que és per la Reina.
—Pugeu a dalt de la nau, triareu d'ella.—
Com dalt de la nau va ser la nau féu vela;
mariner es posa a cantar cançons novelles,
amb el cant del mariner s'ha adormideta,
i amb els aires de la mar ella es desperta!
—Mariner, bon mariner, torneu-me en terra,
que los aires de la mar m'en donen pena.
—Això sí que no ho faré, que heu de ser meva.
—De tres germanes que som só la més bella;
l'una és casada amb un duc, l'altra és princesa,
i jo, pobreta de mi, marinereta!
L'una en porta vestit d'or, l'altra de seda,
i jo, pobreta de mi, de sargil negre.
—No en sou marinera, no, que en sereu reina,
que jo só lo fill del Rei de l'Anglaterra.
Set anys ha que vaig pel món per vós, donzella.

La dama d'Aragó

Segle XVII

A Aragó n'hi ha una dama que és bonica com un sol;
té la cabellera rossa, li arriba fins els talons.
Ai, amorosa Anna Maria,
robadora de l'amor!

Sa mare la pentinava amb una pinteta d'or,

sa germana els hi trenava els cabells de dos en dos;
cada cabell una perla, cada perla un anell d'or.
Son germà se la mirava amb un ull molt amorós,
se la mira i se l'emporta a la fira d'Aragó.
De tants anells que li compra li cauen del mocador.
—Germà, germà, anem a missa, anem a missa major.—
Per prendre l'aigua beneita portava un canonet d'or.
Quan és al mig de l'església els altars llueixen tots.
Les dames quan la van veure tot seguit li han fet lloc,
les dames seien en terra, i ella en cadireta d'or.
Capellà que en diu la missa n'ha perduda la lliçó,
escolà que l'ajudava no n'hi sap tornar raó.
¿De qui és aquella dama que llansa tanta esplendor?
N'és filla del rei de França, germana del d'Aragó;
i si acàs no em voleu creure, mireu-li lo sabató,
veureu les tres flors de lliri i les armes d'Aragó.

La guerra dels segadors

Segle XVII

CATALUNYA, comtat gran, qui t'ha vista rica i plena!
Ara el Rei, nostre senyor, declarada ens té la guerra.
Lo gran comte d'Olivar sempre li burxa l'orella:
—Ara és hora, nostre rei, ara és hora que fem guerra.—
Contra de los catalans ja veieu quina n'han feta:
seguiren viles i llocs fins al lloc de Riudarenes,
n'han cremada una església que Santa Coloma es deia,
cremen albes i casulles, los calzes i les patenes,
i el Santíssim Sacrament, alabat sigui per sempre.
Mataren un sacerdot mentre que la missa deia,
mataren un cavaller a la porta de l'església,
don Lluís de Furrià, i els àngels li fan gran festa.
El pa que no era blanc deien que era massa negre,
lo daven a-n els cavalls sols per assolar la terra,
Lo vi que no era bo engegaven les aixetes,
lo tiraven pels carrers sols per a regar la terra;
a presència dels seus pares deshonraven les donzelles.

En daven part al virrei   del mal que aquells soldats feien:
—Llicència els he donat jo,   molta més se'n poden prendre.—
A vista de tot això   s'és esvalotat la terra.
Entraren a Barcelona   mil persones forasteres,
entren com a segadors,   com érem a temps de sega.
De tres guàrdies que n'hi ha,   ja n'han morta la primera,
en mataren el virrei   a l'entrant de la galera;
mataren els diputats   i els jutges de l'Audiència.
Anaren a la presó,   donen llibertat als presos.
Lo bisbe els va beneir   amb la mà dreta i esquerra:
—On és vostre capità,   on és la vostra bandera?—
Varen treure el bon Jesús   tot cobert amb un vel negre:
—Aquí és nostre capità,   aquí és nostra bandera.
A les armes, catalans,   que us han declarat la guerra!

Bach de Roda

Segle XVIII

Ai, adéu, ciutat de Vic,   bé en mereixes ser cremada;
has fet penjar un cavaller,   el més noble de la plana,
per nom s'anomena Bach   i al Bach de Roda s'estava.
Valeu-nos, Mare de Déu,   la del Roser i la del Carme,
la del Carme i la del Roser,   Mare de Déu, ajudeu-nos.
A les nou hores de nit   el destacament marxava,
se'n van dret al Colom gros,   el terme de Roda estava.
Quan n'arribaren allí,   ells a la porta trucaven:
—Està ací un cavaller?   Voluntaris el demanen.
—No està ací aquest cavaller,   al Mas-Nou de Roda estava.—
Quan ne foren en el Mas   allí a la porta trucaven:
—No està ací aquest cavaller,   que al torrent té la posada.—
Quan ne foren al torrent   allí a la porta trucaven:
—Dieu a-n el Bach que surti   que el Vallfogona el demana.
—Déu los guard, los meus amics,   benvinguts sieu vosaltres.
—No som, no, els vostres amics,   ben contraris us som ara.—
Quan en Bach va sentir això: —Trist de mi! penjat som ara.
—Anem a avisar el Domer,   el Domer de Santa Clara,
que vingui a confessar en Bach,   que sigui el peu de l'escala.

Anem a avisar fusters, fusters i mestres de cases;
que vagin a fer les forques allí a les Davallades.—
El Domer fa de resposta que el seu cor no li abastava.
Els fusters fan de resposta: —No tenim vigues serrades.—
Va respondre el General: —Farem aterrar les cases.—
Van a visitar el Domer, Domer de les Davallades,
que vingui a confessar el Bach que la vida se li acaba.
—Del que et suplic, General, si em daràs terra sagrada.
—No te n'espantis, no, Bach, que ja te'n serà donada.—
Quan és al peu de la forca treu una capsa de plata;
diu que la facin a mans del Pare Rafel del Carme:
—Ell era el meu confessor, la tindrà per recordança.—
Dues filles que tenia als peus se li agenollaven:
—Aixequeu-us, les meves filles, de Déu sigueu perdonades:
no em maten per ser traïdor ni tampoc per ser cap lladre,
sinó perquè he volgut dir: que visca tota la pàtria.

La filla del marxant

Segle XVIII

La filla del marxant diuen que és la més bella.
No és la més bella, no, que altres n'hi han sense ella.
La virondon!
La virondon, quina donzella!
La virondon!
La'n treuen a ballar a la dansa primera.
El ballador li diu: —Amor, sou pesanteta.
—I en què m'ho coneixeu? —Bé és prou de bon conèixer:
la cintureta us creix i el davantal s'aixeca
I el faldellí vermell d'un pam no us toca a terra.
Voleu venir, l'amor, anirem a la font bella?
Tota dona que hi beu queda deslliuradeta.—
Quan ne van ser allà la font torna eixuteta.
De sentiment que en té l'infant li'n cau en terra.
—Colliu això, don Joan, tireu-lo a la ribera.
—Tirau-li vós, amor, que no són coses meves.—
El pecat és tan gran l'aigua torna vermella.

Los pescadors del Rei pesquen a la ribera.
N'han pescat un infant bonic com una estrella.
De tan bonic que n'és lo porten a la reina.
—Calleu, calleu, amor, que en sereu presonera.
A la presó del rei vós sereu la més bella.
Vos hi estareu set anys no en veureu cel ni terra.—
Al cap de los set anys treu lo cap en reixeta.
La veu un passejant que s'ha enamorat d'ella:
—Torneu demà el matí: la veureu vestideta,
vestideta de blanc amb lo butxí darrera,
un Sant Crist a les mans, cantant lo miserere.—
Quan ella va passar davant de casa seva,
en va arrencar un gran crit: —Valga'm Déu, mare meva,
si m'haguésseu casat al cap de la quinzena!

El rapte

Segle XVIII

A la torre xica, a la torre gran,
ja n'hi ha una Pepa que l'estimen tant;
bonica és la rosa, més bonic el ram;
de tant que l'estimen no l'en casaran.
Ja en va a la riera rentar un davantal
per anar bonica el dia de Nadal.
Mentre l'en rentava passa el seu galant:
—Què hi fas aquí, Pepa, què hi fas aquí tant?
—Rento les faldilles, també el davantal,
per anar bonica el dia de Nadal.—
L'agafa i l'en puja a dalt de cavall;
la sella n'és verda, el cavall n'és blanc.
Els carrers de Lleida passa sospirant:
—Per què plores, Pepa, per què en plores tant?
—Ploro pels meus pares i pels meus germans,
que són gent sentida, d'això moriran.
—Si es moren que es morin, ja els enterraran,
les tombes són noves, les estrenaran;
cada cap de tomba un ram posaran;
capellans i frares per ells resaran.

L'hereu de la forca

Segles XVIII-XIX

Quan jo n'era petitet la mare me'n regalava,
me'n donava alguns ouets i alguna nou mastegada;
me'n posava sobre el llit, quan dormia no plorava.
Als set anys filava al torn, als nou ja cardava llana,
als dotze em poso a robar, cosa que la llei no mana.
Als divuit a confessar a un frare que predicava;
al ser a mitja confessió diu mal dels meus camarades.
Un dia, davant de Déu, jo li tiro escopetada:
un dia, davant de Déu, mentre la missa resava.
—Agafeu-lo, que es traïdor, que l'església no li valga.
—No em valga l'església, no, valguin les relíquies santes.—
Jo d'això no em vaig fiar, em valguin les meves cames.
I saltava una paret, set canes ne té d'alçada,
tot això no era res, baix n'hi havia quatre d'aigua.
Sota un rodet de molí jo la vida me campava.
A les dotze de la nit ja trucava ca ma mare:
—D'on veniu vós, lo meu fill? Males ordres corren ara;
diu que heu mort un sacerdot mentre la missa resava.
—Mare, no cregueu això, mireu que us han enganyada,
que si així fos veritat jo no fóra dintre Espanya.—
Estant en eixes raons una carta els arribava,
la carta era per ell, el sobre escrit per sa mare,
que l'en volien fer hereu de la plana de Cerdanya:
«I aquí dalt en un fossar tens una casa parada,
una casa amb tres pilans sense sostre ni teulada,
que de dia hi toca el sol i de nit la lluna clara,
vingui d'allà on vingui el vent sempre et tocarà a la cara.»

Muntanyes del Canigó

Segles XVIII-XIX

Muntanyes del Canigó són fresques i regalades,
més que més ara aquest temps que les aigües són gelades.

Tres mesos m'hi vaig estar sens veure persona nada,
sinó un trist rossinyolet que a l'eixir del niu cantava.
Mes ara em penso que és mort, tres dies ha que no canta.
M'ha pres gran enyorament i una trista mala gana;
ningú no m'entén el mal, ni metges ni apotecaris,
sinó una gentil minyona que l'amor me'n té robada;
me'n té robada l'amor el meu cor i les entranyes.
Al torrent de Sant Martí l'encontrí que sabonava;
jo li'n dic: —Deu me la guard, color de rosa encarnada.—
Ja no me'n torna raó com si l'hagués malparlada;
me la miro de les mans, veure quants anells portava;
me la miro jo dels peus, veure quin calçat portava,
porta sabata amb taló i la mitgeta encarnada.
Me la miro jo del cos, veure quin gipó portava,
porta gipó d'escotí amb un cordonet de plata;
me la miro jo del cap, de quin modo va tocada,
porta una pinteta d'or amb uns lligamets de plata.

Dona Elisabet

Segles XVIII-XIX

Dona Elisabet s'estava al palau amb sos infants;
trau el cap a la finestra, los camps mira verdejar.
Ja en veu el Rei que sortia a cavall a passejar
amb los nobles i los patges que el solen acompanyar.
Així que els perdé de vista veu venir de la ciutat
uns quants cavallers que corren cavalcant en bons cavalls;
les armes, selles i brides relluen més que un cristall;
entre ells veu Don Rodrigo, i això fou mala senyal.
Mana tancar-ne les portes per més segura quedar;
lo portaler no fou prompte i los ha deixat passar.
Quan se creia més segura per la sala els veu entrar;
entren fent la cara trista i saluden menaçant.
—Déu guard, Dona Elisabet, Déu vos lliure de pecar.
—Cavallers, en molt mala hora, en molt mala hora arribau.
—Què és lo que teniu, senyora, que tan mal nos saludau?
Ens coneixeu tal vegada? Lo que hem de fer sospitau?

—Bé vos conec, cavallers, bé vos conec per mon mal;
veig el germà de la Reina que m'és enemic mortal.
—Sí, la Reina ací ens envia per fer-vos tallar lo cap.
—I què he fet jo a nostra Reina perquè em vulga fer matar?
—Diu que del Rei teniu fills, i ella no n'ha tingut mai.
—Si jo del Rei ne tinc fills, Déu sap per què me'ls ha dats;
si la Reina no en té encara, sap Déu si n'hi donarà...
Bé en sabeu vós, Don Rodrigo, bé en sabeu la veritat.
Quan encara era una nina, poncelleta de pocs anys,
demanà el Rei mes amors, i no les hi volguí dar.
Ne féu parlar a ma mare, la mare es posà a plorar;
ne pregà després al pare fent promeses als germans.
Tots li feren de resposta que em matarien abans.
A un monestir me dugueren per poder-me d'ell guardar;
tanta por per la nostra honra i encara no va bastar!
Com me va saber reclosa dins poc temps se va casar...
Vós sabeu com me va traure per portar-me a est palau
on set anys m'ha mantinguda contra de ma voluntat.
—Calleu, Dona Elisabet, deixau-vos de tant parlar;
l'hora assenyalada arriba, lo sol a la posta va.
Ací teniu l'Arquebisbe per si us voleu confessar;
ací teniu lo notari, si testament vos caldrà;
ací el botxí vos espera, que prest vos ha d'escapçar...
Quan sentí això, la mesquina, promptament va contestar:
—Botxins, abans de matar-me deixau-me a la cambra entrar;
los fills del meu cor vull veure, la despedida els vull dar!
Quan eixia de la cambra feia pena de mirar;
ne sortí tota endolada amb un Santcrist a la mà,
punt per punt l'en adorava: «Ell és qui m'ha de salvar!»
Un fill duia a cada banda, lo majoret al davant;
l'infantó que a sos pits cria lo portava a plec de braç.
—No em dol la mort que m'espera, mos fills me dol de deixar.
No té el gran sis anys encara, quatre i tres los dos mitjans,
lo menut encara mama, qui li donarà mamar?
Vos suplic, pel Rei son pare, que els meus fills no prenguen [mal!
—No mancarà qui los cuide; confessau-vos aviat.
—Adéu, fills de la meva ànima, vostra mare han de matar;
adéu, jardinets ombrívols que al Rei plau de conresar;

adéu, cadira de braços on el Rei ve a descansar.
Adéu, fills de la meva ànima, la mare us van a matar!
Asseguda a la cadira l'infantó volgué mamar;
mentre que l'infant mamava lo botxí la va escapçar...
Al verger, al mig dels arbres, l'anaren a soterrar;
com venien d'enterrar-la Don Alonso va arribar.
—A on és l'Elisabet que no em vinga a saludar?
No l'he vista a la miranda d'on me sol atalaiar.—
Abans de pujar l'escala tots sos fills ja sent plorar;
ploren criats i criades, mal los han d'aconsolar.
Quan és a mitjan escala se troba amb lo seu cunyat.
—D'on veniu vós, Don Rodrigo, tan vermell i acalorat?
—He jugat a la pilota, i la passada he guanyat.
—Mentiu pel coll! Ma Isabet veniu ara de matar.—
Se n'arranca de l'espasa i lo cap li-n fa saltar.
—No ploreu, fills de ma vida; vostra mare, a on està?
—L'han colgada dins de terra, la n'han vinguda a matar.
—Ai d'aquells que me l'han morta! Ai de qui la féu matar!
Ai dels qui no ho aturaren i ho podien aturar!...—
Prompte féu desenterrar-la i endolar tot lo palau.
—No l'he coronada en vida, morta l'he de coronar.—
Aquella mort celerada vint-i-nou ne va costar.

BONAVENTURA CARLES ARIBAU

1798-1862

La Pàtria

(Trobes)

Adéu-siau, turons, per sempre adéu-siau,
oh serres desiguals que, allí en la pàtria mia
dels núvols e del cel de lluny vos distingia
per lo repòs etern, per lo color més blau.
Adéu tu, vell Montseny, que, des ton alt Palau,
com guarda vigilant, cobert de boira e neu,

guaites per un forat la tomba del jueu
e al mig del mar immens la mallorquina nau.

Jo ton superbe front coneixia llavors
com conèixer pogués lo front de mos parents;
coneixia tan bé lo so de tos torrents,
com la veu de ma mare e de mon fill los plors.
Mes, arrencat després per fats perseguidors,
jo no conec ni sent com en millors vegades;
així d'arbre migrat a terres apartades
son gust perden los fruits e son perfum les flors.

Què val que m'haja tret una enganyosa sort
a veure de més prop les torres de Castella,
si el cant dels trobadors no sona en mon orella
ni desperta en mon pit un generós record?
En va a mon dolç país en ales jo em transport
e veig del Llobregat la platja serpentina,
que, fora del cantar en llengua llemosina,
no em queda més plaer, no tinc altre conhort.

Plau-me encara parlar la llengua d'aquells savis
que ompliren l'univers de llurs costums e lleis,
la llengua d'aquells forts que acataren los reis,
defengueren llurs drets, venjaren llurs agravis.
Muira, muira l'ingrat que, al sonar en sos llavis
per estranya regió l'accent natiu, no plora,
que, al pensar en sos lars, no es consum ni s'enyora
ni cull del mur sagrat la lira dels seus avis.

En llemosí sonà lo meu primer vagit
quan del mugró matern la dolça llet bevia;
en llemosí al Senyor pregava cada dia
e càntics llemosins somiava cada nit.
Si, quan me trobe sol, parl' amb mon esperit,
en llemosí li parl', que altra llengua no sent,
e ma boca llavors no sap mentir, ni ment,
puix surten mes raons del centre de mon pit.

Ix doncs per a expressar l'afecte més sagrat
que púgia d'home en cor gravar la mà del cel,
oh llengua a mos sentits més dolça que la mel,
que em tornes les virtuts de ma innocent edat.
Ix, e crida pel món que mai mon cor ingrat
cessarà de cantar de mon patró la glòria;
e pàssia per ta veu son nom e sa memòria
als propis, als estranys, a la posteritat.

JOSEP LLUÍS PONS I GALLARZA

1823-1894

L'olivera mallorquina

CONTA'M, vella olivera,
mentre sec alenant sobre la roca,
noves del temps d'enrera
que escrites veig en ta surenca soca.

Jo vinc a recolzar-me
a tes nuades rels, trist d'enyorança,
perquè vulles tornar-me
dels béns que n'he perduts sols l'esperança.

Ton delicat fullatge
que sota lo cel blau l'embat oreja
és de la pau la imatge,
de tots los goigs de la ciutat enveja.

Ta rama verda i blanca
com cabellera d'àngel t'emmantella;
i a ta esqueixada branca
falta pel vent l'arrabassada estella.

Quan jove i vincladissa
creixies sobre el marge de la coma,
xermava ta verdissa
la falç del llaurador fill de Mahoma.

JOSEP LLUÍS PONS I GALLARZA

L'àrab i sa mainada
respirant-ne tes flors pel maig sortien,
i ta oliva escampada
sos fills, per la tardor, la recollien.

Ah, quin dol!, escoltant-ne
del corn aragonès lo toc de guerra,
tallà tos brots, donant-ne
empriu a l'host de la guanyada terra!

I el jorn de la conquista
amb llàgrimes del cor senyant sos passos,
sense girar la vista,
sortí, amb l'infant més xic estret als braços.

Los cavalls trepitjaren
dins lo solc sarraí les bruies tendres
i els ferros enfonsaren
de l'alqueria en les calentes cendres.

Com reposava, a l'ombra,
deslliurat lo baró dels durs arnesos,
mentre els llebrers sens nombre
jeien al sol assedegats i estesos!

I de son puny volant-ne
lo manyac esparver dalt tu es posava,
les ungles encreuant-ne,
i els tendres cims dels branquillons vinclava.

Quan era una alta ermita
aqueix claper de trossejada runa,
lo místic cenobita
aquí s'agenollava al clar de lluna.

Al toc del monastiri,
mans plegades al pit, pregàries deia,
i el cel en son deliri
per lo reixat de ton ombratge veia.

Ara aquí el temps enganya
lo pastoret que embadalit s'atura
i amb flabiol de canya,
gira el ramat que al comellar pastura.

Mentre l'ovella tosa
amb lo clapat anyell entorn apila,
la cabra delitosa
tos tanys novells per rosegar s'enfila.

Arbre amic del que plora,
dosser sagrat d'eternitat serena,
jo et sento grat de l'hora
que m'has aidat a conhortar ma pena.

Tu al cor m'has donat força,
tu apar que em tornes joventut perduda
com de ta eixuta escorça
la saba n'ix que ton brancatge muda.

Jo moriré, i encara
espolsarà el mestral ta negra oliva:
res serà del que és ara:
tu sobre el blau penyal romandràs viva.

TEODOR LLORENTE

1836-1911

Vora el barranc dels Algadins

Vora el barranc dels Algadins
hi ha uns tarongers de tal dolç flaire,
que, per omplir d'aroma l'aire,
no té lo món millors jardins.
Allí hi ha un mas, i el mas té dins
dolços records de ma infantesa;
per ells jo tinc l'ànima presa,
vora el barranc dels Algadins.

Vora el barranc dels Algadins
s'alcen al cel quatre palmeres;
el vent, batent ales lleugeres,
mou son plomall i sos troncs fins.
En elles, mils de teuladins,
fan un soroll que el cor encisa.
Qui oir pogués sa xillerissa,
vora el barranc dels Algadins.

Vora el barranc dels Algadins
l'aigua corrent los camps anega;
en sos espills lo sol llampega,
i trau l'arròs verdosos brins.
Sona el tic-tac en los molins,
i, al caure el sol, caçadors destres
a joca van d'ànecs silvestres
vora el barranc dels Algadins.

Vora el barranc dels Algadins
mourà demà les palmes l'aire,
li donaran els horts son flaire
i sa cantúria els teuladins.
El mas demà guardarà dins
dolços records e imàgens belles;
jo no podré gojar ja d'elles
vora el barranc dels Algadins.

JACINT VERDAGUER

1845-1902

L'Atlàntida

CANT II: L'HORT DE LES HESPÉRIDES

...No hi ha sorrenques vores, ni rònegues carenes;
tot l'herba ho encatifa rosada a bla ruixim,
gronxant-hi entre lianes de nuadisses trenes
la palma escabellada son ensucrat raïm.

Encinglant-se, la cabra esbrota un olm mengívol
des d'un cairell de timba penjada sobre el riu,
i els bisons s'arramaden amb aire germanívol
dels llimoners i mangles al regalat ombriu...

...S'hi acosta entre bardisses de murtra, i ja sos polsos
los aires apetonen mig embeguts de mel;
de bla fullatge i aigües murmuris s'ouen dolços,
i veu descloure en pluges de pedreria un cel.

Los cinamoms a rengles i poncemers altívols
al dolç pes ajupint-se de llur novella flor,
de dos en dos s'acoblen en porxes verds i ombrívols
on guaita el raig de l'alba per reixes de fruits d'or.

Los cirerers s'hi gronxen, de flors viventes toies
on vessaren tota sa flaire maig i abril,
i el fruit ja vermelleja fent goig entre les joies
que s'enfila a penjar-hi d'un cep tòria gentil.

Rieronets hi llisquen i fonts arruixadores,
llurs aigües adormint-se sovint entre les flors,
mentre eixes mig desclouen los llavis a ses vores
per dar a les abelles lo nèctar de sos cors.

Los brolladors escupen un riu per brocs de marbres,
i, esbrinadís al ploure lo ram de fos argent,
jugant l'iris corona lo cimeral dels arbres
i es veu entre ses tintes més blau lo firmament.

Cascades mil esqueixen ses ones de bromera
per escalons de pòrfir i balmes de cristall,
i estols de blanques nimfes desfan sa cabellera
pels remolins d'escuma, seguint-los riu avall.

Pels riberencs herbatges, com un ruixat de perles,
festívol saltirona l'aucell del paradís;
ou-s'hi glosar joiosos sinsonts i esquives merles,
i a estones gemegar-hi lo tord enyoradís...

Rosalia

De matí se'n baixa a l'hort
    Na Rosalia,
a collir los clavellets
    i satalies;
n'ensopega un ros Infant
    que ja en collia:
—Infantó, bell infantó,
    les flors són mies.
—Què en faríeu de les flors,
    Na Rosalia?
—Les volia per Jesús
    que tant m'estima.
—Si les volíeu per Ell,
    jo per l'aimia.
—Si per l'aimia és lo ram,
    dau-li d'ortigues,
que si no me'l dau a mi
    jo us lo pendria.—
Tot prenent-li el ramellet
    lo veu somriure;
bon Jesús, prou les entén
    vostres joguines;
amb les joguines d'amor
    vos coneixia.
—Donau-me les flors, si us plau,
    preneu les mies.
—La flor que volia Jo,
    ton cor de nina.
—Si em dau lo vostre d'infant,
    bé us lo daria.—
Mentre es canvien los cors,
    s'és desfallida,
que ja no pot obeir
    tanta delícia.
Lo traïdor del rossinyol
    canta i refila,

amb cançons i refilets
 tot ho espia.
La mareta, que entra a l'hort,
 plora i sospira
quan la veu entre els rosers
 tan esllanguida.
—Filleta, qui t'ha fet mal,
 ma dolça filla?
—Collint roses i clavells,
 dolceta espina.
—Una agulla tinc d'or fi
 que la trauria.
—Ni que fos de diamant
 serà prou fina.
—Filleta, què et gorirà,
 ma dolça filla?
—Mare, eixes roses i flors
 que m'han ferida.—
Tot espargint-les-hi al pit,
 sent que sospira:
—Doncs que et tornen a punyir,
 ma dolça filla?—
Sa filleta no respon,
 embadalida
amb qui fuig entre els clavells
 i satalies.
Tot fugint-li, riallós
 los ulls li gira.
Lo cel se va asserenant,
 l'herba floria.

Sortint de Cadis

Pel molinet ja sento rotllar-se la cadena,
i al crit de: Llevar àncores! sotraquejar la nau;
al desplegar les veles sento cruixir l'antena,
i en los veïns navilis i en l'apartada arena
 lo trist adéu-siau.

Des del llit d'agonia per la finestra miro;
d'escalonades ones sols la blavor se veu;
les ones, sols les ones i el cel per qui sospiro,
i a la verdosa terra ni menys los ulls hi giro;
ja res hi té el cor meu!

Allà d'allà rienta l'Amèrica m'espera,
mes clos al darrer son mon ull no la veurà,
que ans d'arribar a sos braços, on riu la primavera,
la mar en lo bell fons de sa badanta ossera
mos ossos guardarà.

Oh cel, oh sant desig que l'ànima esperona,
que és dolç des d'eixa terra on som damnats a mort
mirar-te com florida i esplèndida corona!
que és dolç, a cada assalt que la maror nos dóna,
sempre obirar ton port!

La mort de l'escolà

A Montserrat tot plora,
tot plora d'ahir ençà,
que allí a l'Escolania
s'és mort un escolà.
L'Escolania, oh Verge,
n'és vostre colomar:
a aquell que ahir us cantava,
qui avui no el plorarà?

En caixa blanquinosa
mirau que hermós està,
n'apar un lliri d'aigua
que acaben de trencar.
Té el violí a l'esquerra
que solia tocar,
lo violí a l'esquerra,
l'arquet a l'altra mà.

Sos companyons de cobla
lo duen a enterrar.
Lo rossinyol salmeja,
salmeja més enllà;
quan veu l'Escolania,
calla per escoltar.

Lo cant de les absoltes
comencen a entonar;
lo primer vers que entonen
del cel sembla baixar,
lo segon vers que canten
se posen a plorar.
Lo mestre de la cobla
los aconhorta en va,
les fonts ja són rieres,
i les rieres mar.

Oh patges de la Verge,
bé teniu de plorar,
al qui millor cantava
venint de soterrar.
Los monjos també ploren;
sols canta un ermità,
sentint cantar los àngels
i amb ells lo seu germà,
aucell d'ales obertes
que cap al cel se'n va.

Mentre ell canta pels aires,
lo violí sonà.

Lo Noi de la Mare

MENTRES Maria bressava i vestia
son ros i tendre Fillet que no dorm,
perquè no plore, ni en terra s'enyore,
dolça li canta dolceta cançó:

No plores, no, Manyaguet de la Mare,
no plores, no, que jo canto d'amor.

Cada gronxada et daré una abraçada,
cada abraçada un beset amorós;
mes rosses trenes seran tes cadenes,
niu i arcoveta les ales del cor.

Que n'és de bella ta galta en poncella!
Que en són de dolços tos llavis en flor!
són una rosa que els meus han desclosa
sols per xuclar-ne la mel de l'amor.

Feu-li, aurenetes, cançons d'amoretes;
fes-li musica, gentil rossinyol;
si t'és poc fina ma falda de nina,
baixen los Angels del Cel un bressol.

Sien ses ales glasser de tes gales,
sien sos braços coixins de ton cos;
jo per tos polsos ne tinc de més dolços;
per embolcar-te, les teles del cor.

Sien ta faixa, si el Cel no te'n baixa,
quatre palletes de sec poliol,
quatre palletes tot just floridetes
que et servirien de faixa i llençol.

Guarniu-me'l, Àngels, bressau-me'l, Arcàngels,
d'aire bon aire, tot fent-li l'amor;
mística bresca lo Cel li servesca
si en llet de Verge no troba dolçor.

Dels Reis l'estrella claríssima i bella
n'és baixadeta a posar-se en ton front;
quan ells te miren gelosos, se'm giren:
«Quina faldada de perles i flors!»

Totes s'esfloren les flors que t'enyoren,
feia-les nàixer ton riure tan dolç,
tornen reviure si els tornes a riure,
mes, ai!, sols beuen rosada de plors.

Quan se n'adonen los Angels, entonen
càntics de festa que es tornen de dol:
«Amb Tu abans d'hora clareja l'aurora,
amb Tu abans d'hora s'ha de pondre el sol.»

Mentres Maria el bressava i vestia,
veu ses manetes creuades al cor;
prou l'endevina d'amor la joguina,
que Fill i Mare barregen sos plors.
No ploris, no, Manyaguet de la Mare,
que en la creu dura morirem tots dos.

Canigó

Cant V: Tallaferro

Lo comte Tallaferro va com lo vent
volant per les altures del Pirineu.
Tan bon punt ahir vespre deixà l'aplec,
seguiren-lo els fallaires en reguitzell;
són fills d'eixes garrotxes tots cepadencs,
germans de les alzines i dels avets.
Per la Porta Forana baixa a Castell,
se'n puja a Marialles i Collet Verd;
tot faldejant la serra de Tretze Vents,
s'atura a l'ermitatge de Sant Guillem.

Sant Guillem s'està dintre pregant a Déu,
en creu alçats los braços, los ulls al cel.
Trau lo cap a la porta tantost lo sent:
—Oh comte Tallaferro! no us atureu,
que els sarraïns saquegen Elna i Ceret.
Mes veu's aquí una espasa que és de bon tremp:

de Castelló en lo siti   la duia Otger;
Otger moria en braços   d'un avi meu
que de l'espasa féu-li   gentil present;
relíquies de Sant Jordi   té dins la creu.
«No la doneu, li deia,   sinó a un guerrer
que talle el ferro verge   com brots de cep.»
Preneu-la, Tallaferro,   no us atureu.—
Lo comte no s'atura,   deixa el bon vell,
que aixeca el toc solemne   de sometent.
La campana amb què hi toca   no és de gran preu,
no és de coure, ni bronzo,   d'or, ni d'argent,
sinó del millor ferro   d'aquells meners;
en ella no s'hi veuen   colps de martell,
sols s'hi veuen ditades   del penitent.
Un dia anà a la farga   de Montferrer:
—Fargaires, bons fargaires,   així us guard Déu
com jo he feta una ermita   dintre el desert;
les portes són de roure,   l'altar de teix;
sols me falta una clotxa   per son cloquer:
podria en les tempestes   tocar a bon temps,
i en les guerres de moros   a sometent.
Per fer-me-la de ferro   me'n donareu?
—De la fornal preneu-se'l,   està bullent.—
Posant la mà a la fosa,   lo sant se'l pren;
lo pasta com sa terra   lo terrisser,
d'una mitra donant-li   l'aire i caient.
Prometença que feia   vui la compleix,
alçant lo coure als moros,   com al mal temps.

Lo comte Tallaferro   pel camí dret
segueix lo Comalada,   que embranca amb Tec,
i vora les pedreres   de marbre verd,
passa el Pont de la Verge,   puja a Cabrens.
La muntanya es corona   d'un gran castell,
lo castell de tres torres   amb sos merlets;
passa ell prop de les dues   sense dir res;
al peu de la més alta   llança un renec:
—Baixau d'eixes altures,   con llamp de Déu,

que puja un riu de moros per Argelés;
si no baixau vosaltres, pujaran ells
a traure d'eix niu d'àligues los esparvers!—
Diu i ja sent com baixen, baixen corrent,
arrossegant la llança, fent dringar l'elm.
Lo comte no els espera, corre més que ells;
corre cap a Custoges per Sant Llorenç.
Des d'un cim de carenes del Pirineu,
fa ressonar la trompa dos colps o tres.
Quan l'aparta dels llavis, ja són desperts
masovers i masies d'aquells endrets,
i des de la Jonquera fins a Baget
los pobles se remouen en sometent.
Lo comte no els espera, no té pas temps;
ventant esperonada, baixa rabent
des del cim de Custoges a Massanet.
Diríeu que amb mà forta lo vent l'empeny,
lo vent de tramuntana canigonenc.

Oh Mangala de ferro, que don Roland
plantà enmig de la plaça roja de sang!
si el comte no t'arrenca, ningú ho farà.
Lo comte té una espasa que més li val,
d'argent té la creuera, d'acer lo tall;
los moros quan la vegen, tremolaran,
com tremolen les messes prop de la falç.
On Mangala de ferro de don Roland!
a qui té aqueixa espasa tu no li plaus
i esperona a sos hèroes al crit d'avant.
Lo castell de Cabrera los veu pujar,
com serp que s'aforesta, vers Panissars.
Dels Trofeus de Pompeyo passen davall,
que, alçant entre suredes son front gegant,
lo Rosselló dominen i l'Empordà.
Rocabertí, entre penyes mal amagat,
vers Requesens l'exèrcit mira enfilar.
Allí els avets i alzines, roures i faigs
se creuen com les llances en un combat;

lo comte a colps d'espasa va obrint-se pas,
deixant-ne grans esteses ençà i enllà.
Si els moros lo vegessen destralejar,
lo colp no esperarien de sa destral.
Lo comte Tallaferro ja veu ses naus,
lluint la mitja lluna damunt dels pals,
astre de mal auguri per nostres camps,
i exclama amb ulls encesos i braços alts:
—Bon Déu, s'han fet pel moro ports catalans?—
Aquí el Pirene altívol abaixa el cap,
com monstre que s'abeura dintre la mar.
Lo comte Tallaferro timbes avall
davalla com lo núvol del temporal,
prenyat de pedregades, de trons i llamps.

Cant X: Guisla

Camí de Cornellà, lo comte Guifre
va a pendre comiat de la comtessa;
que els ne troba de tristos aquells marges
on al sol de l'amor ahir tot reia!
Los arbres que s'inclinen remorosos,
com si parlassen de son crim li sembla,
i els joiosos aucells que hi saltironen
li apar que esquerps eviten sa presència,
un a l'altre contant-se l'homicidi,
mal de contar amb ses arpades llengües.
Lo virolat verdum ja no hi refila,
lo rossinyol no hi canta, que gemega,
arpa d'on, l'alegria escorreguda,
tan sols la corda del neguit hi resta.
Lo vent que sòpit en lo bosc dormia
se remou tot plegat com una fera,
s'ouen lladrucs sinistres dins lo córrec,
i damunt dels teulats cants de xaveca,
i de núvol en núvol per los aires
rodar lo tro, preludi de tempesta.
Quan de sos avis al palau s'acosta,

veu sa Guisla gentil a la finestra,
entre els dos gerros de clavells que a riure
surten quiscun en sa clavellinera;
endolada la veu com una viuda
i avergonyit abaixa els ulls a terra.
Cada graó que de l'escala puja
lo rega amb una llàgrima coenta;
al capdamunt de tots ella és qui plora,
com un desmai doblant sa hermosa testa.
Les paraules que es diuen són paraules
de punyidora i funeral tristesa:
—Adéu—diu ell—, esposa de ma vida;
a l'arrencar-me del teu cor, se trenca
mon cor emmalaltit, com una branca
que de son tronc un braç cruel esqueixa.
—No te'n deixaré anar, respon sa esposa,
no te'n deixaré anar, ta vida és meva.
Davant l'altar lo jorn del desposori
estimació sens fi no m'has promesa?
—T'estimaré com sempre t'he estimada,
mes, ai de mi!, serà des d'una celda
d'un monestir que sobre l'oratori
de Sant Martí de Canigó s'aixeca.
Allí morir devia en una forca,
menjat per corbs enmig de cel i terra;
a Déu, que em torna compassiu la vida,
bé li puc oferir lo que me'n resta!—
Respondre vol sa desolada esposa,
mes està de neguit sa ànima plena,
sos ulls sols tenen llàgrimes amargues,
muda sols troba algun sospir sa llengua.
Ell en son front lo darrer bes estampa,
l'estreny entre sos braços i la deixa,
de llàgrimes humits los ulls girant-hi,
com l'infantó arrancat de la mamella.
Llavors escala avall un plor ressona
i un xisclet en la sala li contesta;
ploren amb ell los cavallers i patges,

les dames del palau ploren amb ella,
que veu entrar per on surt ara Guifre
l'espectre glaçador de la viudesa,
amb son cabell estès sobre la cara
i arrossegant la mantellina negra,
caiguts sos braços d'ufanós magnoli
que en sa florida esbrosta la tempesta,
i sos ulls d'aranyó i son front de lliri
ennuvolats amb boires de tristesa.
Quan se revé son cor i de ses llàgrimes
cau amansida la maror primera,
al monestir que l'enviudà tan jove
vol portar, virtuosa alguna pedra.
Surt a l'eixida del palau que hi dóna
i amb agulla d'argent i fil de seda
vol brodar una càndida estovalla
de la més fina i preciosa tela.
Les Barres Catalanes hi dibuixa,
sembrant sos entremigs d'alguna estrella,
com si del cel los somnis li vinguessen
entrellaçats amb somnis de sa terra;
sota l'escut posa sa bella firma
i damunt sa corona de comtessa.
A cada punt que dóna sa àurea agulla
al cenobi naixent los ulls aixeca,
deixant caure una llàgrima que en l'obra
se podria encastar per una perla.
Ses donzelles voldrien-la distreure
i a ses dolors son pensament s'aferra
i a sos records més íntims sa memòria,
com a les runes d'un palau una heura.
Tot li parla de Guifre: les muntanyes
a on solia batre's amb les feres,
la font on ella eixia-li a l'encontre,
per vasull oferint-li sa mà tendra,
la verda coromina on flors collien,
lo marge fresc del rieró on s'asseien
mirant les aigües a sos peus escórrer

serenes com sos jorns de fadrinesa,
lo salze que els donà redós ombrívol,
los pins que al cim del comellar gemeguen,
com les vibrants cordes d'un salteri
que l'aspre geni del mestral punteja.
I dels aucells les fonedisses notes,
los bruits misteriosos de la selva,
lo rondineig de l'aire entre les fulles,
ones li són d'un pèlag de tristesa.

De prompte s'ou lo cant d'una minyona,
com en la mar lo cant d'una gavina,
amorosir ses ones amargantes
amb un raig enganyívol d'alegria.
Escolta Guisla la cançó i la troba
en son enyorament massa escoltívola.
—Qui serà —diu— aqueixa dona o àngel
que alegre canta quan tothom sospira?
Voldria anar a veure-la: tal volta
tindria per mes penes medecina.—
Del porxe a l'hort, de l'hort a la boscúria
passeja el feix de ses dolors sens mida.
Totes les flors capbaixes veu com ella,
que n'era no fa gaire la regina,
i li fan aquells arbres més angoixa
on sent més refilets i cantadissa.
Per enjoiar-lo amb raïms d'or i perles,
a l'arc del porxe la sarment s'enrinxa,
l'oritjol filador a l'olm s'enarbra,
braços d'esposa que a l'espòs es lliguen,
i entre ses branques lo colom dels boscos
parrupejant a sa coloma crida
que aplega per son niu algun bri d'herba,
per sa casa de brossa enorme biga.
Lo rieró festeja la nimfea,
somriu a l'astre d'or la margarida
mostrant sobre son pit sa rossa imatge,
segell diví de son bell cor d'aimia;

mes ella mai ha vist lo cel tan núvol,
jamai la terra li semblà tan trista;
oh terra de Conflent! per ta mestressa,
com t'has tornada avui tan enyorívola!

Com viatger que assedegat escolta
lo murmuri de l'aigua cristal·lina,
se n'entra bosc endins, vers la donzella
que entre ovelles i anyells canta i refila,
tot fent rajar lo fil de la filosa,
asseguda a la soca d'una alzina.
Per regalar-se bé amb sa cantarella
camina suaument quan hi arriba,
tan suaument que no doblega el trèbol,
ni fa colltòrcer l'herba que trepitja.
Ja la sent més a prop, ja allí a la vora,
sols la'n separa una frescal bardissa,
ja decantant los sàlics i vidalves
entre vergelles de roser la mira,
com una rosa de pastor que esclata
lluny del verger, al sol i a la celístia.
És son brial de rústega burata
com son caputxó de color d'oliva,
caminadora i blanca sa espardenya
és del cànem més fi, com lo que fila.
La cançó que ella entona és d'esperança
de veure l'aimador per qui sospira;
anà amb los moros a lluitar i prompte
deurà arribar, puix sa bandera arriba.
De la tendra cançó a cada posada
llença un sospir la consirosa Guisla,
assaborint ses notes d'una a una,
per son cor trist rosada d'alegria.
L'angèlica pastora se n'adona
i estranyada de veure-la i oir-la.
—Què té? —diu condolguda a ses donzelles—.
S'haurà plantada al peu alguna espina?
—Me l'he plantada al cor—diu la comtessa—;

tu cantes dolçament i jo estic trista,
jo que só la comtessa de Cerdanya,
d'aqueix bocí de Pirineus pubilla.
Hauries tu trobat en eixos boscos
pels afligits la font de l'alegria?
—Un dia la hi trobí de primavera,
dia de cel que l'ànima no oblida;
mes, ai!, l'enyorament abans de gaire
sos puríssims cristalls enterbolia.
—Qui és, doncs, lo teu gojat? —diu la comtessa.
—És la flor dels donzells d'aqueixa riba;
l'àngel hermós dels cavallers del comte.
Sols vós no el coneixeu que li sou tia?
—Gentil? —diu esglaiada la comtessa.
—Gentil! —respon tot sospirant la nina;
i com pel llamp corsecador tocada,
cau l'esposa infeliç de l'homicida,
sos llavis de carmí tornant-se gebre,
les roses de ses galtes satelies.

En braços se l'enduen ses donzelles
vers lo palau d'on en mal punt ha eixida,
com cadavre vivent cap a la tomba,
des d'on del seu amor la tomba obira.
Plora el Conflent, sos pagesius i pobles,
plora en son niu la tórtora soliua,
i el cel, a on esclata la tempesta,
és, com sos ulls, de llàgrimes font viva.
No pot plorar així Griselda hermosa,
que, senzilla com és, tot ho endevina:
no pot plorar així, que sempre és seca
la més crua tempesta de la vida;
i no podent sa pena desfogar-se,
va a enterbolir sa testa jovenívola
fent-li perdre lo seny, hermosa estrella
que s'acluca en la nit de la follia.

JACINT VERDAGUER

Epíleg: Los dos campanars

Doncs, què us heu fet, superbes abadies,
Mercèvol, Serrabona i Sant Miquel,
i tu, decrèpit Sant Martí, que omplies
aqueixes valls de salms i melodies,
la terra d'àngels i de sants lo cel?

Doncs, què n'heu fet, oh valls!, de l'asceteri,
escola de l'amor de Jesucrist?
On és, oh soletat!, lo teu salteri?
On tos rengles de monjos, presbiteri,
que, com un cos sens ànima, estàs trist?

D'Ursèol a on és lo dormitori?
La celda abacial del gran Garí?
On és de Romualdo l'oratori,
los palis i retaules, l'or i evori
que entretallà ha mil anys cisell diví?

Los càntics i les llums s'esmortuïren;
la rosa s'esfullà com lo roser;
los himnes sants en l'arpa s'adormiren,
com verderoles que en llur niu moriren
quan lo bosc les oïa més a pler.

Dels romànics altars no en queda rastre,
del claustre bizantí no en queda res:
caigueren les imatges d'alabastre
i s'apagà sa llàntia, com un astre
que en Canigó no s'encendrà mai més.

Com dos gegants d'una llegió sagrada
sols encara hi ha drets dos campanars:
són los monjos darrers de l'encontrada,
que ans de partir, per última vegada,
contemplen l'enderroc de sos altars.

Són dues formidables sentinelles
que en lo Conflent posà l'eternitat;
semblen garrics los roures al peu d'elles;
les masies del pla semblen ovelles
al peu de llur pastor agegantat.

Una nit fosca al seu germà parlava
lo de Cuixà: —Doncs que has perdut la veu?
Alguna hora a ton cant me desvetllava
i ma veu a la teva entrelligava
cada matí per beneir a Déu.

—Campanes ja no tinc —li responia
lo ferreny campanar de Sant Martí—.
Oh, qui pogués tornar-me-les un dia!
Per tocar a morts pels monjos les voldria;
per tocar a morts pels monjos i per mi.

Que tristos, ai, que tristos me deixaren!
Tota una tarda los vegí plorar;
set vegades per veure'm se giraren;
jo aguaito fa cent anys per on baixaren;
tu que vius més avall, no els veus tornar?

—No! Pel camí de Codalet i Prada
sols minaires obiro i llauradors;
diu que torna a son arbre la niuada,
mes, ai!, la que deixà nostra brancada
no hi cantarà mai més dolces amors.

Mai més! Mai més! Ells jauen sota terra;
nosaltres damunt seu anam caient;
lo segle que ens deu tant ara ens aterra,
en son oblit nostra grandor enterra
i ossos i glòries i records se'ns ven.

—Ai! ell ventà les cendres venerables
del comte de Rià, mon fundador;

convertí mes capelles en estables,
i desniuats los àngels pels diables
en eixos cims ploraren de tristor.

I jo plorava amb ells i encara ploro,
mes, ai!, sens esperança de conhort,
puix tot se'n va, i no torna lo que enyoro,
i de pressa, de pressa, jo m'esfloro,
rusc on l'abell murmuriós s'és mort.

—Caurem plegats—lo de Cuixà contesta—.
Jo altre cloquer tenia al meu costat;
rival dels puigs, alçava l'ampla testa,
i amb sa sonora veu, dolça o feresta,
estrafeia el clarí o la tempestat.

Com jo, tenia nou-cents anys de vida,
mes, nou Matusalem, també morí;
com Goliat al rebre la ferida,
caigué tot llarg, i ara a son llit me crida
son insepult cadavre gegantí.

Abans de gaire ma deforme ossada
blanquejarà en la vall de Codalet;
lo front me pesa més, i a la vesprada,
quan visita la lluna l'encontrada,
tota s'estranya de trobar-m'hi dret.

Vaig a ajaure'm també: d'eixes altures
tu baixaràs a reposar amb mi,
i ai!, qui llaure les nostres sepultures
no sabrà dir a les edats futures
on foren Sant Miquel i Sant Martí.—

Així un vespre els dos cloquers parlaven;
mes, l'endemà al matí, al sortir lo sol,
recomençant los càntics que ells acaben,
los tudons amb l'heurera conversaven,
amb l'estrella del dia el rossinyol.

Somrigué la muntanya engallardida
com si estrenàs son verdejant mantell;
mostrà's com núvia de joiells guarnida;
i de ses mil congestes la florida
blanca esbandí com taronger novell.

Lo que un segle bastí, l'altre ho aterra,
mes resta sempre el monument de Déu;
i la tempesta, el torb, l'odi i la guerra
al Canigó no el tiraran a terra,
no esbrancaran l'altívol Pirineu.

L'emigrant

Dolça Catalunya,
pàtria del meu cor,
quan de tu s'allunya
d'enyorança es mor.

I

Hermosa vall, bressol de ma infantesa,
blanc Pirineu,
marges i rius, ermita al cel suspesa
per sempre adéu!
Arpes del bosc, pinsans i caderneres,
cantau, cantau,
jo dic plorant a boscos i riberes:
adéu-siau!

II

On trobaré tos sanitosos climes,
ton cel daurat?
mes ai, mes ai! on trobaré tes cimes,
bell Montserrat?
Enlloc veuré, ciutat de Barcelona,
ta hermosa Seu,
ni eixos turons, joiells de la corona
que et posà Déu.

III

Adéu, germans: adéu-siau, mon pare,
no us veuré més!
oh! si al fossar on jau ma dolça mare,
jo el llit tingués!
Oh mariners, lo vent que me'n desterra
que em fa sofrir!
estic malalt, mes ai! tornau-me a terra,
que hi vull morir!

La Rosa de Jericó

En sa cambreta humil
pregant està Maria,
Maria està pregant
mentres lo món dormia.
Lo sol a l'Orient
per veure-la sortia.
Ella no el mira, no,
sol més bonic somnia;
lo sol que està esperant
mai més se li pondria.

En son clavelliner
un roseret tenia,
roser de Jericó
que poncellar volia.
Sola regor que beu
de sos ullets venia,
quan Ella mira el cel
la llum si en baixaria.

Un Angel n'ha baixat
dient-li: —Ave Maria,
lo Senyor és amb Vós
i amb tots los homes sia.—

La Verge li respon:
—Sa voluntat és mia;
sa esclava la téací
que el cor li donaria.—

Sobre Ella un blanc Colom
ses ales estenia,
i amb la claror del Verb
la Verge resplendia.
Lo món s'omple de llum,
lo cel de melodia,
i al test del finestró
la rosa mig s'obria.

Desvetlla't, oh Betlem,
enrama l'Establia,
guarneix-la com pitxer
amb or i pedreria,
que en tu de Jericó
la Rosa floriria.

Entre flors

ENCARA és petit, petit,
l'Infant de la Glòria,
petit com un lliri blanc,
bell com una rosa
dels rosers amb què en abril
Jericó es festona.
La Verge sembla el roser
quan al braç lo porta,
quan lo porta vora el riu
a esbandir la roba.
Per esbandir-la millor
sobre l'herba el posa
entre mates d'iris blau
i margaridoies.

L'Infantó somriu,
la Mareta plora.

Gira al Fill dels seus amors
sos ulls de coloma
cada volta que s'ajup
a la rentadora.
Lo veu en somni suau
com dorm i reposa
al peu d'un arbre d'encens
que li fa bona ombra.
De genolls un Serafí
sos cabells esflora;
voldria besar son front,
voldria i no gosa,
veient que en son jaç florit
l'amor lo deixonda,
fent-li estendre sos bracets
a l'aire del Gòlgota.
Al pendre-la Ella en los seus
de Mare amorosa,
la creu estampada ha vist
en son llit de molsa,
com firma que el Déu infant
en la terra posa.
L'Infantó somriu,
la Mareta plora.

Los cosinets

Jesús i Sant Joan
se'n van
per un boscatge alegre:
que hermosos són tots dos!
l'un ros,
l'altre de cabell negre.

Un ramadet que els plau
s'hi escau

al peu d'unes alzines;
petits són los anyells
com ells;
los prenen per joguines.

Jesús fa de sos dits
petits
pinteta de sa llana,
mentres los va arruixant
Joan
al doll d'una fontana.

Los donen d'herba els brins
més fins,
de péixer quan és hora,
de sa maneta el bell
palmell
fent-los d'abeuradora.

Xopegen dintre el riu
ombriu
de cap entre la fulla;
com és nuet son peu
de neu,
son calçadet no es mulla.

Abans de fer-se'ls fosc
al bosc,
vers Nazaret que els plora
van, com aucells al niu,
on riu
la Mare que els enyora.

Jesús munta l'anyell
més bell,
Joan davant camina;
Jesús porta la creu
de Déu;
Joan una petxina.

Dolça càrrega

Amb son cànter a la testa
ve la Verge de la font,
degotant l'aigua tan llesta
com la suor de son front.

I diuen flors i donzelles
que la miren perlejant:
—Més hi escaurien estrelles
d'aqueixa testa al voltant.—

Sant Josep du un feix de llenya
dels boscos de Nazaret:
és feixuc com una penya
i trampela el sant Vellet.

I Jesús deia a sa mare:
—Donau-me el cànter, si us plau.
—Dau socors a vostre pare—
respon ella amb veu suau.

Sant Josep li responia:
—Jo encara puc un xic més;
donau-li el cànter, Maria;
vostre front no és per tant pes.—

Jesús estén en garlanda
sos dos braços, amorós,
i amb una mà a cada banda
los ajudava a tots dos.

Lo Calze i l'Arpa

De penyores d'amor
Jesús mil me n'ha dades,
me n'ha donades mil,
dues de sobiranes.
M'ha dat un calze d'or

i una arpa d'or i plata;
un calze celestial
per beure sang sagrada,
la del seu cor diví
que pel costat li raja.
Quan n'he beguda un glop
me'n poso a tocar l'arpa,
cantant a terra i cel
l'amor que m'embriaga.
Que sia tan feliç
als homes no els agrada;
m'han pres lo calze d'or
a on ma set s'apaga,
la set d'amor diví
que abrusa la meva ànima.
M'han pres lo calze d'or
i em volen pendre l'arpa,
ressò de les del cel
que cada nit me parla;
amor de mos quinze anys,
de ma vellor companya,
l'esposa del cor meu,
de l'esperit germana.
Quedeu-se el calze d'or,
però deixeu-me l'arpa;
deixeu-me-la tocar
postrat als peus de l'ara,
mentres begau lo Vi
de la sarment sagrada
voltats de llum i encens
dels àngels en la taula.

Tot sia per Déu

La forta tempesta
que em dobla la testa
i el cor me despulla
com arbre de fulla;

la destral ferrenya
que de mi fa llenya;
tot sia per Vós,
Jesuset dolcíssim:
tot sia per Vós,
Jesús amorós.

La malavolença
que té a punt l'ofensa;
los claus i improperis
i afronts i dicteris;
la que escup metzina,
llengua serpentina;
tot sia per Vós,
Jesuset dolcíssim;
tot sia per Vós,
Jesús amorós.

Ma corona aimada,
d'espines tornada;
l'antiga riquesa,
la nova pobresa,
los goigs que s'esmunyen,
les penes que punyen;
tot sia per Vós,
Jesuset dolcíssim;
tot sia per Vós,
Jesús amorós.

Les fletxes tirades
per mans amagades;
l'amic que se'm gira
i al cor me les tira;
les que, ai!, he rebudes
besades de Judes;
tot sia per Vós,
Jesuset dolcíssim;
tot sia per Vós,
Jesús amorós.

Glop-de-neu

Ara veieu!
del Glop-de-neu
la flor petita i ranca
volia ser tan blanca
com la Mare de Déu!

—Enrera, flor superba,
lluny de mi!—
digué Nostre Senyor:
—val més que tu el bri d'herba
que el bestiar boví
trepitja en son camí.—

I aquesta pobra flor
perdé l'olor!

La rosa fugí d'ella,
lo repunxó també,
i l'ardenta rosella
li digué:
—M'estimo més per veïna
la pota cavallina.—

I aquella pobra flor
perdé el color!

Abans era molt útil,
mes ara ja no ho és
per res.
Si un dia era tendrívola,
ja se la menja el sol;
si abans era mengívola,
ni el bestiar la vol.

JACINT VERDAGUER

La formiga

UNA hermosa plana
tinguí per bressol;
com la vigatana
no en veu altra el sol.
Jo fui la formiga
de son pla i garriga,
del mas oreneta,
del camp rossinyol.

Per les torrenteres
que alegre tresquí
del camp a les eres,
de l'hort al jardí,
me nasqueren ales
com a les cigales
i a aquell pla d'Ausona
l'adéu jo doní.

Vegí hermoses terres,
més d'una ciutat,
m'enfilí a les serres
de l'alt Montserrat.
Baixí a Barcelona,
la perla amb què l'ona
enriquí fa segles
l'antic Principat.

Dintre horts que floriren
per encantament,
palaus se m'obriren
plens d'or i d'argent.
En mala diada
ne fiu ma posada,
puix ma vida i somnis
fugiren corrent.

Mes grandeses foren
floretes d'empriu
que naixen i moren,
bombolles de riu.
Fou aquella glòria
vana i transitòria,
com pel lapidaire
rosada d'estiu.

Tot era falsia
dintre aquell palau,
los mots que hi sentia
d'afecte i de pau.
Los ramells de roses
foren de gatoses;
los llaços de murta
cadenes d'esclau.

Dintre aquelles sales
enemic cruel
les frisoses ales
me llevà d'arrel.
Si no hagués deixada
la gàbia daurada,
mai més vos veuria,
ma terra i mon cel.

Jo deixí en mal hora
lo teu pagesiu,
oh poble que enyora
mon coret soliu:
de ma terra amiga
jo fóra formiga:
¡mal hagen les ales
que m'han tret del niu!

M. COSTA I LLOBERA

1854-1922

El pi de Formentor

Mon cor estima un arbre! Més vell que l'olivera,
més poderós que el roure, més verd que el taronger,
conserva de ses fulles l'eterna primavera,
i lluita amb les ventades que atupen la ribera,
com un gegant guerrer.

No guaita per ses fulles la flor enamorada,
no va la fontanella ses ombres a besar;
mes Déu ungí d'aroma sa testa consagrada
i li donà per terra l'esquerpa serralada,
per font la immensa mar.

Quan lluny, damunt les ones, renaix la llum divina,
no canta per ses branques l'aucell que encativam;
el crit sublim escolta de l'àguila marina,
o del voltor que puja sent l'ala gegantina
remoure son fullam.

Del llim d'aquesta terra sa vida no sustenta;
revincla per les roques sa poderosa rel;
té pluges i rosades i vents i llum ardenta;
i, com un vell profeta, rep vida i s'alimenta
de les amors del cel.

Arbre sublim! Del geni n'és ell la viva imatge:
domina les muntanyes i aguaita l'infinit;
per ell la terra és dura, mes besa son ramatge
el cel que l'enamora, i té el llamp i l'oratge
per glòria i per delit.

Oh! sí: que quan a lloure bramulen les ventades
i sembla entre l'escuma que tombi el seu penyal,

llavors ell riu i canta més fort que les onades
i vencedor espolsa damunt les nuvolades
sa cabellera real.

Arbre, mon cor t'enveja. Sobre la terra impura,
com a penyora santa duré jo el teu record.
Lluitar constant i vèncer, regnar sobre l'altura
i alimentar-se i viure de cel i de llum pura...
oh vida, oh noble sort!

Amunt, ànima forta! Traspassa la boirada
i arrela dins l'altura com l'arbre dels penyals.
Veuràs caure a tes plantes la mar del món irada,
i tes cançons tranquiles 'niran per la ventada
com l'au dels temporals.

L'arpa

I

PUJAREN al castell. L'augusta porta
oberta al vent de la tardor estava.
Allà la Reina, deturant sa filla,
signà la mar de l'orient llunyana.
I entraren al palau. Sales immenses
mostraven fondes la buidor que esglaia,
i al so de les petjades, s'estremien
els negres cavallers qui les guardaven.
Ai! aquells negres cavallers de ferro
no mouran mai sa poderosa llança...
Al cruixir de les buides armadures,
la Reina sospirava.

II

Dins la cambra reial, trista i polsosa,
un trone d'or hi resplendia encara;
la Reina hi va pujar, i s'hi va asseure
amb el record de majestat passada.

Allà, baix d'ella, s'assegué la jove,
i mirava amb tristor l'antiga sala...
—Mare, tos fills i ton poder finiren!
—Filla, tu vius per a conhort encara.
—Què resta, mare, d'aquell temps, què resta?...—
La Reina aquí, sense dir mot, plorava;
i fent signe llavores a sa filla,
li va mostrar una arpa.

III

L'arpa era antiga que en els jorns de glòria
davant els reis en el castell sonava:
encara dins la pols d'aquelles cordes
notes dormien de dolçura pàtria.
La jove prengué l'arpa, i tremolosos
els sons primers, com a gemecs, pujaven.
Després va rompre un torrental de notes,
com fonda pena que plorant esclata.
I los ecos fidels que sempre vetllen,
repetiren la veu tan enyorada,
i es movia dins l'ombra una bandera,
i l'òliba xiulava.

IV

Estols de notes màgiques sortien
de dins les mans de la princesa blanca,
com els ocells aletejant nasqueren
de dins les mans puríssimes de l'auba.
Baixos els ulls, la Reina consirosa
bevia el so de l'harmonia estranya,
i per moments parlava com en somnis,
i sos fills que eren morts anomenava...
Tard era ja. La lluna blanca i freda
guaità tranquilament a dins la cambra,
i ningú sap, ai Déu!, fins a quina hora
durà el ressò de l'arpa.

El Gorg Blau

Adéu, tristor encastellada
del pla de Cúber i Almaluig!...
Seguint arreu l'aigua qui fuig
d'aqueixa terra desolada,
sorprèn mos ulls la portalada
d'un Paradís...
L'aigua s'atura a son encís
i com que diga: *reposau!*
—Dolça és la calma del Gorg Blau.

Les colossals penyes bessones,
formant un freu meravellós,
sols deixen caure un raig dubtós
sobre l'estany pur i sens ones.
D'encantament blavors pregones,
com un safir,
aquest estany fan resplendir
i com que diguen: *somniau!*
—Dolç és el somni del Gorg Blau.

L'antic camí tot solitari
voreja l'aigua, recobert
baix del penyal, i sembla obert
per un exèrcit llegendari...
Passant del Gorg al mur contrari
pel rústic pont,
somriu la coma de la font
com un idl·li tot suau.
—Dolç és l'oasi del Gorg Blau.

Sortint del Gorg, per entre molsa,
ramatges, eures i ramells,
l'aigua jugant fa amb els aucells,
seguit, seguit, música dolça.
La neta escuma que ella espolsa
singlota o riu?

Al qui l'escolta pensatiu
com que li diga: *meditau!*
—Dolça és la parla del Gorg Blau.

Per entre flors, per entre espines,
lo que era estany se fa torrent,
i avall, endins, se va perdent
per un rocam com en ruïnes...
No hi troba ja murta ni alzines,
molsa ni flors,
quan allà baix, desfeta en plors,
dins la gran *Fosca* l'aigua cau...
—Ai! com la vida és el Gorg Blau!

Vagant pel bosc

REMOR del bosc, solemne salmodia
del gran pinar desert,
bressa en notes de pau i poesia
mos somnis de despert.

Bressa ma vida qui te sent, corpresa
d'aquell intens encant
amb què un escolta la cançó incompresa
qui l'adormia infant.

Infant m'agombolares, veu difusa,
i jove pensatiu...
Aquí aprenia de cantar ma musa
com au que hi té son niu.

Doncs aquí volen pel ramatge ombrívol
mos somnis i records:
aquí mon cor escolta, i enyorívol
conversa-hi amb sos morts.

Ai! de cada any amb major nombre hi parla;
i aquesta solitud

entre els ausents qui vénen a poblar-la
em veu més abatut.

Temps era temps en què el boscà murmuri,
essent al d'ara igual,
em sonava tan sols com un auguri
de càntic triomfal.

Llavors eix to planyent jo no hi sentia:
sols notes de vigor
de l'arpa muntanyenca recollia
mon jovenil ardor.

Llavors eren les meves recordances
celatges del matí,
i alegre estol de joves esperances
s'alçava en mon camí.

Llavors ma vida desbordant no veia
lo baix ni lo somort,
i fins l'arbre ferit que a mos peus queia
me dava un signe fort.

Oh! sí: la gran pinassa qui tombava
ferida amb la destral,
deia: «Per vèncer la maror més brava,
me'n vaig d'aquest penyal.»

Arbre avesat a dominar tormentes
dins la regió del vent,
venceria les ones turbulentes,
navili prepotent...

Ara els navilis ja no es fan de fusta;
i quan aquest pinar
caiga tallat de la muntanya adusta,
serà llenya a cremar...

Quantes coses pel camp de l'existència
he vist mudar així,
perdent noblesa i triomfal potència
dins lo vulgar mesquí!

Palmes, corones de llorer o roses,
trofeus d'ambició...
virtuts del cel, estrelles mig descloses
per l'abnegació...

Meravelles del món o de l'empiri,
que el cor es proposà:
com quedau lluny de l'impotent deliri
qui us estengué la mà!

Buida jo torn ma vida a ton refugi,
oh vell pinar desert!
Com la teva remor, per més que pugi,
mon pobre cant se perd...

Prou venturós seré si, solitari,
algun somniador
mon cant escolta i consegueix trobar-hi
l'encant de ta remor.

Prou me serà, si per la lluita odiosa
essent com un infant,
oh bosc! dins ta pregària remorosa
sé viure tot pregant.

Tu em faràs veure sota el teu ramatge
que tot mundà atractiu
és com eix ull de sol qui per l'herbatge
belluga fugitiu.

Tu em parlaràs amb veu fonda i seguida
de lo abismal i etern,
dels sers volguts, eixits d'aquesta vida,
vius a l'afecte intern.

Així, nodrint-me com per temps enrera
de ton potent vigor,
si no recobro encant de primavera,
tindré els de la tardor.

Bella aquí és la tardor, que el cap no esfulla
d'alzines ni de pins,
i sols el bosc amb la unció remulla
de núvols gegantins.

Noble tardor en què, si bé es lamenta,
el bosc, canta més fort,
i al vibrar amb l'alè de la tormenta
modula i representa
una marxa triomfal sobre la mort...

Cala Gentil

Sobre la cinta de blanca arena,
que besa una aigua de cèlic blau,
grans pins hi vessen a copa plena
olor de bàlsam, ombra serena,
remor suau...
Oh dolç estatge de bellesa i pau!

Un aquí troba la llum més clara,
les colors vàries de to més viu;
pura delícia de tot s'hi empara,
i sol o lluna mostrant la cara,
tot hi somriu...
Oh de mos càntics inefable niu!

Per puigs i serres s'acaramulla
frondós boscatge de verd etern,
que eixa floresta de vària fulla
la tardor trista mai la despulla
ni el fred hivern...
Oh Paradís que apar al món extern!

Si aquí s'acosta qualque mal dia
de nuvolades amb negre estol,
sols hi du tendra melancolia,
com una verge sense alegria
        que en pau se dol...
Oh bon refugi de callat consol!

Aquí, ben jove, pensí abrigar-hi
un niu d'humana felicitat:
després la tomba vaig somiar-hi
a on tindria més solitari
        repòs més grat...
Oh lloc per vida i mort fantasiat!

És que en la calma de tals paratges
tan dolç és viure, veure i sentir,
i vora l'aigua de purs miratges,
al ritme eòlic d'aquestes platges
        tan dolç dormir!
Mes jo tal sort jamai dec posseir.

Què hi fa? D'aquesta cala opalina
prou el misteri n'hauré gustat,
mentre ara, a l'hora que el sol declina,
m'hi sent corfondre dins la divina
        serenitat...
Oh dolç moment, o glop d'eternitat!

A Horaci

Príncep afable de la docta lira,
mestre i custodi de la forma bella,
tu qui cenyires de llorer i murta
        doble corona:

ara tolera que una mà atrevida
passi a mon poble la que amb tal fortuna

tu transportares al solar de Roma
cítara grega.

Aspra i ferrenya sonarà en ses cordes
fines la llengua de ma pàtria dura;
mes també noble hi sonarà: ma pàtria
filla és de Roma.

Filla de Roma per la sang, pel geni,
clara i robusta com sa mare antiga,
guarda en ses terres per llavor de glòria
cendra romana.

Sí: dins sa terra el cavador atònit
ossos i marbres i joiells hi troba,
armes, monedes i penons que ostenten
l'àguila augusta.

Bella ma pàtria és, ademés. Viuria
sens enyorança ta divina Musa
dins eixa terra que cenyeix la blava
mar de sirenes.

Illa és galana, a on el sol de Grècia
brilla puríssim, i d'ardenta saba
pròdig, li dóna amb el raïm alegre
l'àtica oliva.

Deixa, doncs, ara que dins ella evoqui
clàssiques formes i l'antiga Musa,
just amb sos propis ornaments, ma pàtria
veja somriure.

Ara que folla la invocada Fúria,
febre als poetes inspirant, ungleja
l'arpa plorosa, i entre fang destil·la
fonts d'amargura,

oh! com enyora mon afany les clares,
dolces fontanes del Parnàs hel·lènic!...
Mestre, amb ta bella, cisellada copa,
deixa-m'hi beure.

Deixa que tasti la sabor antiga
que omple tes odes i dins elles dura
com un vi ranci de Falern que guarden
àmfores belles.

Nèctar poètic amb què el cor s'anima,
febre i deliris d'embriac no dóna;
dóna la calma de l'Olimp, la sana
força tranquil·la.

Qui de tal nèctar troba el gust, no cerca
l'or, ni les armes, ni el domini frèvol:
l'art és sa vida, que entre goigs o penes
guarda segura.

Ah! pugin altres a palaus que habiten
grogues les ànsies amb l'afany hidròpic,
negres insomnis que en un llit de plomes
posen espines.

Vagen al fòrum, on febrosa turba
crida i s'empaita disputant la presa
que la Fortuna dins la pols humana
llança per riure.

Puga jo, a l'ombra del nadiu boscatge,
seny i bellesa agermanar, oh artista!
seny i bellesa que amb la lira formen
digna aliança.

Sí: que a tes obres el bon seny, Horaci,
guia la dansa de gentils estrofes,
tal com Silenus, el vell gris, guiava
dansa de nimfes.

Elles, ben àgils i formant corona,
donen al ritme la lleugera planta:
riuen les Gràcies, i se sent l'efluvi
d'alta ambrosia.

A Virgili

Oh suavíssim, immortal poeta!
«meitat de la meva ànima» et diria,
com un jorn te digué l'amic Horaci,
si tant gosava qui de lluny t'adora.
Qui no t'estima si et coneix? Ton estre,
ton art suprem admiració ens imposen;
però encara promou més simpatia
ton esperit, que en misteriós efluvi
la flor eterna de ton vers exhala.
Ton esperit corprèn. Té l'hàlit verge
de les selves balsàmiques, l'augusta
pau de les blaves ombres que s'estenen
de puigs altívols, mentre el sol declina
i munta el fum de les humils cabanes...
Té la frescor del rou, la unció que duen
les plantes de virtut benefactora,
la sanitat del camp en ple consorci
del bon treball i la feconda terra.
Té el vel de la celístia, el tendre càntic
de Filomela dolçament planyívol,
l'efusió de les fonts, la llum serena
de l'estel dels pastors a la vesprada.
Rei de la solitud grata a les Muses,
també cantares heroismes èpics
de primitius guerrers, un alt origen
fantasiant per la superba Roma.

Així regares del gran riu homèric
l'ample terrer llatí. Dins l'espessura
de la mítica selva tu collires

aquell ram d'or que, com a ceptre màgic
de poesia, te donà l'entrada
per l'espectral imperi de les ombres.
I més que aquell avenc, tu feres veure
les fondàries del cor, vivent abisme
que penetra ton cant. L'afecte tràgic
de la púnica Reina, la mort noble
dels dos joves amics tu consagrares
amb tal encant, que encara avui ne dura
viva corrent de llàgrimes... Ah! sempre,
damunt horrors, grandeses i batalles,
damunt jocs, infortunis o ventures,
ta poesia escampa son misteri
de sentiment. Un no sé què dolcíssim
de bon cor i de gràcia fa tes obres
incomparables dins l'edat antiga,
oh Rei gentil de la tendresa humana!

No en va l'oracle sibil·lí digueres
a l'imperi romà donant l'anunci
d'un naixement meravellós. L'aurora
d'un nou ordre de segles descobrires
des del cim de ton geni, i va nimbar-te
un tendre raig de la claror futura.
Per això fou que dins el gran eclipsi
del món gentil, tu sol ja romangueres
tot lluminós; i sols pogué la fosca
transfigurar-te, per servir de guia
al vident d'altres mons Dant Alighieri.
Per això arreu les canviant centúries
t'adoren al passar, i tu fas sempre
de guia i confident al cor poètic
que és capaç de sentir-te i pelegrina
per camins de dolor o d'esperança...

A Cabanyes

Com una brosta de llorer novella,
naixent d'antiga rel que estava oculta
entre pedres ciclòpiques i marbres
de clàssica ruïna,

sobre l'august abatement s'aixeca,
evocant heroismes, amb sa fulla
de to metàl·lic i apuntada forma,
a tall d'ínclita llança;

talment sorgí, malaguanyat poeta,
ta solitària inspiració, nodrida
de noble saba i amb l'aspror i força
de ta nadiva terra.

Ardit, auster i vigorós ton geni,
era bé el geni de ta pàtria dura
que amb sa lira de bronze s'adquiria
del vers la independència.

Tu, desdenyant banalitats sonores
i fàcil pompa buida, sols cercaves
intensitat, elevació, noblesa,
que escolta qui n'és digne.

Sols qui n'és digne. Ni tirans altívols,
ni baixa turba afalagar volgueres...
Jamai a l'or venut ni al pler que embruta
rendires homenatge.

Fins execrares la més docta lira,
si amb so d'adulació fou profanada,
si va corrompre amb sensual mollesa
la fibra de son poble.

Així, fent-te de l'art un sacerdoci,
el foc sagrat ne mantenies, i altre
ardor no t'inflamà, mes que amor pura
i entusiasme magnànim.

Del món hel·lènic adorant la forma,
tu l'esperit d'altra època sentires,
i modulares a una verge el càntic
de sospirants estrofes.

Fins més allà de la grandesa humana,
el pur crisma assolint de l'Evangeli,
en l'altar el vessares quan ta Musa
volà nimbada amb l'iris...

Sublim nasqueres; mes la humana glòria
te fou negada, car l'edat caduca
del classicisme bord no comprenia
ta clàssica noblesa.

El manllevat idioma, resistint-se
a les audàcies de ton estre indòmit,
violències en patí, que no tolera
son geni d'altra raça...

Ah! la llengua materna te calia
per abocar-hi el cor... Mes eixa parla
desdenyada, envilida, corrompuda,
ja l'art la creia morta.

Oh cantor sense llengua! així passares,
obscur i pensatiu, en curta vida...
Després l'oblit d'immerescut silenci
cobrí la teva tomba.

I aqueix oblit immerescut perdura,
malgrat l'esforç inútil d'algun savi,
mentre la folla multitud aclama
vulgaritats indignes.

Oh jove atleta de la forta lira!
que eres bé el geni de la pàtria dura,
ara que en glòria ta materna llengua
retorna a vida nova,

per què no tornes tu? Per què en l'esplèndid
ressorgiment que a ton terrer esclata,
alçar no tornes jovenil la testa,
com fresc botó de lliri?

Ai! tu que amb tal imatge te planyies
de que els hèroes passats no revinguessen,
tampoc mai més has de venir a l'obra
que t'assignava el geni.

I romandrà ton buit... més buit encara
essent inadvertit; i mai ton poble
sabrà lo que perdé quan tu morires
abans d'ell recobrar-se.

Tu, que a la pàtria arravatat, pogueres
almenys deixar-hi ta mortal despulla,
de ton doble esperit l'hereu suscita
potent sobre ton poble.

I no manqui a ta raça la corona
que amb temps i millor sort cenyir devies,
de Tarraco en l'Acròpolis sagrada,
Píndar de Catalunya!

Al Poeta que em féu present de fruites saboroses

SOTA un parral que pampolós verdeja
per les columnes jòniques de marbre,
tot clapejant de soleiet i d'ombres
bellugadisses el mosaic de l'atri,
cal posar ton present, jove poeta!

Oh! quin present de fruites saboroses!
Són de Tempé frescal? Són de l'Arcàdia?
A quin hort les collires? Bé pot fer-se'n
a les tres Gràcies delicat obsequi,
que de fruites més sanes i exquisides
ningú en presentarà. Veniu rioleres,
oh petita Pandara, oh jove Ixena,
per oferir-ne les primícies pures
a les Gràcies mateixes, coronades
amb rou d'eterna joventut! No hi manqui
Methymna amb sa gran copa a on fulgura
la netedat... No hi manqui la parella
de Lamon i Alidé, vellets benignes,
per honrar-nos la llar amb la constància
d'amor, que és foc sagrat i dura sempre...
Mes del festí poètic vaja enfora
l'entonament aparatós. Que hi sia
senzill i noble tot, com l'art hel·lènic.
Convidem-hi els amics. Cada un que porti
son present escaigut amb cor placèvol.
Jo sols hi podré dur de ma garriga
qualque bresca de mel, però mel pura
que pren l'abella als romanins estèrils,
mel com ells olorosa i ben daurada,
com rajolí del sol qui daura l'Illa!

Comiat

Per un cel matinal tot blau i rosa,
jo veia un temple de puríssim marbre
blanquejar entre el verd de la ribera,
damunt les clares ones.

Ses columnades de gentils estries,
al perfilar-se paral·leles, feien
conjunt harmoniós, com el cordatge
de la sagrada lira.

Esculpit el frontó, damunt el pòrtic
serenitat irradiava augusta,
com el front galeat i sereníssim
de Pal·las Atenea.

Era allò, vist en fora, el santuari
de l'Art suprem. Com en seria esplèndid
l'interior! Quin càntic, quins oracles
allà ressonarien!

Jo prou volguí pujar-hi; mes vaig perdre
l'incert camí; m'abandonà el coratge;
i l'esglai me digué: «Per què t'esforces,
somniador inútil?»

Després... el temple aquell perdí de vista,
i ja mai més he somniat muntar-hi.
Però a voltes, encara, per ma ruta
girant-me, el veig enfora.

El veig, i deturant-me a contemplar-lo,
ja per mi inassequible, en don indici
a l'esforçat jovent que canta i puja
les costes de la vida.

Oh vosaltres que un jorn entreu al temple,
no us deman per a mi ni una memòria;
mes ah! gravau-hi lo que jo hi volia:
el nom de nostra pàtria!

Les Matines

Sospira el jove fra Anselm,
sospira, prega i dejuna,
quan veu de son monestir
l'observança decaiguda.
Ni per les festes majors
ja hi ha salmòdia nocturna:

només l'òliba, de nit,
s'hi sent per la volta muda.
Sospira el jove fra Anselm,
plorant de zel que l'abrusa.
Vigília del Fundador
així l'abat importuna:
—Pare meu, ni sols anit
per vigília tan augusta
les matines cantarem
com la regla preceptua?
—Fra Anselm, ja vos he dit prou
que es farà com s'acostuma:
bona regla és la costum
que en bones raons es funda.
—Pare meu, pel nostre Sant
qui mai tingué llit de fusta,
i sols rendit d'oració
dormí damunt llosa dura...!
—Fra Anselm, cansats i rendits,
de bon dormir afreturen
aquells qui prou han cantat
quan l'església no està buida.
—I què dirien els morts,
si veien lo que ara s'usa?
—Fra Anselm, anau a cantar
amb els morts, si vos ajuden!...

Fra Anselm se n'entra pel chor,
tot solet dins la foscura...
Dorm en silenci el convent
i les Cabrelles se'n munten.
Quan sona la mitja nit
cap frare sent l'hora justa;
mes ja los desperta tots
un ressò qui los conturba.
Del chor i l'orgue mesclats
és l'harmonia robusta
que per claustre i corredors

vibra, s'escampa, s'allunya...
Els frares qui van sortint
de les cel·les, ja s'ajunten,
i tremolosos d'espant,
a penes si es fan pregunta.
Cap al chor se'n van units,
mes al portal ja s'aturen:
les portes tanca qualcú
sense clau ni tancadura.
Muts de terror senten ells
la gran salmòdia nocturna,
baix d'una arcada arraulits
per on aguaita la lluna.
I los versicles del salm
continuen, continuen,
com ones d'un mar immens
qui vers l'infinit bramula.
L'orgue hi encrespa damunt
ses notes brillants qui munten,
com sobre un mar oratjós
rompents de sonora escuma.
Darrera cada Nocturn
les tres lliçons es modulen,
i de primatxers ja morts
se sent la veu coneguda...

Així antífones i salms,
himnes i càntics s'ajunten,
fins que en deliqui suprem
el *Benedictus* se'n puja,
se'n puja estàtic, volant
entre l'encens qui el perfuma.
Quan la *Salve* de la fi
l'estel de l'auba saluda,
per si mateixa en el chor
s'obrí la porta feixuga.
Els frares vius, esglaiats
van a guaitar-hi tot d'una.

El que veuen allà dins
la sang conglaça i atura.
Veuen frares, ciri encès
i acalada la capulla,
qui se'n van de dos en dos
i vers la cripta s'allunyen.
Així com van arribant
del vas a la boca obscura,
els ciris apaguen ells
i lentament s'hi sepulten...

Postrat, allà, enmig del chor,
sols un frare continua.
És fra Anselm, però difunt
ja el mostra l'alba que apunta.

JOAN ALCOVER
1854-1926

La Serra

«Copeo, copeo, copeo, traïdor:
roseta encarnada,
si t'he agraviada
jo et deman perdó...»

Qui me du l'estrofa, plena de perfums
abella brunzenta de la soledat?...
Quan de ma finestra, a encesa de llums,
estenc la mirada per damunt ciutat,
i l'ànima mia s'enfonsa llunyana,
dins la serra immensa
que l'illa travessa, que l'illa defensa
de la tramuntana,
llavors de la serra surt una cançó,
surt una harmonia que es torna visió:
«Jo venc a parlar-te d'una vida d'or,
de la vida lliure que enyora ton cor;

som la camperola que presents te du,
jo venc de la serra, mes no som per tu.»
Oh flor de muntanya, fina morenor,
o la pageseta que és una pintura
        i té la cintura
        com un gerricó!
L'aviram la volta amb gran voleteig,
quan de matinada crida son estol;
amb capell de pauma se guarda del sol,
quan rega els bellveures vora el safareig.
Per servir als pobres fumants escudelles,
confitar codonyes, adobar gonelles
o guarir les nafres, no hi ha millors dits;
        canta codolades
        i sap contarelles
        d'alicorns i fades
        i poals florits.
Al fons de la cambra porta a la padrina
el vas ple d'escuma de la llet que muny;
        encar és fadrina,
mes serà madona d'un terme de lluny.
La nit del dissabte, se posa a escoltar
i el cor d'alegria li bat en secret
quan dins la salvatge negror de l'estret
on la coma acaba, sent un eguinar
        que ella coneix bé.
És l'euga ensellada del pubill qui ve.
Arriba a la clastra, bota de la sella;
escomet els amos, escomet la filla,
        s'asseu devora ella;
        i encara no brilla
        l'estel del matí
reprèn la tornada pel mateix camí.

I llavors la fosca de la nit, que minva,
i tots els paratges, ecos i llumets,
els torrents qui bramen al peu de la timba,
el matí que esclata en mil saluets,

els galls que desperta, les penyes que daura,
els bous que pasturen, el parell que llaura,
les viles disperses en la vall sublim,
el boc que corona la roca del cim,
el gorg que no es mou
dins la penya brava,
com gota de rou
dins una flor blava,
les dones que renten i la que entrecava,
olivars, pollancres, vinyes, sementers,
molins i masies i castells roquers,
pel jove qui passa, plena de dolçor
de la festejada l'ànima xalesta,
tot és una festa
que canta d'amor.
Oh esquerpa cadena de puigs gegantins!
Oh la visió pura que ve d'allà endins,
flor de rustiquesa
que em du l'enyorança de la jovenesa!
Si per amoixar-li la cua penjanta
m'inclin' a la jove, ella se decanta...
«Copeo, copeo, copeo traïdor:
roseta encarnada,
si t'he agraviada
jo et deman perdó...»
Ella se decanta i desapareix;
i mentres s'allunya i se converteix
en llum solitari lo que era visió,
en llum solitari dins la majestat
de la serralada,
tota silenciosa i tota nimbada
de serenitat...
encara ressona
la veu argentina
d'aquella fadrina
que serà madona:
«Jo som la pagesa que presents te du;
jo venc de la serra, mes no som per tu.»

Oh esquerpa cadena de puigs gegantins!
Ginebrons balsàmics, estepes i pins;
sitges que negregen sota l'ausinar;
soleiada ardenta que besa el pinar;
ombra esmaragdina del fullatge espès;
càntics de revetlla que arriben al mar,
de l'església oberta com un ull encès;
mules trotadores
que cascavellegen
per la carretera
del coll en avall;
falles que flamegen,
seguint la primera
de les balladores
en la nit del ball;
soledat feresta
on sembla que udola
d'obscur fratricidi la gòtica gesta;
trilleig de campanes que el vilatge endola;
endolats que resen i de dos en dos
cap al cementiri segueixen la caixa;
garrofers que freguen amb la branca baixa
les veles de carros que van an el cos;
tonada del batre, cadència moresca;
mèl·leres que broten per dins la verdesca;
famílies que volten la font de salut,
i fruites que es fonen dins la boca fresca
plena de rialles de la joventut;
musa cançonera, vella rondallaire;
sanitosa flaire
de la pagesia;
llumeneret blau
que l'ànima atrau
de la minyonia...
sou l'exquisidesa, sou l'encantament
on l'ànima hi sent
de la pàtria mia.

Miramar

SEMPRE visquí vora del mar,
mes fins avui no el coneixia;
sobtadament, a Miramar,
m'ha revelat sa fesomia.

Sembla somriure i alenar,
com una verge qui somnia;
de món a món sembla passar,
com una immensa correntia.

Vénen la flota i el fibló,
i del fantàstic horitzó
no s'interromp la pau eterna.

Sols, en els ulls del pelegrí,
vibra quelcom de gegantí
quan passa l'ombra de Blanquerna.

La Relíquia

FAUNE mutilat,
brollador eixut,
jardí desolat
de ma joventut...
Beneïda l'hora
que m'ha duit aquí.
La font qui no vessa, la font qui no plora,
me fa plorar a mi.
Sembla que era ahir
que dins el misteri de l'ombra florida,
tombats a la molsa,
passàvem les hores millors de la vida.
De l'aigua sentíem la música dolça,
dintre la piscina guaitàvem els peixos,

collíem poncelles, caçàvem bestioles,
i ens fèiem esqueixos
muntant a la branca de les atzeroles.

Ningú sap com era
que entre l'esponera
de l'hort senyorívol,
fent-lo més ombrívol,
creixia la rama d'antiga olivera.
Arbre centenari,
amorós pontava la soca torçuda,
perquè sense ajuda
poguéssim pujar-hi.
Al forc de la branca senyora i majora
penjàvem la corda de l'engronsadora,
i, venta qui venta,
folgàvem i rèiem, fins que la vesprada
la llum esvaïa de l'hora roenta,
de l'hora encantada.

Somni semblaria
el temps que ha volat
de la vida mia,
sense les ferides que al cor ha deixat;
sense les ferides que es tornen a obrir
quan veig que no vessa,
ni canta ni plora, la font del jardí.

Trenta anys de ma vida volaren de pressa,
i encara no manca
penjat a la branca
un tros de la corda de l'engronsadora,
com trista penyora,
despulla podrida d'un món esbucat...
Faune mutilat,
brollador eixut,
jardí desolat
de ma joventut.

Desolació

Jo só l'esqueix d'un arbre, esponerós ahir,
que als segadors feia ombra a l'hora de la sesta;
mes branques una a una va rompre la tempesta,
i el llamp fins a la terra ma soca migpartí.

Brots de migrades fulles coronen el bocí
obert i sense entranyes, que de la soca resta;
cremar he vist ma llenya; com fumerol de festa,
al cel he vist anar-se'n la millor part de mi.

I l'amargor de viure xucla ma rel esclava,
i sent brostar les fulles i sent pujar la saba,
i m'aida a esperar l'hora de caure un sol conhort.

Cada ferida mostra la pèrdua d'una branca;
sens mi, res parlaria de la mitat que em manca;
jo visc sols per a plànyer lo que de mi s'és mort.

Col·loqui

LA MUSA

Per què de mi et recordes
i a l'arpa d'altre temps les mans allargues,
i, tot mullant les cordes
de llàgrimes amargues,
com pluja d'estels d'or
solquen els rims la fosca de ton cor?

EL POETA

És mon desig que un raig de poesia
il·lumini mes llàgrimes; voldria
trobar al fons de l'ànima quelcom
d'eixa punyent i fonda melodia
que fa aturar tothom,

perquè en la pietat dels qui passessin
i el càntic escoltessin,
com a l'entorn del violí qui plora
demanant caritat en nom de Déu,
duràs almenys sobre la terra una hora
la vida de mos fills, que fou tan breu.

LA MUSA

La plenitud de vida no comença
ni arriba l'home a sa virilitat
sens que fermenti en l'ànima el llevat
de l'íntima sofrença.
Sia ton cor el ferro espurnejant,
damunt l'enclusa del dolor, sonant...

EL POETA

A mos infants no tornarà la vida
el broll de foc i el ritme dels martells
sobre el metall de l'ànima enrogida;
no em plany de ma dissort, els plany a ells.
Si a l'espona del llit,
quan se glaçava el cos, quan l'agonia
els ulls enterbolia
del jove moribund, li haguessin dit
de part de Déu: —Minyó, te'n vols anar?...
ell, què hauria respost? —Me dol deixar
ma família, la terra a on nasquí;
és prest; la vida riu; eixa amarganta
copa de fel, decanta-la de mi;
jo me somet, ta voluntat és santa;
però, si et plau, Senyor, deixa'm aquí...
No pogué ser; i se tancà la porta
de ma casa, una nit, sens que ell tornàs,
i el duien a romandre al mateix vas
de sa germana morta.

JOAN ALCOVER

LA MUSA

Mes tu deus a la vida ton tribut.
No sents la host qui se canta a si mateixa,
i avança menyspreant la multitud
dels morts que tomben i els ferits que deixa?

EL POETA

Mai la vegí tan bella com és ara,
la vida d'aquest món,
que d'un encís crudel tota s'amara
per a parlar-me dels que ja no hi són.
Plorar!... També plorava
Jesús davant la tomba de l'amic.
Ran de la fossa com un arbre estic,
que hi beu tota la saba.

LA MUSA

Mes, l'arbre ha de fruitar

EL POETA

Jo vull que l'oli
del fruit amarg, com esprémuda oliva,
cremi tot en la llàntia que aurioli
dels dos adolescents la imatge viva.
Si la força del geni m'és estranya,
tan gran com ell s'aixeca mon dolor,
i jo puc llavorar l'alta muntanya
per esculpir-hi un monument d'amor.

Dol

I

Sé d'una vella consirosa
a qui sos fills varen deixar
per la fortuna fabulosa
de l'altra banda de la mar.

JOAN ALCOVER

Com la grisor d'un ull d'oracle,
mira la fonda solitud,
esperant l'hora del miracle
que li retorni el bé perdut.

Com ella guaita la marina,
mon pensament, vetlla, abocat;
mes la finestra a on s'inclina
s'obrí davant l'eternitat...

Arriba un jorn que nostra vida
ja no veu res en l'avenir,
mes, a l'hivern rejovenida,
en la dels fills torna florir.

Tèbia dolcesa els ulls amoixa
de pressentir la tendra mà
que en acabant l'última angoixa,
piadosament els tancarà.

I de llur vida l'auriola
ens sembla veure en el futur,
que nostres cendres agombola,
assoleiant el vas obscur.

Però si cau llur jovenesa
i se'ns acluca l'ideal,
¿què n'ha de fer de sa vellesa
l'àrida soca paternal?

Cap a l'abisme que ens espera
mon pensament amolla el fruit,
com el brancam d'una figuera
tota penjada sobre el buit.

Llum de records passa allà enfora,
pluja d'estels en la negror.
No me'n sé anar, no, de la vora
de mon terrible mirador.

Com en el fons d'un vell retaule,
llisquen els dos adolescents;
passen, ulls clucs, sense paraula,
com a somnàmbuls somrients.

Passa la flor de l'amor mia,
passen en creu aquelles mans
que ma tendresa cobdicia
per a besar-les com abans.

De la foscor mai explorada
pugen alens d'oratge fred,
que ma existència amenaçada
fan tremolar com un llumet.

¿Cal defensar la flama incerta
d'aquest llumet feble i morent?
Per a tancar la porta oberta,
cal que forcegi contra el vent?

Entri la ratxa que em perfuma
amb la fetor d'un món podrit;
¡munti l'oreig que du l'escuma
de les rompents de l'infinit!

II

Ombra divina, protectora
de l'aliança dels dos mons.
Jo torn a tu; mon cor enyora
les oblidades oracions.

Aquí tot parla de l'imperi
a on sojornen els difunts;
aquí batega el gran misteri
que vius i morts escalfa junts.

Sols la fredor d'aquestes lloses
calma la febre de mon front,

davant les úlceres descloses
en l'Enclavat en creu d'afront.

Els qui duim l'ànima ferida,
com els captaires afollats,
entre el tumulte de la vida
ens hi trobem desemparats.

Mes, en el temple que il·lumina
com un estel la llàntia d'or,
l'eternitat s'hi sent veïna,
afalagant el nostre cor.

I els endolats, al peu de l'ara,
sentim els morts més avinent,
i a eixugar el plor de nostra cara
ve la carícia de l'absent.

Record de Sòller

AMIC, teixiu aquesta visió de la infantesa...
Ja coneixeu la vila d'ombrívols carrerons,
la rica vall de Sòller, entre serrals estesa,
on totes les vivendes tenen un hort al fons.

Era senyor de casa el somni de la sesta;
la posadera em feia senyal de que emmudís,
posant-se el dit als llavis; una verdor xalesta
pel portaló guaitava com auri paradís.

L'hort m'oferí refugi, dosser la verda branca
del taronger; en l'herba me vaig tombar; l'eixam
d'insectes, com espurnes, brunzia per la tanca,
i em feia pessigolles al front l'espès herbam.

Eren les verdes tiges profunda columnada;
filtrava, arran de terra, l'esguard per allà endins;

dansaven les corol·les de fulla acarminada,
com baiaderes entre pilars esmaragdins.

Llavores un misteri per mi se va descloure,
torbant la fonda calma del cor adolescent:
entrà una joveneta amb els cabells a lloure,
que un raig de sol feria com nimbe resplendent.

Amagatall cercava per treure's una pua
del cos; a totes bandes girà l'ull inquiet;
s'alçà la falda roja, mostrà la cama nua
que més amunt tenia una blancor de llet.

Mon cor, davant la casta nuesa, va suspendre
son ritme; una calrada bullenta vaig sentir;
i l'esglai que sentiria la bergantella tendra
que es creia tota sola, si s'adonés de mi!

I el nin va tornar home... ¿Quin esperit dins una
espina de figuera de moro va saltar
a l'abscondit ivori de l'Eva, tan dejuna
de dar-me el fruit de l'arbre simbòlic a flairar?

Mai més l'he retrobada; i veig com aquell dia,
fa quaranta anys, la nina que no em coneix tampoc
i el món d'una edat nova, inconscient m'obria,
incendiant la porta sense percebre el foc.

Amic, teixiu aquesta visió de la infantesa,
vós que caceu libèl·lules en la presó del rim,
vós que preniu les ales amb tanta subtilesa
que no se perd un àtom del matisat polsim.

JOAN MARAGALL

1860-1911

Les minves del gener

ELL PARLA

...Anit eixí de casa teva, aimia,
tot neguitós i malcontent de mi.
Que coses que et vaig dir, que no volia!
Que coses vaig callar, volent-les dir!
Al matí el malestâ encara em durava.
Era un matí emplujat com pel febrer.
Déu meu, aquest hivern que mai s'acaba!
I aquesta primavera que no ve!
He trobat els passeigs arreu fangosos,
sadollats per la pluja de la nit;
els brots tendres brillaven temorosos
al bell damunt del fosc brancatge humit;
i tot d'una, volant a la ventura,
com lleu companya de mon greu afany,
he vist creuar l'espai, balba, insegura,
la primera oreneta d'aquest any.
Jo l'he vista arribar, vola que vola,
fins al balcó del blanc palau discret,
i allí aturar-se arrupideta i sola,
guaitant poruga i tremolant de fred.
Guaitant poruga les desertes planes
del cel desemboirant-se lentament,
enyorant-hi el volar de ses germanes,
que ha deixat endarrera incautament.

ELLA

También ha vingut — pobre aucellet,
tot arraulit,
a mon balcó — cercant redós.
Mes jo li he dit:

— No temis ja — lo que és passat,
aixeca el vol:
el cel és blau, — els arbres verds,
i brilla el sol. —
Així mateix — dic a l'aimat:
— Oblida ahir:
diga'm avui — amb cor lleuger
lo que em vols dir.

ELL

Com asserenes mon neguit,
com fuig mon dol!
Ets el cel blau, — ets l'arbre verd,
ets el meu sol.

Pirenenques

III

BEN ajagut a terra, com me plau
el veure davant meu en costa suau
un prat ben verd sota d'un cel ben blau!

I en les albes la gran bellugadissa
de les fulles d'acer que el vent eriça
amb tants reflects de llum enlluernadissa.

I el sol estès pertot. I el rec com cau
escumejant avall la costa suau
del prat ben verd sota del cel ben blau.

Tots els membres caiguts, tot jo per terra,
buidat de tota força i sens desig,
la pensa a poc a poc se'm desaferra...

I em vaig trobant tan bé an allà entremig,
i em va invadint com una immensa pau,
i vaig sent un tros més del prat suau
ben verd, ben verd sota d'un cel ben blau.

El Mal Caçador

La missa matinal
la diuen allà dalt
així que es fa de dia.

La missa de l'estiu
el capellà la diu
amb les portes obertes.

S'oeix de tots costats
quan enflaira els serrats
el ginestar de Corpus.

El caçadô es daleix.
De fora estant l'oeix
amb un genoll a terra.

Al bell punt d'alçar Déu,
li bota allà al bell peu
la llebre endiastrada.

S'esventa el gos lladrant,
la llebre fuig botant,
i el caçadô al darrera.

«Corres i correràs.
Mai més t'aturaràs.»
Aquesta és la sentència.

«Doncs, corro i correré.
Mai més m'aturaré.
Alegre és la sentència.»

S'allunyen amb el vent,
perdent-se en un moment
els crits, la fressa, el rastre...

JOAN MARAGALL

Passen dies i nits...
Pels marges reflorits
ha tornat Corpus Christi.

La missa matinal
la diuen allà dalt,
les portes són obertes.

En un vent de visió
passa el mal caçador
entre lladrucs i fressa.

Se gira i veu l'altar,
i al peu el capellà,
i en alt veu l'Hòstia càndida.

Passa i es perd al lluny...
La boirina de juny
cenyeix l'horitzó immòbil.

Roden les estacions,
revénen els plançons:
cada any, cada any ve Corpus.

Cada any torna a passar;
cada any torna a mirar,
cada any, la missa augusta.

Cada any els capellans
tenen més cabells blancs
i aixequen més els braços.

Cada any l'Hòstia es va alçant,
el temple es va aixafant
i l'Hòstia puja, puja...

Passen més anys i més,
el capellà no hi és:
l'Hòstia va sola en l'aire.

Amunt... amunt... amunt...
La volta perd el junt,
la llum del cel s'hi filtra.

L'Hòstia s'hi va acostant...
El temple es va esquerdant...
El caçador no para.

Ve un any, la volta cau
i s'obre el gran cel blau
damunt de l'Hòstia blanca,

que s'alça lentament...
Al ser l'estiu vinent
floreix el temple en runes.

Se'n va pujant al cel...
El caçadô, amb anhel,
cada any, cada any la mira.

L'Hòstia per 'nâ al zenit,
té l'espai infinit,
i ell, per caçâ, encisat,
té el temps, l'eternitat.

Joan Garí

I

A la muntanya miracle,
una llegenda ha florit:
la llegenda del diable
i de Fra Joan Garí.
Fra Joan fa penitència
enfilat a dalt d'un cim.
Li duien una donzella
que tenia els mals esprits.

Montserrat, muntanya santa,
la muntaya de cent cims.

II

Fra Joan dintre la cova
estava fent oració:
Riquilda se li presenta
vestida de temptació.
Fra Joan clou les parpelles,
mes la veu contraclaror.

Montserrat és ple de boira:
Riquilda és un raig de sol.

III

Després del pecat tan gran
ell resta bocaterrosa.
Riquilda és timbes avall,
Montserrat és net de boira.
Fra Garí veu els abims
i les cames li tremolen.

Si prova de redreçà's
cau de mans una altra volta.
Joan Garí ja no és un sant,
Joan Garí ja no és un home,
que és una fera dels camps
que per Montserrat pastora.

IV

Al cap d'anys de terrejar
sent una veu d'innocència:
«Aixeca't, Joan Garí,
la teva sort és complerta:
ja pots alçâ els ulls al cel
que ja els tens prou plens de terra.»

Joan Garí s'alça de mans
com un ós quan se redreça.

El comte Arnau

III

—Treu-te la capa —li demana ella—.
Treu-te la capa, que et veuré més gran.
—Treu-te tu el manto, que et veuré més bella.
—No, que só l'abadessa de Sant Joan.—

Canta una alosa de la part de fora,
per la finestra entra el sol brillant,
el cel és blau i resplendenta l'hora:
el comte i l'abadessa es van mirant.

—Treu-te tu el manto, que et veuré més bella:
sense toca et voldria i sense vel.
—De genolls jo et voldria en la capella:
tan gloriós, faries goig al cel.

—Prô a mi el cel no em fa goig més que si el miro
des de la terra sobre meu obert:
me plau trobar-lo, quan els ulls hi giro,
buit i silenciós com un desert.

El cel és el repòs de la mirada,
i és el repòs del braç i el pensament;
perxô, ajagut a terra, el cel m'agrada
i m'adormo mirant-lo fixament.

—Altre cel és per mi la tenebrosa
capella on un altar brilla tot sol:
el cos humiliat sobre una llosa,
l'ànima deslliurada aixeca el vol.

I de la terra i d'aquest món s'oblida,
sospirant per la mort que ha de venir.
—En tos llavis gruixuts, de mort al dir,
com hi oneja suaument la vida!

—Mes, són fang. Quan per sempre s'hauran clos,
vindran els cucs i se'n faran pastura.
Vull amagrî els meus llavis i el meu cos
per fer-me tornar l'ànima més pura.—

Canta una alosa de la part de fora,
per la finestra entra el sol brillant,
el cel és blau i resplendenta l'hora:
el comte i l'abadessa es van mirant.

—Adalaisa, tu que ets tan vividora
i que els ulls els tens plens de voluntat,
i aquesta àvida boca prenedora,
i en els teus aires tanta majestat,

¿com és que ara malparles de la vida,
per la que estàs tan fortament armada?
No t'escau la mirada esmortuïda
sota l'arc de la cella ben poblada.

Escaurà bé a tes pàl·lides germanes,
tristos cossos per sempre immaternals:
per elles són les fantasies vanes
de vagues resplendors celestials.

Però tu, performada criatura,
delícia de la terra, torna al món!
Romp el cordó que injuria ta cintura!
Arrenca't, Adalaisa, els vels del front!—

I avança Arnau hermosament; prô es gira
airosa ella an el Sant Cristo nu,
i signant-lo an el comte, li diu: —Mira:
aquest encara és més hermós que tu!—

Canta una alosa de la part de fora,
per la finestra entra el sol brillant,
el cel és blau i resplendenta l'hora:
el comte i l'abadessa es van mirant.

IV

Totes les veus de la terra
criden contra el comte Arnau
perquè, volent Adalaisa,
sense ella se n'ha tornat.

—«Fill de la terra, — fill de la terra,
comte l'Arnau:
per una imatge
t'has deturat,
per un cadavre,
tu que en fas tants!»
—«Com el Sant Cristo — no n'he fet cap.»
—«Què té el Sant Cristo? Què té el Sant Cristo,
comte l'Arnau?
És fusta morta: — no pot brotar.»
—«Ai, sí, que brota! — Ai, sí, que brota!
Valga'm Déu, val!
Quina mirada — ella li ha dat!»
—«Quina mirada, — quina mirada,
comte l'Arnau,
quina mirada — deu havê estat!»
Ell vol esclafir la rialla,
fa un gran crit i arrenca el plor.
Al rugit del plor que arrenca
clamorós el comte Arnau,
totes les veus de la terra
se dispersen udolant.

VI

Totes les veus de la terra
aclamen el comte Arnau
perquè de la fosca prova
ha sortit tan triomfant:

—«Fill de la terra, — fill de la terra,
comte l'Arnau,

ara demana, — ara demana:
qué no podràs?

—Viure, viure, viure sempre:
no voldria morir mai;
ser com roure que s'arrela
i obre la copa en l'espai.

—Els roures viuen i viuen,
prô també compten els anys.

—Doncs, vull ser la roca immòbil
entre sols i temporals.

—La roca viu sense viure,
que res la penetra mai.

—Doncs, la mar somovedora
que a tot s'obre i dóna pas.

—La mar s'està tota sola,
i tu vas acompanyat.

—Doncs, ser l'aire quan l'inflama
la llum del sol immortal.

—Prô l'aire ni el sol no estimen
ni senten l'eternitat.

—Doncs: ser home sobre home,
ser la terra palpitant.

—Seràs roure, seràs penya,
seràs mar esvalotat,
seràs aire que s'inflama,
seràs astre rutilant,
seràs home sobre home,
perquè en tens la voluntat.

Correràs per monts i planes,
per la terra que és tan gran,
muntat en cavall de flames
que no se't cansarà mai.
El teu pas farà basarda
com el pas del temporal.
Totes les veus de la terra
cridaran al teu voltant.
Te diran ànima en pena
com si fossis condemnat.»

La fi del comte Arnau

ARNAU

—La terrenal via infinita
deixeu-me córrer ben fidel.
Mireu que us porto la collita:
«Pare nostre que estau en lo Cel.»
Só com un cep amb molta fruita
que es dobla al pes de sa dolçor:
no em veremeu, que encara en lluita
vaig aprenent la llei d'amor.
Porto en mi els fills i gent estranya,
porto l'aimada sobre el cor;
i la muller, que m'acompanya,
me canta el cant de vida i mort.
Per l'encontrada més obscura
de tant de pes vaig carregat:
sento al damunt com me madura
l'amor degut i no pagat.

ADALAISA

—Qui semblant fruit arribi a heure,
li amargarà el mateix que fel:
amor que es paga com un deure,
ni grat te'n sento, queda-te'l!
Que trist amor! Quina altra cosa
la generosa voluntat

que salta el marge i la resclosa
com un torrent que ve sobtat!
Ai! No era aquesta, no era aquesta
la que m'havies tu promès
per dur-me al món com a una festa
i corre-hi sempre i sempre més?

ARNAU

—Corro de nit, corro de dia;
veig a tothom, no em veu ningú:
veig l'esperit que a dintre els nia
i com treballa en cada u.
Els veig, la cara somniosa
del son terrer, que es van alçant;
sento la veu misteriosa
que els va cridant, que els va cridant.
De tant en tant paren l'orella:
no saben què és; miren entorn;
veuen la terra que és tan bella
i mig rient baixen el front.
Mes han de fer ben tost per viure:
el dia és curt, la feina és gran...
I van perdent aquell mig-riure:
els uns del tot, altres no tant.
Jo passo entre ells sense fer nombre
ni entre els vivents ni entre els esprìts,
com un ensomni, com una ombra,
com un despert entre adormits.

LA MULLER

—En el bon temps, a casa nostra,
jo feia igual que ara fas tu:
tu sota el cel, jo sota un sostre:
per a una mare tot és u.
Quan els infants i les criades
eren dormits, ja de nit gran,
jo recorria les estades
com un fantasma vigilant.

Jo veia els somnis i figures
volar damunt dels fronts dormits;
tocava el rostre a les criatures
per si eren freds o bé enardits.
Veia en llur jaç a les serventes
(el de la dida vora el bres)
en positures diferentes,
i en llur son encara més.
Hi havia aquella forta Assumpta
(que terres lluny era el marit)
que s'adormia cella junta
i amb una mà damunt del pit.
Després, aquella joveneta
que era un xic rossa i tan humil,
tenia sempre una rialleta
i entorn del cap el braç gentil.
Però les altres, aplanades,
pel gros treball de tot lo jorn,
boca terroses o badades,
eren com mortes a l'entorn.
I, per la casa tenebrosa
tornant al nostre llit retret,
m'hi esmunyia silenciosa,
vetllant encara ton son inquiet.

ARNAU

Ditxosa tu, que així visqueres
rica d'amor, muller lleial,
i per l'amor de mil maneres
dintre la vida universal!
Mes... ai de mi! jo que vivia
per mi tot sol i els meus delits,
i ara, mort-viu, haig de fer via
com un despert entre adormits!

LA MULLER

—Ara ho veieu, les nostres filles,
com no éreu filles de l'amor!...

JOAN MARAGALL

LES FILLES

—«Fills i filles, llops i guilles»,
solíeu dir, pare i senyor.

ELS MOSSOS

—També ens en dèieu de ben grosses
mentre ens robàveu les suors.

ARNAU

—«Mossos i mosses, alans i gosses»
fou de mes dites la mellor...
...Totes les veus de la terra
se fan sentî an el comte Arnau,
li van movent eterna guerra
per els camins de la gran pau.
Són com a mar esvalotada
que de molt lluny se fa present
amb la clamor de ses onades
tota la nit en gran turment;
són com el vent de les altures
que d'un sol crit omple l'espai;
són com el plor de les criatures,
que no té fi ni en tindrà mai;
són el Dolor, rei de la terra,
que en tot pit d'home es fa sentir...
El comte Arnau se desespera,
perquè vol dir-lo i no el sap dir.

Però l'esposa fila i canta,
dalt a mig aire del cel blau.
El comte Arnau tot s'hi decanta
per si la sent cantar suau.
Mes a sa veu altra es conlliga
que mai s'hi havia conlligat...
que va cantant la cançó antiga
amb una nova pietat.
És una veu encara viva.
No ve del cel, ni ve dels llims:

ve de la terra, tan festiva,
amb verd als camps i amb sol als cims.
En un pendís de la muntanya
hi ha una pastora de l'ull blau
que, tot cantant la cançó estranya,
se'l va estimant, el comte Arnau.
Un campanar sona en l'altura;
les gents se mouen pels sembrats;
esquellejant salta i pastura
l'escampadissa dels ramats...
I la pastora enamorada
canta que canta la cançó:
li ha mudat tota la tonada
i ha redimit el pecador.
Que des de que ella l'ha cantada
amb altra veu, amb altre acord,
ja no hi ha ànima damnada...
La cançó ha mort, la cançó ha mort.
Seguiu el pla, seguiu la serra,
vila i poblat, per on vulgueu:
la cançó és fora de la terra
i ja mai més la sentireu.
Alguns diran que la sentiren;
altres ni en tenen cap record;
quins l'oblidaren, quins ni l'oïren...
La cançó ha mort, la cançó ha mort.
Jo, d'una vella ja afollada
pel pes dels anys, la vaig sentir
ja sense to, a glops, trencada...
I aquella vella es va morir.
Cantant, cantant, nasqué la infàmia,
i descantant, la redempció:
el Comte Arnau tenia l'ànima
a la mercè d'una cançó.
Lo que la mort tanca i captiva,
sols per la vida és deslliurat:
basta una noia amb la veu viva
per redimir la humanitat.

La fi d'En Serrallonga

—Pare, absoleu-me: só cansat de viure.
—T'escomet a bona hora el cansament.
La teva via s'ha acabat i ets lliure
d'anar-te'n al repòs eternalment.
Mes, abans d'adormir-te i reposar-te,
cal que et recordis dels teus grans pecats:
tots aquells que jo puga perdonar-te,
també de Déu seran-te perdonats.
—El primer pecat meu és l'orgull, pare:
jo só aquell que he tingut un rei al cos;
mai he pogut sofrir que algú em manare:
fer la llei a tot déu era el meu goig.
Perxò he tingut tant odi al rei d'Espanya
i li he fet la guerra jo tot sol.
Ell la terra ens ha omplert de gent estranya
i manar-nos-ho tot és lo que vol.
Doncs, jo li he dit: «No em plau!» I, via fora!
he anat pel món com m'ha vingut a pler,
he fet lo que he volgut, lliure a tota hora,
i no he obeït llei, ni rei, ni rê.
I, tant se val!, és una bella cosa
fer tremolar tothom i estar segur!
Cap respecte en ma via m'ha fet nosa,
mai he baixat la testa per ningú...
—Mes, ara...
                    —Mes, ara que ja sé que compareixo
en presència del Déu omnipotent...
—Te'n penedeixes?
                              —Sí, me'n penedeixo.
—Doncs, sia't perdonat.
                                        —Amén, amén...
—Quin altre pecat tens?
                                      —La ira, pare
Quan m'encenc no tinc fre ni aturador,

me giro contra el món, Déu i sa Mare,
i tot voldria dur-ho a destrucció.
Pare, he estat crudel: moltes vegades
m'he delitat vegent rajar la sang;
he vist alçar-se a mi mans ajuntades
i segar-se genolls caient al fang.
I jo me n'he rigut, perquè em plavia,
i, podent perdonar, no he perdonat...
És una cosa dolça i fa alegria
veure un 'nemic als peus ben manillat!
I fer mal! I fer mal! Allò era viure:
destruir sols per gust i per voler;
sentir plorar tothom i poder riure...
Ser com rei de dolor... És bell, a fe!
—Fill meu! Fill meu! Això és massa malesa;
això és un mal esprit que tens al cos:
encara en parles amb la vista encesa
en foc d'infern!...
—No, no!... Ja ve el repòs.
Doncs, ara que ja sé que compareixo
en presència de Déu omnipotent...
—Te'n penedeixes?
—Sí, me'n penedeixo.
—Doncs, sia't perdonat.
—Amén, amén...
—També he tingut enveja i mala bava
per corrompre la glòria dels demés:
allí on jo he conegut que no arribava,
no he volgut que cap altre hi arribés.
D'aquell que em feia ombra o bé respecte,
m'he gaudit fent-ne córrer males veus,
i, tot fingint-li acatament i afecte,
li anava segant l'herba sota els peus.
De lo que no he entès, n'he dit mentida,
dels fets més grans que els meus, n'he dit rampells,
he volgut sols un pes, sols una mida:
la meva: els que en passaven, pobres d'ells!
Rebaixar, rebaixar, fins que es confonga

tothom en un mesquí i humil estol,
i al damunt En Joan Sala i Serrallonga,
sent més que tots i governant tot sol.
—Mes, ara...
—Mes, ara, que ja sé que compareixo
en presència de Déu omnipotent...
—Te'n penedeixes?
—Sí, me'n penedeixo.
—Doncs, sia't perdonat.
—Amén, amén...
—He estat avar: mai he tingut de sobra,
sempre he anat per més al camí ral;
per molt que posseís, sentia'm pobre
i amb la por d'anâ a raure a l'hospital.
Ai! La cobdícia no em deixava viure,
era roí pels altres i per mi:
per un parell de bous, per una lliura,
hauria fet deu hores de camí.
Veure'm dinê apilat me consolava;
mes fruir no podia'n altrament
que pensant a quants altres els mancava
allò que era per mi un bon passament.
«Això és ben meu —pensava—; això no falla:
els altres, si misèria o fam vingués,
que es pengin!» I, llavores, ni una malla
hauria dat a un pobre que passés.
—Mes, ara...
—Mes, ara, que ja sé que compareixo
en presència de Déu omnipotent...
—Te'n penedeixes?
—Sí, me'n penedeixo.
—Doncs, sia't perdonat.
—Amén, amén...
—La peresa, la gola i la luxúria
ben cert que foren mos pecats més xics;
prô algun cop m'ha plagut deixar la fúria
dels combats, lluny d'amics i d'enemics.
Me n'anava a fer cap a la masia

oblidada en el fons d'alguna vall,
i m'entaulava en bona companyia,
menyspreuant tota lluita i tot treball.
Llavores jo me'n reia de la guerra
i dels meus que es batien, capsigranys!
i tant se me'n donava que la terra
la manessin els propis o els estranys.
Ben menjat, ben begut, plavia'm jeure
a bona ombra per fer la migdiada,
cantant cançons d'amor que fan distreure,
o escoltant els aucells en la brancada.
Si llavores passava alguna mossa
revinguda de cos, jo la cridava,
ella venia a mi, la deshonrava,
i encara se'n tenia per ditxosa.
—I goses riure?
—Era cosa bona...
—Mes no ho és pas a l'hora de la mort.
—Bon menjar, bon oblit i jeure amb dona:
mai havia trobat millor conhort.
—Mes, ara...
—Mes, ara, que ja sé que compareixo
en presència de Déu omnipotent...
—Te'n penedeixes?
—Sí, me'n penedeixo.
—Doncs, sia't perdonat.
—Amén, amén...
—I el tracte amb Na Joana, no és injúria
que clama també a Déu Nostre Senyor?
Acusa't!...
—Pare, no: no fou luxúria,
sinó una veritable estimació.
És cert que jo, en ses carns, moltes vegades
hi he enterrat tant de força i de voler!
Mes eren llaç d'amor ses abraçades
i coronat de seny son front serè.
La Joana m'ha estat reina i esclava;
molts cops ella pensava per tots dos;

quan jo estava adormit, ella vetllava;
ella m'ha fet valent i poderós.
M'ha ajudat amb l'esguard, amb la paraula;
si ha calgut, amb la força del seu braç;
cada migdia m'ha llescat pa a taula
i cada vespre m'ha alegrat el jaç.
En paga, jo li he estat amant sol·lícit...
D'això també me n'haig de penedir?
—Fou un amor desordenat i il·lícit!
—Doncs... tant se val!... me'n penedeixo, sí!
—Tens algun pecat més dins teu?
—No, pare.
—De tots els que m'has dit i els que has comès
contrit demanes perdó a Déu?
—Sí, pare.
—I et sap greu de tot cor d'haver-lo ofès?
—Sí.
—Doncs en nom de Déu omnipotent,
Pare, Fill i Esperit Sant, t'absolc. Amén...
—Moriré resant el Credo;
mes digueu an el botxí
que no em mati fins i a tant
que m'hagi sentit a dir:
«Crec en la resurrecció de la carn.»

En la mort d'un jove

Te'n vas anâ amb aquell ponent dolcíssim...
Caigueres, lluitadô, al marxâ a la lluita.
Somreies a la força dels teus muscles
i glaties per guerres i corones,
i tot de cop t'has esllanguit per terra
amb els ulls admirats...

Ai, la Mort, i que n'ets d'embellidora!
Aquell teu primer vel, quan el llançares
damunt de l'hèroe en flor, tots somriguérem
sota els plors estroncats, que una serena

va començâ a regnâ en el pit i el rostre
del moribond. L'alè anava i venia
suaument emperesit, fins que esperàrem...
I no tornà... Llavores esclataven
més alts els plors al Cel... Ell ja no hi era...
Prô a fora, al camp, era un ponent dolcíssim...

Endreça

SENYOR! Deu consol a qui plora
i torneu-li el plô al qui no pot plorar,
i doneu-li pau a l'ànima inquieta
perquè us sàpiga esperar.

Diades d'amor

V

TOT l'estiu l'he enyorada dintre el cor
i ara l'han vista els ulls que resplendia
amb el novell infant ja al braç, i fort.
L'he vista molt de lluny a ple migdia:
ella alçava l'infant davant del sol
i el besava en la llum que els revestia.

Haidé

ELLA digué son nom: llavors la vella,
que li era a la vora, va dir: —Per quin sant és?—
I respongué l'amiga amb els ulls riallers:
—Això rai, tant se val, la santa és ella.—

I

Ella és la santa d'ella perquè és bella,
i Déu li ha fet la gràcia de llançar llum entorn;
ella és el sol del seu propi jorn
i de sa nit l'estrella.
I té la gràcia al cos tan abundanta,

que en ella naix i mor tot lo que fa:
ella és el cant, si canta,
ella és la dansa, si li plau dansar.
I com que del dansar n'és tan amiga,
el meu seny la veu sempre que graciosament
ondula el seu bell cos sense fadiga
com creat en l'encís del moviment.
Els meus ulls van seguint-la mentres dansa
obedients al pas del seu cos bell;
i si reposa, tot me meravell
com si es trenqués la llei de sa criança.
Mes llavors, en la llum del seu mirar
i de ses galtes fortament rosades,
i en l'onada del pit a l'alenar
i el repòs de ses formes tan amades,
retrob el ritme que creguí perdut
i a mon esprit per sempre s'hi reposa
com en una absoluta beatitud.

II

Ella de sa hermosura és generosa
i me'n féu tot el do que jo en volia.
M'ha donat sa paraula graciosa
alenanta de prop, que m'invadia.
I les mirades dintre les mirades,
el pit tot somogut, la galta ardenta,
parlàvem amb les boques inflamades
de qualsevulga cosa indiferenta.
La paraula sols era la musica
del gran voler que el pit ens agitava:
jo resseguint sa cara, tan bonica!
ella en mos ulls veient com m'inundava.
I talment la inundà l'ànima meva
de sa bellesa la potenta onada,
que a l'alçar-me ubriac de vora seva
i trobar-me privat de sa presència,
ja no trobí en son lloc ma consciència,
enduta per la forta rierada.

Represa de Haidé

L'AMIC me deia: —En aquesta hora dolça
(era un diumenge al caure de la tarda)
és quan se'm torna més potenta i viva
la memòria que servo d'aquella altra.
Torna a invadir-me aquell amor d'un dia,
com si tingués davant la que el causava;
la torno a veure amb aquell gest tan propi,
la boca, els ulls movent-se-li en la cara,
i aquell mateix vestit que duia a sobre,
i el lligat dels cabells, i tot lo altre.
Torno a sentir sa veu i lo que em deia,
tornen a mi els seus mots i l'alenada,
i torno a defallir com defallia
sota l'encís de sa presència ràpida.
¿Per què, per què me fou tan tost represa
un cop m'havia ja sigut donada
i jo poguí conèixer-la per meva
com cap me fou ni m'ho serà cap altra?
«—Quantes —diràs—, al món, que mai has vist,
perdudes per ton cor sense recança!»
Prô aquesta l'he tinguda dintre els ulls
i una eterna enyorança m'hi ha deixada.
Quan veig una aigua que reflecta el cel
tan clarament, i la verdor dels marges,
penso en son rostre, on tot lo món hi és
tan transparent que se'n pot veure l'ànima.
Tiro una pedra a l'aigua davant meu,
que tota es torba i tremolant s'eixampla:
així son rostre, al caure-hi mon esguard,
en un pasme de goig se dilatava.
Si miro un arbre, commogut pel vent,
parpellejant en la blavor dels aires,
penso en sos ulls, parpellejant així
quan volia i dolia ans de parlar-me...
...Ara sóc com la dida d'un infant

que tot just l'hi han tret, i en té enyorança,
i diu si no l'hi deixarien veure
ben d'amagat que no dirà paraula.
Juga l'infant amb la finestra oberta,
corre d'ací i d'allà dintre la cambra,
fent a tots la mateixa rialleta
que tant solia fê a la qui el criava;
i allà a la reixa hi ha una cara trèmula
que contra els ferros plora i riu i calla
tot menjant-se amb la vista la criatura,
d'aquell antic amor tan descuidada!
Així mon esperit està a tota hora
contemplant en l'absència la manyaga
que em té tan lluny del pensament i es gira
a tothom amb aquella bona cara.
Jo la veig que s'aixeca i que s'inclina,
i que va i ve de l'un indret a l'altre,
i es posa al llit, i dorm i es desensonya,
i està sempre de mi tan oblidada!
Mes mon sentit està en contínua vetlla
d'aquell record que dintre meu restava,
i aquelles gràcies, en son rostre juntes,
cerco disperses per tants rostres d'altres.

Haidé

—Ja no em plau ni el dansar ni l'alegria
perquè qui m'ha de veure ja no em veu.
¿On són aquells ullets que em perseguien
i no em deixaven tot lo dia arreu,
que jo em sentia tan acompanyada
com si ja no visqués sola per mi,
com si la meva vida fos doblada
i tot lo meu tingués un segon fi?
I, perxò jo em polia i m'esmerava
i sabia del cert que no era en va,
que tot mon resplendor s'aprofitava
perquè hi havia algú que em contemplava

tenint-me com un sant en un altar.
Mes, ara, què en treuré d'ésser bonica
si he perdut mon mirall de bonicor?
Més d'un esguard en mon esguard se fica,
prô amb altra ardència, que amb aquella no.
Aquella era una ardència de puresa
que feia una gran llum sense cremor.
Ara conec com he sigut aimada
per lo que enyoro els ulls de l'aimador.—

Com una flor, sempre més
el teu amor en ma vida
hi ha deixat una fragància
que ja no em serà esvaïda.
Com una flor, sempre més
el teu amor en ma vida.

Ves qui t'ho havia de dir,
cara fresca i colorada,
per un breu instant d'amor
tota ma vida enflairada.
Ves qui t'ho havia de dir,
cara fresca i colorada.

Jo porto el teu pensament
com al front una corona
que m'ombreja bellament:
ningú sap l'encantament,
prô tot lo món se n'adona.
Jo porto el teu pensament
com al front una corona.

Hauré de fê un gran sospir
per emportar-me les aures
d'aquest cel a dintre el pit.
Ai, sol! que els cabells li daures.
Hauré de fê un gran sospir.

I ara adéu... El somni meu
mai més tornarà a florir.
Ara adéu... però no adéu,
lo mellor teu resta en mi.
Ara adéu... però no adéu...

Vistes al mar

V

Una a una, com verges a la dansa,
entren lliscant les barques en el mar;
s'obre la vela com una ala al sol,
i per camins que només elles veuen
s'allunyen mar endintre...

Oh cel blau! Oh mar blau, platja deserta,
groga de sol! De prop el mar te canta,
mentres tu esperes el retorn magnífic,
a sol ponent, de la primera barca,
que sortirà del mar tota olorosa.

La fageda d'En Jordà

Saps on és la fageda d'En Jordà?
Si vas pels volts d'Olot, amunt del pla,
trobaràs un indret verd i profond
com mai cap més n'hagis trobat al món:
un verd com d'aigua endins, profond i clar;
el verd de la fageda d'En Jordà.
El caminant, quan entra en aquest lloc,
comença a caminar-hi a poc a poc;
compta els seus passos en la gran quietud
s'atura, i no sent res, i està perdut.
Li agafa un dolç oblit de tot lo món
en el silenci d'aquell lloc profond,
i no pensa en sortir, o hi pensa en va:

és pres de la fageda d'En Jordà,
presoner del silenci i la verdor.
Oh companyia! Oh deslliurant presó!

Oda nova a Barcelona

—On te'n vas, Barcelona, esperit català
que has vençut la carena i has saltat ja la tanca
i te'n vas dret enfora amb tes cases disperses,
lo mateix que embriagada de tan gran llibertat?

—Veig allà el Pirineu amb ses neus somrosades,
i al davant Catalunya tota estesa als seus peus,
i me'n vaig... És l'amor qui m'empeny cap enfora,
i me'n vaig delirant amb els braços oberts.

—Oh! detura't un punt! Mira el mar, Barcelona,
com té faixa de blau fins al baix horitzó,
els poblets blanquejant tot al llarg de la costa,
que se'n van plens de sol vorejant la blavor.
I tu fuges del mar?...
—Vinc del mar i t'estimo,
i he pujat aquí dalt per mirar-lo millor,
i me'n vaig i no em moc: sols estenc els meus braços
perquè vull Catalunya tota a dintre el meu cor.

—Altra mar veus enllà, encrespada i immòbil,
de les serres que riuen al sol dolçament:
per copsar tanta terra i tanta mar, Barcelona,
ja et caldrà un pit ben gran, amb uns braços ben ferms.

—Com més terra i més mar, i més pobles obiro,
a mesura d'amor el meu pit s'engrandeix,
i me sento una força que abans no tenia,
i sóc tan tota una altra que fins jo em desconec.

—Corre enllà, corre enllà, corre enllà, Barcelona,
que ja et cal esse' una altra per ésser la que deus;

perquè ets alta i airosa i fas molta planta,
però bé et falta encara molt més del que tens.
Ets covarda, i crudel i grollera,
Barcelona, però ets riallera
perquè tens un bell cel al damunt;
vanitosa, arrauxada i traçuda:
ets una menestrala pervinguda
que ho fa tot per punt.

Alces molts gallarets i penons i oriflames,
molts llorers, moltes palmes,
banderes a l'aire i domassos al sol,
i remous a grans crits tes espesses gentades,
per qualsevulga cosa acorruades
entorn de qualsevol.

Mes, passada l'estona i el dia i la rauxa
i el vent de disbauxa, de tot te desdius;
i abandones la via i la glòria i l'empresa,
i despulles el gran de grandesa.
I encara te'n rius.

Te presums i engavanyes alhora
amb manto de monja i vestit de senyora
i vel de la musa i floc relluent;
prô mudes de pressa, i amb gran gosadia
la musa i la nimfa i la dama i la pia
s'arrenca el postís i la veu disfressada,
i surt la marmanyera endiablada
que empaita la monja i li crema el convent...
I després el refàs més potent!

Esclata la mort de tes vies rialleres
en l'aire suau:
esclata impensada, i segura i traïdora
com altra riallada escarnidora...
Riallades de sang!
El fang dels teus carrers, oh Barcelona,
és pastat amb sang.

I tens dreta en la mar la muntanya, ai! que venja
amb son castell al cim, i amb la revenja
mes ai! en el flanc!

Tens aquesta rambla que és una hermosura...
i tens la dolçura dels teus arravals,
on, tan prop de tes vies sonores
i al mig de les boires del fum i ses marques,
camps de blat en la pau dels patriarques
maduren lentament els fruits anyals.
I allí, a quatre passes, febrosa de sobres,
més ampla que l'altra, la Rambla dels pobres
tremola en la fosca ses llums infernals.

Prô ni el baf ni la pols de tos llots i desferres,
ni els pals i filferres
que t'armen a sobre la gran teranyina,
ni el fumar de tes mil xemeneies,
ni el flam de les teies
que mou la discòrdia i abranden l'incendi,
són bastants a posar vilipendi
an aquest cel que tens tan dolç i blau
que tot s'ho empassa i resol i canvia,
i ho torna en oblit i consol i alegria:
mil cops la perdessis,
mil cops més tornaria a tu la pau.
A la part de Llevant, místic exemple,
com una flor gegant floreix un temple
meravellat d'haver nascut aquí,
entremig d'una gent tan sorruda i dolenta,
que se'n riu i flestoma i es baralla i s'esventa
contra tot lo humà i lo diví.
Mes, en mig la misèria i la ràbia i fumera,
el temple (tant se val!) s'alça i prospera
esperant uns fidels que han de venir.

Tal com ets, tal te vull, ciutat mala:
és com un mal donat, de tu s'exhala:

que ets vana i coquina i traïdora i grollera,
que ens fa abaixâ el rostre,
Barcelona! i amb tos pecats, nostra! nostra!
Barcelona nostra! la gran encisera!

Cant espiritual

Si el món ja és tan formós, Senyor, si es mira
amb la pau vostra a dintre de l'ull nostre,
què més ens podeu dâ en una altra vida?

Per'xò estic tan gelós dels ulls, i el rostre,
i el cos que m'heu donat, Senyor, i el cor
que s'hi mou sempre... i temo tant la mort!

Amb quins altres sentits me'l fareu veure
aquest cel blau damunt de les muntanyes,
i el mar immens, i el sol que pertot brilla?
Deu-me en aquests sentits l'eterna pau
i no voldré més cel que aquest cel blau.
Aquell que a cap moment li digué «—Atura't»
sinó al mateix que li dugué la mort,
jo no l'entenc, Senyor, jo que voldria
aturar tants moments de cada dia
per fê'ls eterns a dintre del meu cor!...
O és que aquest «fê etern» és ja la mort?
Mes llavores, la vida, què seria?
Fóra l'ombra només del temps que passa,
la il·lusió del lluny i de l'aprop,
i el compte de lo molt, i el poc, i el massa,
enganyador, perquè ja tot ho és tot?

Tant se val! Aquest món, sia com sia,
tan divers, tan extens, tan temporal;
aquesta terra, amb tot lo que s'hi cria,
es ma pàtria, Senyor; i no podria
ésser també una pàtria celestial?

Home só i és humana ma mesura
per tot quant puga creure i esperar:
si ma fe i ma esperança aquí s'atura
me'n fareu una culpa més enllà?

Més enllà veig el cel i les estrelles,
i encara allí voldria ésser-hi hom:
si heu fet les coses a mos ulls tan belles,
si heu fet mos ulls i mos sentits per elles,
per què aclucâ'ls cercant un altre *com?*
Si per mi com aquest no n'hi haurà cap!
Ja ho sé que sou, Senyor; prô on sou, qui ho sap?
Tot lo que veig se vos assembla en mi...
Deixeu-me creure, doncs, que sou aquí.
I quan vinga aquella hora de temença
en què s'acluquin aquests ulls humans,
obriu-me'n, Senyor, uns altres de més grans
per contemplar la vostra faç immensa.
Sia'm la mort una major naixença!

Al cim

El sol se n'anava
quan jo hi he arribat.
La copa dels pins ja era negra,
prô el tronc tot daurat.

El cim, tot vermell del sol, que es ponia
una mica a ponent del Montserrat;
i la muntanya santa resplendia
d'un encès morat.

Mes el sol ha tombat la carena
i tot s'ha apagat.

He baixat. Per la terra enfosquida
no restava ni un rastre de sol;
i al bell fons de la Vil·la Joana
començava a cantâ un rossinyol.

Nausica

Primer acte

ULISSES

ALTRE perill fugit, altra aventura
després de tantes... El furor de Troia,
tan gran com fou, ja dintre meu sols resta
com un record llunyà i confós. Ma vida,
tan plena allí, tot just hi començava:
lo que em semblava fi era principi,
i el que creguí toc de retorn sols era
senyal de la partida. Lo de Troia
era empresa de tots: lo que en seguia
per a mi, fou de mi tot sol; la guerra
fou la guerra cabdal de Grècia tota,
prô mos treballs són els treballs d'Ulisses.
Hi ha hagut prou temps, des de que en ells em trobo,
perquè tants reis hagin tornat dispersos
a llurs palaus i hagin regit llurs terres
en pau molts anys; i alguns encara s'hagin
enfonsat en l'imperi de les ombres.
Agamemnon!... Aquiles!... Aiax!... mísers!
Vostres testes altives colltorçaren-se,
a vostres ulls no brilla el sol; i encara
Ulisses va pel món i l'alegria
del retorn a la pàtria, que ja és morta
o fallida per tants, sols per mi resta
dolça a venir al bell lluny de l'esperança.
Mes ara ja és a prop: un déu m'ho dicta
dintre el cor. Jo et veuré, muller, Penèlope,
tan suau i segura en ton afecte;
i a tu també, fill meu, que ja deus ésser
un home gran com jo; i a vós, mon pare,
de reveure-us tinc fe damunt la terra,
que éreu fort com un roure. Mes ¿vosaltres
m'espereu, a mi, encar? I, en ma figura,

¿hi trobareu aquell que en la memòria
deveu tenir altrament? Ulisses,
t'has fet vell, prô has viscut: la sort accepto
de grat; que si algú ara redonar-me
pogués els anys que he anat per tantes terres
patint i aimant, i amb odis i amb victòries,
i tanta experiència de les coses,
i lo que he après i lo que he fet...; si em deia
algú: —¿Vols tornar a viure els anys que foren,
i viure'ls en tes terres i en ta casa,
en pau amb la muller i el fill i el regne?—
jo li diria: —No: la sort accepto,
accepto mos treballs i les angúnies
i la imminent vellesa, perquè em trobo
més ric de mi, més ple del món, més ànima.
I tu, tendra princesa, tu, l'última
de tantes deves o mortals que foren
dolces a Ulisses, tu com cap m'ets cara,
perquè has vingut a mi amb les mans obertes
i amb tota la innocència. Tu no esperes
de mi ni aquella força poderosa
del braç reial, ni ma famosa astúcia,
ni els delits de l'amor, que tot ho ignores.
No saps que sia rei! que sia Ulisses;
i, fins veient-me obscur i miserable
i monstruós, quan totes fugirien
tu te'm poses davant, dreta i serena,
amb l'admiració als ulls, el riure als llavis,
i fins, lo que és millor, un xic tremolosa,
sols perquè et surt del cor, on els déus regnen.
O dolça criatura!...

NAUSICA

Vine, vine,
Estranger, que ja a punt tenim la marxa
i et durem a ciutat; mes no en el carro:
no fos cas que la gent que t'hi veiessin

amb nosaltres, diguessin, tot girant-se:
—¿Qui és aquest foraster que ve amb Nausica,
d'un aspecte tan noble i admirable?
Potser és el seu promès, i ella a la costa
l'ha anat a recebir; potser és un príncep
d'una terra llunyana, que venia
per fer-la sa muller, i ella ho callava;
potser és un rei, i en cas qui sap si fóra
un déu baixat del cel per posseir-la...—

Segon acte

ULISSES

Aquella tarda, Circe, l'encisera,
la dels cabells rullats, aspres i rossos,
em prengué per la mà, i, allí a la vora
de la nau, que enllestia's per la marxa,
em digué: —Has passat perills molt grossos,
però cap com aquest que ara t'espera.
Arribareu a un punt de la mar blava
molt prop de la mansió de les sirenes,
que són unes estranyes criatures
mig dones i mig peixos: ajagudes
s'estan en un bell prat de la marina,
i atalaien de lluny les naus que passen;
i, quan en veuen una que s'acosta,
es posen a cantar. I et dic que tenen
un cant tan dolç, tan dolç, que qui l'escolta
oblida de seguit tota altra cosa
i se n'hi va de dret: mai més, al míser,
el veurà de retorn la llar en festa,
ni la muller el rebrà dintre els seus braços,
ni els fills li saltaran entorn ditxosos;
sinó que, amb el cant llur, les enciseres
l'atrauran sens remei fins a tenir-lo
i endur-se'l enllaçat cap a llurs coves,
on el devoraran; i d'això viuen.

Quan t'hi acostis, als companys de pressa
els taparàs amb cera remollida
les orelles; mes tu, si vols, escolta
el cant, fent-te lligar en el arbre mestre,
i digues an els teus que no et deslliguin,
encara que plorant els ho preguessis
fins a ésser ben lluny de l'encontrada.—
Així em parlà amb l'amor l'encantadora,
i varàrem la nau i férem vela.
Arribats a l'indret que em deia Circe,
vaig fer com ella m'ensenyà; i, encara
no havien acabat bé de lligar-me,
caigué el vent, la mar tota s'ablania
restant com adormida, els meus plegaren
les veles, i amb els rems bateren l'aigua,
per cap més so ni cap més plec moguda.
Llavors començà a oir-se un cant dolcíssim
de moltes veus, tan fines i acordades,
que a mi em semblava entrar en els camps elisis.

Terç acte (El port)

NAUSICA

Ha estat dintre l'infern, ell, l'únic,
i ha vist les ombres de les gents que foren,
la de la seva mare. Ell la volia
abraçar, i ho provà per tres vegades,
i diu que cada volta se'n tornava
els braços buits al pit, i no estrenyia
res més que l'aire fosc...

DAIMÓ

Resteu, resteu en vostra llar, donzella,
enc que ara us sembli trista i desolada.
Serveu la visió gran del pas de l'hèroe
davant dels vostres ulls: tota la vostra
vida en serà il·luminada; i, sia

vostra sort quina sia, sempre, sempre,
en pau reclosa, o bé pel món enduta,
en calma, en tempestat, en la vellesa,
en dolors, en salut, en malaltia,
sempre tindreu a dintre el cor la dolça
memòria gran d'aquest moment i hora
en què heu aimat a un hèroe en puresa,
i la seva presència fugitiva
haurà signat per sempre més, des d'ara,
vostre cor jovenil, bla com la cera,
amb segell immortal.

MARIA-ANTÒNIA SALVÀ

1869

Libèl·lula

FLOR viva de l'aire,
libèl·lula atzur
volares rondaire
per sobre del mur.

Tota esgarrifança,
tota il·lusió,
son blau d'alegrança
llançant a baldó,

la meravellera
s'emmeravellà;
mes tu, l'encisera,
fugies enllà.

El pi ver

A la terra dels avis i del pare,
tota ella amb so de pins murmuriosa,

joia del cor i de l'esguard delícia,
s'aixecava un sol pi de pinya vera.
Alt i esvelt, son vigorós ramatge
el fruit color d'aram tot just traïa
massís, ferreny com un puny clos d'atleta
a nostra mà d'infants inabastable.
Amb sos enginys en Miquel Pou l'havia:
el garriguer colrat, fill de la brosta,
abocava el sarró de pell de cabra
i queia en nostres mans la bella pinya.
Quin goig en treure el pa! Car ella en rebre
l'hàlit del forn, a poc a poc, flairosa
de la reïna pròdiga es badava,
i ens lliurava el tresor que tant delíem:
aquells pinyons granats de closca dura
i sanitós bessó, que en masticar-lo
ens deixava les boques untuoses.
Prou el pi ver les tales respectaren;
cap destralada no l'atuiria:
una ventada abraonant-lo amb fúria
al pedregam el va ajupir de testa.
I àdhuc tot ajupit i en sa vellura,
un fruit migrat adés i ara ens dóna.

El Florer

Boticel·li hauria
aviat pinzells
per posar en ta via
danses d'Amorells,

dolça reconada
d'infantil delit,
tota encatifada
d'un herbei florit.

Cor de minyonia,
ulls d'enamorat,

per a tu tenia
nostra bella edat.

Res de Boticel·li
no sabia encar
quan a *Santi bel·li*
s'esqueia jugar;

però ja ens atreia
ton secret esquer.
—Nostre llavi et deia
de nom «El Florer».

Gerdor hivernenca

Aigua fina, gotellina,
tany de murtra, nova rel.

Cau, pausada, l'aubaïna
que ha pintat un arc-en-cel.

La taronga mandarina
guaita fresca, com un gel.

Cau, pausada, l'aubaïna,
la vedella fa el bruel.

Rosa vera, blat que brina,
pluja fina, cel fidel.

Recobrament

Em plau tancar les portes del passat
al rosec sospirós de l'enyorança,
obrint el cor al sol de l'esperança,
a l'oreig eternal de bat a bat.

Drecera amunt, té el senderó que em guia
floretines i rou cada matí,
que els ulls meravellats em fan obrir
com si fruís del món la primeria.

L'amplària de cel que m'encisà
s'eixampla fins a fer-se indefinida,
cada nou jorn enlaira un poc ma vida
i tots em parlen d'un joiós demà.

Sé que en xuclar la terra ma llangor
l'esperit immortal restarà lliure,
i amoroseix mos llavis el somriure
d'una mai estrafeta serenor.

Res de quant estimí no m'és absent;
tot quant al món m'ha fet bona escomesa,
es revesteix per mi de jovenesa
al sol auguri del recobrament.
Oh joia del ponent!

GUERAU DE LIOST

1878-1933

Eucarística

No us goso a parlar
(tampoc no en sabria).
Deixeu, si més no,
que canti una mica.

Clareja tot just
que torno de missa.
Les flors del camí
em fan cortesies,
el gall matiner

em dóna el bon dia,
el raig de la font
tremola i no frisa,
s'esblaima l'atzur
clapat de boirines,
que us duc en el bres
de l'ànima mia.
Del vostre sojorn,
Senyor, no só digne.
Us duc i no us veig:
la fe us endevina.
La mare tampoc
(misteri de vida)
l'infant no capeix
i el sent que es congria.
Jo em sento arborat
de dur-vos a dintre.
De res no tinc por:
só fort com l'alzina.
No em bat el senglar,
ni em puny la bardissa,
ni el fred no em deté,
ni el foc no em retria,
ni els lladres de bosc,
ni els lladres de vila,
ni el mal esperit
(la creu li faria).

El seny no us capeix,
ni us lluca la vista,
ni us copsen els dits,
ni us flairen narines,
ni us trobo en el tast,
ni us ouen oïdes...
L'amor, que és humil,
l'amor els suplia.
Bé prou capiré
per tota la vida

en veure-us segut
en alta cadira
omplint l'univers
com una celístia.
Oh gaudi! L'amor
serà com junyida.

El sol, que és manyac,
es lleva a les cimes,
al prat s'esbandí,
s'eixuga a l'artiga,
festeja els conreus,
s'atura a l'eixida.
El sol és eixit
que torno de missa.
Al porxo m'assec:
la taula convida.
Es sent la remor
d'un fil d'aigua viva.
El sol fa lluir
la fusta polida,
els vasos mig plens,
el càntir d'argila,
la coca amb pinyons,
la plata de figues,
gemades encar,
i un braç de cadira.
El blanc tovalló
de fil estenia:
s'hi marquen els plecs
com feixes petites.
Començo tot just
i es mou la cortina.
La dona somriu
si em mira no em mira,
que m'entra l'infant
a dar-me el bon dia.

Sigueu-hi, Jesús,
que us porto de missa.
Seguem al capçal:
beguda faríem.
La dona ens serveix
com una fadrina.
Ens toca l'infant
i ens dóna el bon dia:
Sigueu-hi, Jesús,
per tota la vida.

Ofrena rural

Dona Maria d'Arimells,
única aimia
del Cavaller Guerau, sense castells
fora d'un casolà castell de poesia:
més fort que tres segells,
vostre llavi em segellaria.

De l'era estant de Liost,
s'albiren dotze carenes.
Al capdavall d'un llargarut congost,
una cala s'adorm, jaç de sirenes.
Nosaltres tenim al rost
perdius que d'un rosari de fusta passen denes.

Entre gatoses un camí s'esmuny,
arrecerat del sol a mitja tarda.
Mena al serrat on us trobí pel juny,
entre fonolls parada i olivarda.
Un ginebre llampat no gaire lluny
com un senglar felló feia basarda.

La vostra casa presideix la vall.
Com d'una griva l'aterrada tofa,
de la teulada minva l'esquenall

i, plomissal dispers, cada paller s'aclofa.
L'arc de l'eixida fa el darrer badall
i té la pollancreda el ritme d'una estrofa.

El casal de Liost és un castell roquer
escamarlat sobre un penyal que s'esllavissa.
Cingla el penyal, com si fos un corser,
un alzinar, dura malla ferrissa.
Al front llueix com una divisa un esparver
que roquerols esplomissa.

La casa d'Arimells diu que s'esbalaí,
flairosa de les herbes de la prada.
A l'ombra eixuta d'un pi
prospera la llocada.
La casa d'Arimells té la vida al molí,
que li manté l'anomenada.

Si el casal nostre és el castell del sol,
de vostra casa en dic el palau de la lluna.
L'un és la llum, el vent, l'estol
d'un alzinar sense vedruna.
L'altra és farina a casa i boira al corriol
i fullatge caduc a la llacuna.

Llebres pasturen pel vostre quintar,
llebres d'esquerpa tirada.
Si les aborda el ca
i les erreu de bursada,
no trigaran gaire a collar
pels rasos de Liost on l'herba és arranada.

Liost amunt la fageda subtil
vibra del vent de l'altura.
S'entertolliga d'espàrbols el fil
que una argentina moixera tortura.
Passa el tudó viril
que en un pollancre d'Arimells s'atura.

Com seguiria, l'esguard,
d'aquell tudó la volada tan neta!
La meva amor, si pogués, celaria covard,
en el seu pit, decorada naveta.
I li diria: —Cap al tard
vés a l'ampit d'aquella finestreta.—

Vós sou, Dona Maria d'Arimells,
de mon castell poètic sobirana.
Per Vós no té cantells
la graciosa parla catalana.
Els mots en vostre llavi són joiells
i cada gemma grana.

Ací teniu, mal fet,
un enfilall de rústegues pedretes.
El vostre Cavaller, retret,
no gosa a barrejar-se amb els poetes.
Ells tiren flors, amb un aire discret,
i, el Cavaller, sagetes.

Moments de cirerer

II

Ara que el verd verdeja,
cirerer fullat,
es vincla el forcat
i la goma vital hi perleja,
cada fulla juga amb tu
com una maragda prima.

Al pit de l'atzur ben nu
l'or del matí regalima.
Una cirereta hi lluu,
una cirereta sola.
La merla que es banya al rec
com una sageta hi vola...

Oh cirereta, robí
il·lusori!
Oh merla groga de bec,
negra merla de setí,
estoig amb tanca de vori!

Font de l'Oreneta

VOLDRIA ser enterrat al peu
d'aquesta font que endegà el pare.
Té campanetes arreu,
d'aquelles que plaïen a la mare.
Un aire ben senzill
hi porta els sorolls de la vila
i neteja de brossa l'espill
d'aquesta font tranquil·la.
Sovint amb el germà
hi fèiem un atur, suats de la cacera.
En el seu bassol clar
es mirava el llebrer, vanitós que era.
El berenar posava la muller
a la taula que fa aquesta roca.
L'ombreja un castanyer:
damunt la seva casolana soca
un dístic em plauria del meu Josep Carner.
La gent ara en diu
la «Font de l'Oreneta».
Vora la teva font, fes, oreneta, niu:
faràs, demà, companyia al poeta.

La nova amor

NÒDUL saborós de cada setmana:
dissabte vespre, diumenge matí;
dissabte, lluna casolana;
diumenge, solell diví!
Dissabte urgent,

vigília de festa!
Anima i casa neteja la vívida gent.

En arribar els marits de Barcelona,
troben la feina llesta
i les mullers que fan rodona
al voltant de l'autòmnibus que esbufega xacrós
i patriarcal s'esbatana
per despenjar marits de dos en dos
de la portella i la finestra i la barana.

Cada muller rep el marit
(de Barcelona ve pansit)
amb la mirada humida
del record temperat de la lluna de mel.
I no crida.
I és pacífic el cel
i convida
a l'amor casolana.
I l'estol dels encontres apar una sardana.
I el marit besa el front de la casta muller.
I jo sé
que al refrec de la sina endevina l'espurna
que l'incendi promet de la joia nocturna.

Jo també fui marit.
De la plaça del poble fugia, esmunyit,
cap a casa, a muntanya.
I darrera el turó convingut
la meva amor acut,
la petita muller de fèrtil entranya.

Ara sóc al turó.
No veig senyal de mà ni mocador;
l'estelada només i la carena,
i l'alzina de vora el camí,
ferrenya i pura,
i una alba de lluna plena.

I m'estreny la natura,
odorant de ginesta i romaní,
amor de nova mena
humida piament de serení.

I no se'n falta gaire
de si caic dolçament,
com si la rústica flaire
m'enterbolís el pensament.
Oh càustic aire,
beat alè de Margarida absent!

Sàtires

XVII

Nupcial

(Vivent Madona Guida)

Senyor, la dona d'ornament posares
i cordial ajut.
Ella enrama i vesteix les nostres ares
i serva, lúcid, el pairal escut.
Ella és a taula provident i tria
de cadascú la part.
De casa estant ens mena amb el seu art
i és fonedissa com l'estel diürn.
Però, en venir el capvespre taciturn,
és més que mai amorosida i pia
i el nupcial anell arbora en el seu dit
com l'estel immutable de la nit.

(Morta Madona Guida)

Senyor, la dona d'ornament posares
i cordial ajut.
Ella encarnà l'ombra dels pares

i, amb la nissaga, torna el bé perdut.
Quan és al llit malalta per morir,
el ceptre empunya de la llar:
la Santa Creu. Sacerdotal, així,
l'ullada pura
en cada fill atura,
meravellada perquè el veu encar.
Es tímida, la dona,
de massa amor que ens té,
però la teva crida, Senyor, paterna sona,
i apaivagada ens besa, Madona, el cop darrer.

XVIII

De la Mort que ve i se'n torna

Oh Mort que t'insinues
tan enginyosament
que, en descobrir tes conques nues
i aquella mà raptora del nostre pensament,
ja ni volença trobo per confegir l'esment!

Si la tenebra afues,
ennavegant-me en el desori,
com l'esparracaria, las de mi?
Si te l'emmenes, perquè jo no mori,
quan ella ja em cuidava entenebrir,
i es fon, a poc a poc, la teva mà,
arrosegant-la, pel collar,
de tort;
en descloure a la llum la somorta palpebra,
enllà, esvaint la tenebra,
ton arreveure sona, segur com una crida,
i et faig acatament, oh Mort,
fent esperar la Vida.
Abans que la muller sol·lícita m'agenci
posant en joc la vívida aptesa dels seus dits,
la meva gent, esfereïts,

l'orella paren al silenci
que es fa darrera teu, madur,
com si la cambra s'exhaurís de tu.

De la visita que em feres
com l'alzina d'un freu restaria llampat?
No vull que mes pregueres
t'ofenguin ploraneres,
però, de ton veïnatge,
em sento com si Déu m'hagués petjat,
car tu li fas de patge
portant, a tall de glavi, la doble eternitat.

L'enyorament angèlic, d'ara endavant, tindré
d'aquell vident que un dia gustava el cel tercer?
Si un agulló l'agullonava,
d'ara endavant, oh Mort!, caldrà
mesura en el vegetar,
purificant l'ànima esclava.

XIX

De la impossible unitat

Quan maquinal, la serventa forçuda
porta, en pitxer de cristall de Venècia,
un ram d'orquídies amb ferma passa
i, rera d'elles, sorruda, s'escuda;
quan la fadrina escomet la facècia
d'esbiaixar la frenètica plaça

amb un infant, recalcat, com un càntir,
en la duresa del pit que no estreba,
i el risc amb àgil correguda escurça
sense que el bruit ciutadà l'ataranti;
amb l'ai! al cor seguim (del viure treva)
el pas calmós i la ràpida cursa.

Així la por de morir m'ennuvola
i a la pica del seny una corculla

d'exhauriment, arrapada, prospera.
Cada mot se m'esquitlla per la gola
com la bravada d'una casa sulla;
s'adorm la sang com rovell de gotera;

com una jàssera que es polla, inútil,
l'ossada cruix sota l'adversa prova;
amb el trepig, la carn esfulladissa
perd la frescor de la pell inconsútil,
com la manyaga blancor d'una alcova
cau a bocins quan el mur s'esllavissa.

Frágil també sóc de l'ànima, dona.
Sota el vestit de cenyida costura
d'on només surten les mans i la testa,
flairo ta pell inconsútil que entona,
com un aroma de fruita madura,
la transparència vital que hi resta.

Volta, l'esguard, de flamígeres noses,
la nuditat que la vesta perfuma.
Deu-me, Senyor, la mirada que passa
com un ocell per damunt de les roses
o la mirada que tètrica exhuma,
contraverí, la secreta carcassa.

Crucificat l'Home-Déu, no predica
l'analogia de l'home i la fembra,
la humanitat de tota criatura?
Adhuc l'ocell té de l'home una mica:
sota la mínima tossa remembra,
son esquelet, ma divina estructura.

L'esgarrifança de buidor que em gela
no l'apaivaga un erotisme ascètic,
daler de sobreviure lluny del Pare.
Dual, Senyor, la humanitat anhela
una barreja d'home-dona atlètic.
I de la carn la desfeta prepara.

Ai! La furtiva unitat del connubi
és un esclat generós d'egoismes,
treva carnal que la lluita esperona.
El sagrament dignifica l'efluvi
amb la divina unció dels carismes.
Només la mort, ço que anhelem ens dóna.

XX

Comiat de l'Ànima

Si el vent de mort visita el clos
on l'Ànima es complau com un ocell en l'herba,
i el ritme de la sang enerva
com doll que volatilitza el vent,
l'Ànima serva,
com una flama divergent del cos
talment.
Si el contacte li falla,
pren comiat amb una revifalla,
i amorosida, gairebé deslliure,
nimba la faç malalta,
amb englantines a la galta
i violes de bosc en el somriure.
I, esperançada, escruta,
amb ulls de Fe, la paorosa ruta.

Anima, adéu. El foc estima
de l'obrador perfet.
Avida t'obriràs perquè l'àcida llima
exhumi el teu secret.
Ço que podies ser en la terra
caldrà que siguis a la fi.
Ço que la vida esguerra,
la mà del foc ho torna a confegir.
Grumoll encara tèrbol de sutzures,
brolla del foc, duríssim vas,
cristall de facetes pures,
mirall de la Trina Faç.

Del cos amic la polsina
esdevindrà foc follet,
fatuïtat de joguina,
esgarrifança de fred,
fins que, al so de la trompeta
de la resurrecció,
la terra serà més neta
com un tinell d'emperador.
Per la Divina Paraula
et serà parat el cos.
Ell serà com una taula,
i tu com pitxer de flors.

La muntanya magnètica

MUNTANYA, terra vella i sempre nova,
mà que hi sent, que es rabeja en l'infinit:
la terra plana, que amb el cel no es troba,
el retroba en la punta de ton dit.

Ai d'aquell home que et trepitja nua!
L'ànima el deixa, tel·lúric anhel.
Si una sirena té, d'esquer, la cua,
tu el jugues en el dit, cèlica arrel.

I tremoles, compacta i fugitiva.
Si l'home et toca d'una aresta viva,
tombaria llampat de ton senyal.

Pres en ta mà, que el projectava enlaire,
es dissoldria en tu, com el cantaire
d'un vívid cementiri vertical.

La tia Carme

COIXINET de cretona, amb quadrats en maduixa
i una floreta verda al mig de cadascú,
apte, si tinc migranya o se m'adorm la cuixa
o em cal passar tres dies en dejú.

Ta vegetal blanesa m'adorm com una falda:
el caparró s'hi posa confiat.
Amb una olor d'herbetes que no escalda,
em crida a flor d'orella ta casta netedat.

Cada petit de casa ve un dia que t'estrena.
Si me n'exclamo no et troben enlloc.
Val més que et deixi, car l'instint que et mena
farà que aviat tornis, si no em moc.

Coixinet, coixinet, no vull estar-me
d'esmentar la velleta que amb ulleres et féu,
la velleta que es diu Tia Carme
i que de fer-te servir li sap greu.

Era fadrina, i endreçada i neta.
L'horrible mort l'estirà d'una mà.
Amb la mà lliure donà l'animeta
a l'Angel del capçal i no se li tacà.

Però, son cos anyívol,
impropi esdevenia en la foscor del clot.
Tornat mata d'espígol,
s'alliberà en perfum, ja que servar no pot.

Ara torna a ser neta la vida dels terrossos;
ara el cos enterrat, torna a ser net.
Com un esquei fulguren els seus ossos
i l'animeta pot mirar-se l'esquelet.

Elegia

SOBREVENEN uns dies que la vida
és com un cel de perla.
Amb pàtines de mentida,
és una cornucòpia que vibra consentida
el cor, i no s'esberla.
Encara no s'esberla.

L'amor és tasca d'home fet, gustosa
de sa dolor, reïna premiosa.
Caducitat prevista,
joventut refosa,
d'una i d'altra equidista.
De mort i de vida equidista.

En arribar a la maduresa,
cada record té dolçor de tristesa.
Cada record té una història llarga.
Nua com la fornal que la circumda encesa,
Tetis encar visita nostra farga.
Atenea d'ulls d'òliba patrocina la farga.

Lucidesa que l'ànima fadiga
de tan enllà que es projecta!
Amor de posta que vesteix l'amiga,
més que gentil, perfecta!
Hora foscant, l'amor no triga.
Ja sento l'eguinar de sa quadriga.

Si és plenitud d'amor, senyal de posta,
la joia nupcial serà nocturna.
L'home ja fet, a la muller s'acosta
com si fos ella l'urna
de la vida mortal. I, d'una ambosta
cull amor i dolor, equívoca resposta.

Perduda nit, dissipada rutina,
si l'acidesa del misteri
no regala de l'hora vespertina,
si de la lluna l'encanteri
les animetes enfarina,
i és l'amor ensucrada farina.

Nit d'immemorial prestigi
si, darrer vel de l'esposa,
velluta de gebres d'atzur la collida rosa

i valora el vestigi
de la caducitat que arreu es posa.
Així el ritme latent clarifica la prosa.

Quan l'esposa s'immuta
i, amb pànic a l'esguard, es fon enduta
d'un germinal oreig, oblació nefanda,
en sa mirada impersonal, comanda
la llisa llum o la tenebra hirsuta?
Fan, vida i mort, una mateixa ruta?
Fútil amor de les parelles tendres,
tórtora pia:
la vera amor no gosaria prendre's
el goig que la dolor no coneixia.
La vera amor s'ajoca en llit de cendres,
Fènix constant, roserar de les cendres.

Quan el teu cor serà branca de mirra

Dona, sé el gust de la teva presència:
la testa, rosa dels vents invisibles,
el pit d'argila que pateix, arbori,
amb un arranc de braços que s'eleven.

Dona, sé el gust d'abraçar-te, i la nosa.
Dona, sé el gust de fugir, d'enyorar-te.
Si el teu record suplirà la conversa,
saber-te lluny no supleix el tenir-te.

Dona, sé el gust de la mort que separa,
alliberant de sospites de canvi.
En el sagrat epíleg de l'incendi,
cendres i fum s'espiritualitzen.

L'enyorament esdevé permanència.
Compenetrats, el diàleg és íntim.
La teva ment triaria per falda
quan el teu cor serà branca de mirra.

El vent de les altures

CIMAL, llenca florida d'ulls i orelles,
clavada al cel com una punta d'ala,
oberta als vents com una mà sensible!

Com un esglai de la collada acústica,
trepig de vent, ens diu que el vent s'atansa,
per carreranys de comares i congostos.

Com un senyal de cavaller adversari,
esclata sibilant i s'obre via
amb una flingantada de dicteris.

Bèsties, homes, amb igual paüra
s'acoten al presagi que no falla.
I les cases acluquen les finestres.

L'esgarrifança ressegueix les fulles,
i enfollides les deixa, en plena dansa
que els branquillons eriçonats reprenen.

Les branques la duran al paroxisme
i els troncs, a la muntanya l'encomanen
amb esgarips de parteratge còsmic.

Trencadissa de fustes consentides,
estremiment de fustes que serraren,
remor minvant, d'un caos que s'ordena.

La muntanya dels morts

II

OH si dels morts la corrua serena
pogués reveure com una carena:
en cada roure copsar un esperit;

sota l'obaga, penombres del Pare;
i en la solana —materna de cara—,
aquell escalf de quan era petit!

En la cascada que vibra d'escuma,
el sacsejar de la palma que exhuma
l'exuberant pietat d'un germà;
en el flotó de violes marcides,
aquell esguard de les tènues vides
que, primerenc, ens somriu i se'n va.

Oh els enyorats en l'estada conjunta
del meu record! Al qui em fes la pregunta:
—Si vols que tornin—, diria que: —Sí—,
per renovar l'efusiva presència
i per deixar-ne, refeta en l'absència,
la vida nova que tenen en mi.

I tots en mi, com una host taciturna
que entre penyals i covals s'encofurna,
muntanya amunt pujarien plegats.
Llur créixer d'ales faria musica.
Jo ploraria, tot sol, una mica,
i els seguiria amb els ulls aclucats.

JOSEP LLEONART

1880-1951

L'oreig

L'OREIG que em volta em fa una companyia
que m'arrecera de la gent.
Cap d'aquests vianants no m'enraonaria
com l'amic sense cos, amarat de silenci:
l'oreig que forfolleja, que s'abat un moment
sobre la meva nuca, i que en allò que pensi
infon l'esgarrifança, i refresca els meus polsos,
i, mut com és, ens dicta els mots més dolços.

JOSEP LLEONART

Arriba sense pressa i em floreja la cara,
es cargola, s'allisa,
i entre pit i camisa
refà l'alè cansat, i ens cura adesiara
per uns moments, dels nostres mals d'arrel.

L'oreig sense figura és més subtil que un vel,
o que la llum en un mur blanc, o que l'olor
dels llessamins enmig d'una nit clara,
quan som enamorats d'alguna il·lusió.

Un captard de l'estiu, per a ombrejar-me, seia
sota les tílies: baixes, amb la muntanya al fons;
jo no sé de quins deutes de l'ànima em desfeia
al toc de l'oratjol, ple de benediccions,
però sentia el goig d'una pau sense mida,
i no sé de quins dubtes que ens entelen la vida
em lliurava de sobte. Com que no deia un mot
i era a l'ensems dolcíssim, l'oreig condescendent
es conformava en tot
a les cabòries del meu sentiment,
i em lliurava de mal. Era quelcom de mi
quan jo era jove; i caminava amb mi
i a estones es fonia.

Passava gent i gent...
Jo era oblidat de tot, sinó d'aquell sospir del vent
que, més que la meva ombra, em feia companyia.
Jo era feixuc, i ell àgil, i més fi
que, darrera el cristall el color d'or del vi.
I em posava al seu pas, com quan fem via
prop d'algú que és més jove, i em sentia
caminador com ell;
i era sobre el meu cos com un màgic mantell
i com una sang nova dins les venes.

Vaig retornar al meu clos.
Era una d'aquelles nits serenes

que sembla que no tinguin endemà.
Vaig obrir la finestra per guaitar
el gran reialme, que s'omplia
d'un tremolor de fulles i d'estrelles;
i les coses del món eren tan belles
que aquells moments m'hauria
conformat a restar sol amb l'oreig al món,
i que hagués perdurat la nit pura i deserta,
i ens haguéssim trobat en la ciutat de Déu
com algú que es desperta.

JOSEP CARNER

1884

Aigua suau

Cau dolçament, oh pluja, aquest matí;
demà al matí ja hi haurà més d'un bri
en els teulats, on viuen els poetes.

Aigua suau fa créixer les herbetes.

Posa al Neptú de nostre vell jardí,
damunt sos rulls, el teu verdet més fi;
que no el coneguin les marines pletes.

Aigua suau fa créixer les herbetes.

Que s'eixamori la que jo volguí;
no en el seu front, ni en el cabell diví,
sinó en el cor lliurat de les sagetes.

Aigua suau fa créixer les herbetes.

El rat-penat

El rat-penat recorre els vespres, atansat
a la sev'ombra. Bat
grisos besllums d'aigua lleugera.
Amor, miro l'escuma, dempeus a la ribera,
i veig, lliscant, un'ombra: no mai el rat-penat.

Què en sé d'aquells auguris de nit que hi ha en ma pensa
encofurnats, secrets?
Cal, perquè hi faci coneixença,
que em mostri, quan em mires, el pas de ma temença
la palpitació de tos ulls inquiets

Cançó de la divina lassitud

No em donis pas una rosa desclosa
de tos cabells o del fi davantal:
jo vull tenebres, no el foc de la rosa.
Dona, més val.

No vulguis dir la paraula damnada
que dues vides per sempre nués;
treu-me el record amb quieta cantada.
Dona, val més.

Ah! no cobegis que plori i que mori
per la fretura d'un cos immortal:
tanca mos ulls amb la destra d'ivori.
Dona, més val.

La deixa

En la mort del Bisbe Torras i Bages

Oh Pare i Mestre, que te n'has anat
pels camins de l'eternitat!

Oh Pare!, anit passada t'he sentit
com anaves alçant-te en l'infinit,—

sota els braços junyits l'ànima closa;
tancades les parpelles.—Quina cosa
volies dir-me a mi, dir-nos a tots?
O era que tos llavis tan devots
el Rosari passaven, rosa a rosa?
Ai, ja no hi era la mirada clara,
en ta ferrenya cara
que lluí tota dolça amistat
al fred palau, en nua terra avara,
quan anàvem, com a fills, a ton costat.
—Mes ja per la celístia on te movies
sobtadament els braços estenies;
jo queia, dins mon freu,
de genollons en terra
per rebre, com les planes i la serra,
la teva ombra de Creu.

Oh Catalunya, camp ara mateix sembrat,
navili nou, a dins el port lligat,
casal encara moll, tot just embanderat,
infant al caire de la humanitat,
infant tot sol i adormissat...
Sigues en pau, que Ell t'ha senyat.

Al temps de delit

Al temps de delit
que l'arç tot florit
per son verd vestit
poc es desficia,
camino amb un dol
que m'he fet tot sol
per si el ventijol
em consolaria.
Mil vagues tremors em fan companyia.
De color de perla
són els aiguarells.

És l'hora dels iris, nats en una esberla,
cenyits de coltells.
Veus allà la griva, veus ací la merla,
en els arbres tímids del Divendres Sant;
i una clariana de cel blau que encara
no s'ha fet ben clara
i un núvol plorant.
I la Primavera cercant que sa joia
trigui encar més d'un pensarós matí,
no vol en son front veure't decandir,
gris nimbe suau d'angoixes de noia.

Plany

I

L'UNA de l'altra lluny nostres estades,
de sobte, un any, anava a tu, de nit:
en gai insomni, a taules desparades,
cobràvem tot el goig endarrerit.

I ara el dol de tes cambres desolades
com d'una malvestat em fa contrit;
a la fi m'espolien tres anyades
d'aquell fruit amatent no mai collit.

Lassat que só per la minvent sendera,
sols buit estreny la decebuda espera.
De tu, però, mal deslligat encar,

veig que un somrís, fet d'altra llum, m'invita;
i mig en un estel em dónes cita,
mig devora xiprers, davant la mar.

IV

El vas recera la jaent despulla,
àrid senyal de ton departiment.
Tos endolats t'enyoren onsevulla:
la llum els torba, no els respon el vent.

Però el meu esperit és la curculla
on hi ha ta veu, per a mi sol brunzent.
La mort ens deixa, amb sa corbada fulla,
a mi, ferit, i ton secret, vivent.

D'ara endavant, mentre el meu dia duri,
de tot un caire no sabré florir;
i no podem, per més que el fat en curi,

jo del tot viure, tu ben bé morir;
ni vindrà marciment al teu murmuri
fins l'hora fosca de la meva fi.

Cançó del goig perdut

On és anat el goig que jo tenia,
on és anat?

Sota d'un bosc que no coneix el dia
de tot camí me n'era jo oblidat.
O goig d'amor, que etern em prometia!
tot pel meu goig ho havia abandonat.
Com un ocell sobre la mà el tenia
i el meu palmell no es fóra mai lassat.

On és anat el goig que jo tenia,
on és anat?

Ah! si pogués endevinar sa via,
ah! si creuant el cel hagués cantat!
O goig d'amor, que etern em prometia!
Què faré jo, quin viarany prendria,
que a tot arreu hi trobo soledat?
Aire subtil, aire de melangia,
digue'm si has vist el meu ocell daurat.

On és anat el goig que jo tenia,
on és anat?

JOSEP CARNER

Els Pollancs de França

Pollancs de la França de vora els camins,
pollancs de les prades, pollancs dels jardins,
s'acosten, s'allunyen per cada costat,
n'hi ha que travessen o fan un quadrat.

És Déu qui els amoixa i és Déu qui els empeny:
tots duen un ordre, tots tenen un seny.
Cloent la quintana hi serven tresors;
fent via amb qui passa li donen esforç.

Un d'alt, s'encimbella, del rengle desprès;
dos, febles, s'atansen i proven el bes.
D'obscura fontana tres miren el clot:
adoren la menta i el seu bromerot.

I tots, com la boira lleugers en el vent,
fan dolça la terra i el cel més atent
—la terra solcada d'ombreig benestant
i el cel amb sos núvols de borra brillant—.

Triomf de l'altura, plaer d'un recó,
ells són sentinelles en tot horitzó.
I fins si la França fos tota pecat,
encar vetllarien l'honor del passat,
emblemes on frisen les velles virtuts,
més alts que les llances dels dies perduts.

I, amics graciosos del Somni Diví,
cad'un serva l'àngel que un home traí;
i en rengs que s'adiuen com versos rimats
van junts a la missa i a fer de soldats.

Nabí

II

...L'ÀNIMA meva en solitud, desborda.
Oh erm! Dins mi s'animen converses quan m'atreus.
Més que el brogit la quietud eixorda:
tot cor és ple de veus.
Jonàs no porta noves de Déu. La calma blava
de l'aire, a mes orelles consent d'endevinar
el vol de l'àngel que amorós em sol parlar:
em manca, però, l'àngel que mut m'acompanyava
amb un plec segellat a dins la mà...

V

Bell era de veure
altre cop el batre exaltat,
la pressa
del petit en l'il·limitat,
l'ocell en els aires,
el peix en el ròdol marí,
la gran vastedat que com la del cel no podríeu
saber, mesurar ni tenir;
bell era de veure que el fàcil s'eixampla
i enllà l'impossible se'ns fa transparent.
Ocell, tu que et daures del dia,
i peix que degotes l'argent,
un goig en el cor se us aboca,
llampant i lluent.
Oh joia
del petit en l'il·limitat!
Enfora de greus agonies
jo em veia al gran aire llençat,
del clos de la fosca tornat
dins una llargada de dies...

VI

JONÀS

...Jo més em temo que mon Déu declara
un pobre enuig de bon passar.
Qui sap si encara ens baixarà a acotxar
dolç i més dolç, a tall de mare.
Però d'Ell sé una cosa: que ell m'arbora,
que el món no fóra més si Ell em deixés.
Tu, ¿què mai adoraves en l'aurora,
que tot seguit no és?

DONA

Servia l'alba amb la libació
de les rosades,
i amb flors no encara a bastament badades
i sense taca ni pugó.
Car l'alba inspira amb fonedís auguri
el brot de cada nou començament,
la sorpresa de cada pensament
i l'encís de l'amor abans no duri.
Oh delicada decebuda fe!
Oh inútil cura de sos dits de rosa!
De tota bella cosa
tant com llarg el desig, és curt l'alè.
I sort si, com l'aurora, la bellesa
traspunta i fina sobre el món esquiu:
mai abastada ni escomesa.
És ben pitjor si viu.
Marcida al bat de l'aire
ella, l'alada, d'immortal costum,
acabarà com la captaire
que s'humilia o maleeix la llum.
Arran del tracte, la viltat comença.
Tu sola ets pura, tu que passes lleu,
oh gràcia fugint sens defallença,
gemec dels homes i sospir d'un déu!...

La Xarxa Pesquera

VULL anar a la pesquera en nit de lluna,
quan tot serà pintat d'encantament;
amb la rosa al capell, com signe d'una
ànima fresca, abandonada al vent.

Dansarà com podrà la barca bruna:
estel ni calafat no n'han esment.
Jo hi aniré pescant, a la fortuna,
paraules en neguit de pensament.

I com que amor es passa de soldada,
mai no serà l'art meva carregada
del peix que se dol en cuejants combats.

La xarxa des d'avui encomanada
tindrà un miler de resplendents forats
sense senyal de corda pels costats.

Fe

A una dolor que va al dellà del seny
fa només l'Impossible cara tendra.
El pur palau esdevingué pedreny:
els murs són aire, el teginat és cendra.

I, lladre d'aquest lloc desposseït,
palpant, caient, a poc a poc alçant-se,
el descoratjament roda en la nit,
rapicer del record i la frisança.

Jo sé d'on ve l'inesgotable foc
que animarà la morta polseguera.
Veig l'últim monument en l'enderroc.

Jo pujaré, sense replans d'espera,
cap al camí de l'alba fugissera
pel tros d'escala que no mena enlloc.

MIQUEL FERRÀ

1885-1948

En la mort d'En Prat de la Riba

No és somni; és ja per sempre a l'altra part del mur!
Anorreats, l'ull fixe en el portal obscur,
restem plorant el qui s'allunya.
Dins una llum serena d'església triomfant,
a l'altra banda, a rebre'l ix ja l'estol brillant
dels morts preclars de Catalunya.

Entre les ombres cares, estels del patri cel,
en llur esguard la calma del satisfet anhel
ixen el Bisbe i el Poeta.
Ja és dins el mateix nimbe la faç del President,
la faç que tots amàvem, tranquil·la i somrient...
I en nostres mans l'obra mig feta!

Davant la noble vida sagrada a l'ideal,
tota bondat se torna respecte i dol mortal;
calla l'enveja desarmada.
Hi ha en l'aire una viudesa qui ens omple d'estupor.
I el nostre cor desborda d'un dolorós amor...
Oh, Catalunya idolatrada!

JOSEP M.ª LÓPEZ-PICÓ

1886

L'ofrena

TAL com la mare a la qui han tret del pit
el seu infant, d'enyor tremoladissa,
espia dintre casa la nodrissa
amb ulls que guspiregen de neguit;

i la sabeu darrera de la porta
a tot instant, que el temps no li fa tard,
com si fos muda, amb abrigall d'esguard
servant el goig que l'altra se li emporta:

així jo sóc, i així la meva vida,
muda, amb el cant encès en la mirada
i amb el pressentiment de la dissort,

com la nodrissa va espiant la Mort,
que se m'enduu la joia ben amada,
deixant-me sol, amb l'ànima entristida.

Sonet dels recomençaments

SENYOR Dolor, serà una nit callada
que vós vindreu a demanar per mi.
Per escrutar si prest jo us vull seguir,
semblarà cada estrella una mirada.

L'atenció del cel serà admirada
de veure com abans de sê a la fi
he sortit jo mateix a mig camí
i la mà que em donàveu he besada.

Senyor Dolor, després caminarem
fins a la font que vós sabeu. La bona
virtut de l'aigua, que en constant mudança

resta immutable de sa temperança,
menarà la conversa que tindrem,
en la qual vull parlar-vos d'una dona.

Com dins la nit...

Com dins la nit, quan ens desvetlla el vent
més fort que el son, i fins a nostra vora
la clara veu arriba del defora
viva i sonant damunt el món dorment,

i, d'altra cosa sense haver esment,
s'enduu el desig, arremorat a fora
fent-li oblidar la humanitat de l'hora
que el trontollar d'un carro ens fa present;

d'aquesta guisa, quan l'amor s'atansa
i m'arremora amb tal daler pregon
que fora d'ell jo no sé res del món,

com un trontoll de carro en llunyedança
sento la Mort que m'adverteix el límit
de l'humanal desig, tornant-me tímid.

Ressò de caramella

Hauria dit que estava sol;
sol de mi, sol dels altres, al carrer.
I em preguntava: —És cert que estigui sol?
és cert que estiguis al carrer?

Potser reclòs amb els meus llibres,
arrecerat contra la fluïdesa
del temps que passa; protegit per llibres,
imatge enduta en fluïdesa.

Hauria dit que sento el pic
d'algú que vol entrar. No veig ningú,

ni pas ni porta. No he sentit el pic,
i jo mateix no sóc ningú.

Girar els fulls, obrir la porta:
El temps, els llibres, jo mateix, tot passa.
—Sóc jo: sóc tu. ¿No vols obrir la porta
a l'ombra del record que passa?

—Sóc tu i els altres, sóc el temps
dels dies que han estat on eres tu;
a penes rastre esvaïdís del temps
on et descoloreixes tu.

Els morts...

Els morts, els morts, els morts a sota terra
i pluja a llur damunt, llisquent deixalla
amb què el daler d'anar amunt davalla
i torna a llur repòs a moure'ls guerra.

Penetra l'aigua, amoroseix l'argila;
un nou desig de forma pren els cossos.
Reïx la sembra, terra endins, dels ossos
i, amunt, l'estol de tots els morts vigila.

Els morts, la pluja, els morts. No sé res més
sinó el vençut desistiment que obliga
la trèmula caiguda de la pluja.

I a terra el gran dolor, ara i adés,
que esberla gleves i alça la fatiga
dels morts, amb pressa de llavor que puja.

Epíleg de l'Experiència Vital

El món és tot fora de mi:
els anys, l'atzar, la vida incerta;
i jo, sense moure'm d'ací,
com si el paper fos la finestra oberta,
esguardo, escolto, sento el devenir.

JOSEP-SEBASTIÀ PONS

1886

Adéu-siau, oh torre gran...

Adéu-siau, oh torre gran de llosa,
centaures afrontats de marbre rosa,
mates d'herba d'amor, com un record
eixint d'un munt de terra, als peus d'un mort,
i vós, campana abandonada,
que us capteniu sense aixopluc
per a mirar en la davallada
l'eternitat d'un camp de bruc!
Adéu-siau, eterna Serrabona,
l'àngel hi gira santament
segles avall, en una estona,
el full d'un llibre transparent.
Si és estroncada la pregària,
si han soterrat els llavis de la fe,
amb sa puresa originària,
l'alè del bosc aquí pervé.
Quan és la intel·ligència tan incerta,
Lluc i Joan, Marc i Mateu,
evangelistes sants de Déu,
els morts dormen davant la porta oberta,
com les ovelles de l'andà,
i veig tota la clina vesprejar
en l'amplitud pura i deserta.

Pels morts

Els olius emmagrits com la cigala
s'estan negres i clars sens moure l'ala,
i la vinya té un aire moridor.
Pels morts aquest repòs de la tardor.

Un vol inacabable d'ocells gira.
Amb un foc de sarments la vinya expira
i l'alè de l'estany dispersa el fum.
Pels morts aquesta absència de perfum.

Camí

Quin delit era el teu, camí del Riberal!
Ella amb el seu mirar ple de llum m'esperava.
Tremolar de palanca al pas de la canal.
L'arbre, escorça vermella, al fons s'emmirallava.
Camí del riberal dins l'abandó geliu.
Quan l'heura davallant pel marge s'esmunyia,
sota cada ventada on s'allisava el riu,
la neu que porta el vent en sa roba es fonia.

JAUME AGELET I GARRIGA

1888

Pressentiment de l'alba

Ja l'òliba es remou en la foscor
tota picada d'humitat de l'horta;
penja l'entranya de la lluna morta,
degotant, groga i roja, a l'horitzó.

Els rierols cap a l'albada enduts
blanquegen, en la fosca, enmig d'arbredes.
Lluen els còdols com estels caiguts.
Les ramades groguegen a les cledes.

Oh nit bullent, tenebra cristal·lina!
Silenci que s'eleva com un fum!
Ara, darrera l'ombra s'endevina
l'alterosa muntanya de la llum.

CARLES RIBA

1893

Estances

LLIBRE PRIMER

I

T'HA enquimerat la gràcia fugitiva
d'un desig i ara ets deserta, oh ment.
Ai soledat sense dolç pensament
i foll traüt sense paraula viva!

Però ¿què hi fa, si dins el teu oblit
la inquietud pregonament perdura?
Encara el goig sobre la carn s'atura,
duent l'anunci d'algun cant no dit.

I ell és el foc sagrat que et perpetua
damunt les cendres del desolament;
no vulguis calma en ton oblit, oh ment,
oh folla que has gosat mirar-te nua.

5

JOIA, callada endolcidora:
que tímida véns a prop meu!
Toques el sentit com un lleu
alè i la ment encar t'ignora.

Tant de temps que ja hi dorm l'orgull
desert de l'antiga ruïna!
Fes-ne ta casa i il·lumina,
Joia, el silenci que s'hi acull.

Em cals ben ardida i ben forta:
són tantes vies que davant

sol·liciten el vol errant
del sospirar que Amor em porta,

totes calitjoses d'oblit
i gelebrides de paüra!
Però ta presència fulgura
més forta que el fred i la nit.

Joia, amiga lenta i novella,
veu sense so, respir ardent:
envaeix el desolament
que ara és sol a parlar-me d'Ella!

Sigues ma consellera tu,
la comptadora de mes hores;
incendia d'Ella mes vores,
Joia, i vesteix-me'n el cor nu.

10

ULLS meus, ulls que viviu goluts damunt mon rostre:
per vosaltres la imatge d'Ella, dolça a servar,
és davallada al cor, i llum tan pia hi fa
que ja no hi val l'or d'aquest sol que és glòria vostra.

¿Com la carnal recança del goig que amb l'hora fuig
a la bella carn d'Ella us té oberts encara,
si veure-la caduca i fonedissa amara
tot pensament d'amor amb metzina d'enuig?

Ulls meus, closos em fóssiu amb porta de tenebra,
i el vostre esguard girat endins, de cara al cor,
portant a la fidel imatge que no mor,
i a l'adoració que l'estreny, i a la febre,

aquesta coneixença tan viva del sentit,
tan corporal, però ja lliure de paüra:
la mort faria de la bella carn pastura
sense que en tremolés la imatge dins mon pit.

19

El Temps, fill de la Mort, espia i mai no és las.
Ai Mort, així et diu sempre el teu moment quin és!
El goig que atresorem ens fa covard el pas;
així a mig camí ens sortiràs,
lladre armat, com si el nostre bé mai t'aprofités.

Si el trist despullament m'espera a mi segon,
Amor, no em pesis morta damunt dels pensaments:
¿què hi hauria entre tu i els altres morts que hi són?
(¿Ni què ara entre tu i cap dels meus vivents?)

Jo vull ton cos llunyà en un país d'oblit:
un freu d'absència que no domi cap conjur.
I a la nit jo diré, mirant el cel florit:
Així passà son esperit
a ser un nou astre etern damunt del món obscur.

22

Amor, adesiara sento mon pensament
que un sacre horror l'assalta en sa tranquila via:
a l'un costat vas tu, la usada companyia;
però ens volta una turba pàl·lida i vehement.
Tàcites ombres, òrfenes de fesomia! L'alba
neix plena de records; d'elles, ni el nom se salva
de dins la mar udoladora del present.

Amor, elles amaren també, i de ventura
fou el llur pit desesperadament avar;
¿no sents —cendra tornà llur pit— el secular
heretatge de joia que dintre l'aire dura
difús? Les ombres vénen de llur estatge mort
no a pregar una minsa almoina de record,
ans a captar de llur tresor la dolça usura.

Amor, l'innúmer deute clama de dins l'abís!
Vivim dels juraments, els sospirs, les besades

infinites de tantes gèneres escolades!
També un dia la casa clara i el verd país
seran buits de nosaltres i sonors d'altres vides
ignorants que jo i tu, ombres engelosides,
en cada cosa amada ventem un flam d'encís.

24

Hem estat com la gent nada a la riba erma
davant l'innumerable somriure de la mar;
la gran temptació a poc a poc desferma
les voluntats ardides del trist costum avar.

I un dia se'ls enduu, com d'una revolada,
ells, amb els seus records, els seus déus i els seus cants,
per si descobririen una terra daurada
enllà de les tenebres profundes i onejants.

Davant l'esguard errívol dels nauxers d'aventura
la verge mar es pobla d'illes amb ports fidels;
mes cap dolçor terral no iguala llur fretura:
sempre demanen una ruta nova als estels.

I més s'estimen la infinita mar deserta,
i els vents que s'escometen pels volubles camins;
de la sonora lluita la nau son vol concerta:
tal nostra vida, Amor, d'un combat de destins.

38

Pensament de la mort, agre ferment
que la naixó de tot meu pensament
—flonja i tímida massa— vivifiques,
i me'n fas, cor endins, un nodriment:

tu restes, fosc entre ombres fredoliques,
dins la pensa deserta, de les riques
pastures consumides renovat,
i les novelles maines multipliques.

¿D'on hi vingueres? De quin primer estat
de mort impútrida o d'oblit nonat
ets rara perdurança, que la vida
mateixa que t'assetja i et combat

sustenta de sa pròpia força ardida,
pel repòs que promets entraidorida?
I quan davant de tu obri la mort
la porta a la tenebra indefinida,

què faràs per durar i ser encara fort,
pensament de la mort? ¿El teu conhort
suprem serà de fondre't dins la immensa
ona d'eternitat? ¿O del record

múltiple que dormia dins la pensa
fer-ne un nou pensament sense fallença?

LLIBRE SEGON

Uns wiegen lassen, wie
Auf schwankem Kahne der See.
HÖLDERLIN

6

FELIÇ qui ha viscut dessota un cel estrany
i la seva pau no es mudava;
i qui d'uns ulls d'amor sotjant la gorga brava
no hi ha vist terrejar l'engany.

I qui els seus dies l'un per la vàlua de l'altre
estima, com les parts iguals
d'un tresor mesurat; i qui no va a l'encalç
del record que fuig per un altre.

Feliç és qui no mira enrera, on el passat,
insaciable que és, ens lleva

fins l'esperança, casta penyora de la treva
que la Mort havia atorgat.

Qui tampoc endavant el seu desig no mena:
que deixa els rems i, ajagut
dins la frèvola barca, de cara als núvols, mut,
s'abandona a una aigua serena.

7

Hi ha estones que el pensament
és sol i ert com una timba
desesperada sota un vent
que mai no s'atura ni minva.

L'eternitat dels anys difunts
i els que han d'ésser comptats encara
travessen la buidor que brunz,
empentejant-se, amb una rara

fúria d'exèrcit comandat
pel pànic: així, quan fa via
Déu sobre el món, l'home astorat
perd la rialla i fugiria.

Sols tinc una esma que és llavors
que sóc i visc el que em pertoca;
que no em val ser gasiu d'esforç
i creure'm ferm sobre una roca

tranquila, amb l'amor i la llar
i el meu jardinet. Tot navega:
cada vaixell, és tot el mar
que li fa força i l'arrossega.

I quan una onada de dol
o de goig ens bat i ens inclina,
no és res el que és nostre sol:
dins la nostra fusta mesquina

ressonen homes i ciutats,
tot el temps sens fi que ens circumda.
Cal fer rem, per no ser negats
dins la vida abstracta i profunda.

8

Que jo no sigui més com un ocell tot sol,
ales esteses sobre un gran riu
per on davallen lentes barques de gent que riu
a l'ombra baixa del tenderol,
i el rai que el muntanyenc mig nu, enyoradís,
mena amb fatiga cap a ciutats
que estrenyen l'aigua lliure entre molls oblidats
d'haver-hi comes verdes amb arbres i ramats
i un cloqueret feliç.

La vida passa, i l'ull no es cansa d'abocar
imatges clares dintre del cor.
...Tot en mi torna somni: nuvolet d'ombra i or
que flota i fina lluny de la mà.
Qui endinsa en el seu cor com un minaire avar,
qui de recança ulls clucs es peix,
tenen més que no jo, que, estrany a mi mateix
i alt sobre els altres, guaito l'ona incessant com creix
i minva cap al mar.

¿Quin moviment humà pot encara desfer
l'encant, llançar-me sang i sentits
a la presa, que és nostra, afanyada, entre els dits,
o al cant, que d'home a home va i ve?
¿O ha d'ésser mon destí el de l'ocell reial
que un tret, per folga, tomba del cel,
i l'aigua indiferent l'endú, vençut rebel,
cobrint-se amb l'ala inútil els ulls buidats d'anhel,
sense un plany pel seu mal?

13

Fuges, quan per haver-te
donaríem, en una nit obscura,
l'estel que riu, armat, en un tombant,
i en una mar incerta,
un port daurat de vinyes al voltant,
i en un silenci d'odi, el cant
d'una noia pura.

Ens deixessis almenys,
oh bella altiva, un somni dolç de tu
entre els ulls i la visió infinita
del món! Però ens estrenys
amb soledat, presoners de la fita
mirada teva, que l'habita
de lluny, sense tu.

Però si fossis nostra,
si daves —uns instants només— tos braços
al nostre coll, cenyint l'ardent engany
de creure encès ton rostre
per un amor com el que d'any en any
hem après —fet de dolç afany
i de tristos passos,

si te'l lliuràvem— tan
silenciosament atresorat!—
¿quina força immortal ens restaria,
deslligats de l'encant,
per ressorgir damunt la febre impia
i l'animal malenconia
i la soledat?

19

La Fúria adormida

¿De quin pensament devorat
fins a la viva sang
era tan dolçament vinclat,
Fúria, el teu jove flanc,
que semblaves dormir després
d'un amor sense mal
ni tendresa entristint el bes,
simple en son pur excés
d'alegria animal?

¿No ho sabràs, i perquè els meus dits
sobre els teus lassos rulls
han lliscat, a penes ardits
missatgers dels meus ulls,
sortiràs d'aquest son, com d'un
silenci del teu foc,
llebrera del desig profund,
certa d'un cor a punt
—mon cor— per al teu joc?

Talment parlo a una dona, oh nu,
oh bell Remordiment,
i et corono de somnis, tu
que només ets ardent,
content de sofrir braç a braç
amb el teu pler més fort
i refer-me un somni voraç
amb el que em deixaràs
no tocat per la mort.

21

Nu en repòs:
després de l'amor.

Ara és sola entre el foc de tes roses secretes
i l'atònita llum

la nua blancor— ah, les divines desfetes,
en ta blancor, del tacte que a exhaurir-la es consum,
las de tantes delícies tretes!

Mos ulls són un silenci esclau del teu repòs,
i els fats s'inclinen, mentre
l'ànima, en tu, es reprèn i somia el seu cos,
el teu cos! i el retroba feliç entorn del ventre
pur— emanat talment del goig que s'hi és clos.

Ordre ingenu de flor! Pels seus pètals divagues
al grat del somni lent;
que records en la tendra massa encara embriagues,
tu amb tu,— oh! que ets tan present, i el pensament
ja te m'allunya en miratges vagues!

27

Aire crepuscular

VANES flors del dia, les hores
collides lentament per llur
sola beutat al pur atzur,
que en decora ses rases vores!

Puix que el llarg camí no consent
el tan fràgil bagatge, cada
dia més amb mà resignada
dins els llacs rosats del ponent

us llançaré: caiguda encesa,
cercle que dilata el seu or
del cor de la nit al meu cor,
de ma nuesa a sa nuesa!

Un nu i uns ulls

IV

Refiada gran solitud,
cos, d'un astre amb sa fantasia,
cos nu! Inscrit dins l'absolut
de sa unitat! Oh poesia

sense alba, de sobte present
com per a sempre més! Intacte,
secret, remot, indiferent
en la puresa del seu acte

de llum — oh esclat que de sa llum
mateixa fuig, creant-se d'ella!
I que és sense temps, si en el rumb
vagarós d'una meravella

o d'un desig no és pres — reflex
aturat sobre els fluids batecs.

Palmera darrera el balcó; en despertar

La nit, amb la profunda fuga
dels seus ocells damunt tes branques
vers un dolç orient de blanques
aurores, no t'ha fet poruga

ni menys necessària al meu cor,
palmera, columna fidel
sobre qui pesa el primer cel
que m'és tornat, quan súbit mor

el déu dels somnis que em tenia,
i em trobo, nàufrag, no sé on
del temps i de la melangia;

però hi ets, noble forma, hi són
tos raigs contra el dia — oh quiet
triomf d'un pensament perfet!

Cante hondo

Jo no sabia que el silenci
pogués de sobte obrir-se fins
al centre glaçat, i els camins
tenir un sol caminant que llenci

un crit, tots un sol plany que va
a cercar l'esperança, mentre
l'home espera i ignora que entre
l'abisme i el cel es perdrà

el seu plany — l'hi prendran les mortes
mares cansades, per també
fer-ne llur plany, que d'elles ve
a constrènyer les closes portes

del temps ple, i els rostres vivents,
i els cors flotants als quatre vents.

Ilicet

A flor dels ulls, enlluernada,
la festa ha dit el mot darrer;
la nit, tenaç desheretada,
ens espera dreta al carrer.

Tornem al llindar, gairebé
com si fóssim sense mirada;
caldrà cada cosa refer
del que era en nosaltres pensada.

Virginal, portem a les mans
un somni partit en dos trossos;
¿saps quin és d'ara, quin d'abans?

Pròxims tots dos, tots dos distants!
Així un amor viu en dos cants
i una soledat en dos cossos.

Per amunt la brancada...

Per amunt la brancada pura
I en els ulls el món oblidant-se
I en els teus braços l'esperança
L'aigua corre i el temps s'atura

L'aigua sofreix i el temps sospira
Som vells com la fulla i com l'ona
Com el somni que ens empresona
Entre tu i jo una rosa expira

A la rosa i a tu estimada
He donat tardor i primavera
Com una mirada lleugera
En la nit a una ombra pensada

Cançó en la calma morta

Melangia encalmada!
Ni vent ni pena viva
per despertar les veles
d'aquest dia sense illes!
El temps és sols estesa,
l'estesa sols fugida
dels ulls cap a un enllà
que els venç i no els omplia.
L'hora ve sense onada,
resta sense agonia:
com una morta nua
sembla més nua i trista.
No tenen pes ni ales
paraules que diria:
foren dins l'aire un aire

a penes més sensible.
La nit haurà vingut,
i me n'adonaria,
no pel pas que acompanya
ni la guia que brilla,
ans perquè em voltarà
talment de mi sortida,
com si sobrés de mi
i no volgués ¡aquir-me:
de mi, amb el destí
i els noms que ja no el signen,
i amb l'esperança negra
i amb la memòria trida.

Tannkas

XXVI

TAMA-NO-O

FILL de maragdes,
ànima, fil de somnis!
Si et trenques, sigui
com en un rapte, l'últim,
més dolç, de la memòria.

XLII

AVUI que l'aire
té el crit d'abril i una alba
d'ocells que tornen,
com l'ametller enyoro
ma flor precipitada.

LVIII

POESIA REDIVIVA

(*En el centenari del Gaiter
del Llobregat*)

¿DE quina força
t'armà el sospir, de quines

veus el silenci,
que, incert dels vents, no dubtes,
fènix, mai de la flama?

LX

BRANCA SOBRE EL TORRENT

Que pura brilles
amb tanta flor, inclinada,
branca, dins tanta
quieta llum de l'aire,
a tanta fuga d'aigües!

LXI

ROSA

No ets secreta
ni oferta: ets la deessa
que, de sa verge
sola ventura armada,
prova el mortal misteri.

LXX

Conec la flama,
no a mi mateix que hi cremo;
la gelosia,
no el vent antic que sembra
dins meu la flor nocturna.

Elegies de Bierville

V

Clou-te, cúpula verda per sobre el meu cap cristal·lina!
Aigües de curs discret, brisa que a penes ets més
que un moviment del silenci, imiteu la manera senzilla
com la meva sang ara s'oblida i jo sé.

L'inacabable somni del món endolceix una a una
ses onades entorn del malencònic jardí.
Dins la meva ànima en pau sóc el nàufrag que en l'illa profunda
on reneix de la mar, súbitament reconeix
la seva pàtria antiga; i no en té sorpresa; el crepuscle
fa més pur el sender — oh pueril! oh reial!
que l'ha tornat a prendre, envellit i nu, però en flama
més a cada pas, més alentint cada pas
perquè vol la nit i arribar a l'esposa secreta
com esperat d'un esclat sempre imminent de l'enyor,
i ésser l'un per a l'altre un do amorós del misteri
—nit amb joia dels ulls, nit més enllà de la nit!

CLEMENTINA ARDERIU

1893

L'obstinada

L'ORGULL de la victòria contreu son llavi humit,
son tors es dreça encara i és en tensió son pit;
de l'última embranzida, cruel i mesurada,
l'irat fuet tremola a dins la destra alçada.
Ha flagel·lat el rostre d'aquell ardit infant
que, tot encès de joia i al ritme clar d'un cant
prometedor de glòria, se us apareix a voltes,
pren vostres preferències que abans anaven soltes,
i dolçament les lliga, fent-vos del goig esclau.
Mes ella, l'obstinada, de pit retort, el frau
pressent i, cada volta que el lleu infant la cerca
vestint nova disfressa, la troba tan enterca
que creu invulnerable l'estança del seu cor;
oh pobre cor que et migres dins la fredor de mort
d'aquesta carn que et volta!

Via Àpia

Ni sola amb mi ni acompanyada.
Era el diàleg sorprenent
de dos que senten igualment
i callen. Tota una fillada
de pensaments vam engendrar
i caminàvem Via enllà.

I fins també callava l'aire.
—Oh aquell moment que es pon el sol
i res no gosa moure el vol
en una treva de no gaire!
Quan la paraula va venir
portava un ròssec sense fi.

En cada pedra que mirava
tanta d'història m'ha llampat;
i una amargant serenitat
de l'olor dels xiprers lliscava.
Fórem tots dos tocats d'oblit
en el capvespre beneït.

La imaginada via lenta,
la sang dels màrtirs esponjant,
se'ns torna tota palpitant.
L'ombra de Pere, que valenta!
I Roma ens dóna el seu alè
senzillament, com qui no re.

Mentre nosaltres —¿ho diria?—
com per a fer el lligam més fort
entrellaçàvem mots de mort.
La nostra mort, que apareixia
al fons de la immutable via.
Enllà, més lluny, vora el pedrís
on finirà l'amor feliç.

Desassossec

Em donen aigua tèrbola
—jo veig el vi daurat.

No sento la campana
—al cor em va sonant.

Per l'aire, quina angoixa!
—els arbres són fruitats.

Quin rendiment tan pobre!
—més rica sóc que mai.

Si cal que jo naufragui,
em llançaria al mar.

Ventada

Però encara no és passada,
oh cor meu!
Ha vingut escabellada,
tota urc.

Per la força —ai com crida!—
se m'enduu;
sense alè, atemorida,
menjo pols.

L'amistat arremolina
— bo i dolent;
res d'amiga ni veïna
ni cel blau.

Només l'ombra que no em deixa
dintre els ulls;
em debato amb mi mateixa
i em faig mal.

La ventada té cobertes
multituds:

com un camp li som ofertes,
— tristes flors!

I esgarrifa la dallada
que va fent
amb la Mort aparellada:
quanta sang!

Basarda

Basarda,
m'afolles la tarda:
em prens els camins
dels somnis. Mesquins
ocells de mal caire
voltegen per l'aire.
Adéu, tendra llum,
adéu, el perfum
de la primavera!
Enguany, barroera,
malmenada ve.
I jo no tindré
repòs de la tarda,
perquè la basarda,
amb sos fils
subtils,
posà en mes oïdes
remors maleïdes.

JOAQUIM FOLGUERA

1893-1919

El silenci

Sota el temor de la paraula inica,
i un xic gelós d'aquesta solitud,
sense musica ni cap foll traüt,
només callant Et lloaré una mica.

Mercè divina, Tu faràs més rica
l'hora present: em donaràs virtut
amb Ton alè dins el callar golut
que del plaer de callar s'amplifica.

VENTURA GASSOL

1894

Les tombes flamejants

Fou una pàtria. Va morir tan bella,
que mai ningú la gosà enterrar:
damunt de cada tomba un raig d'estrella,
sota de cada estrella un català.

Tan a la vora de la mar dormia
aquella son tan dolça de la mort,
que les sirenes dia i nit sentia
com li anaven desvetllant el cor.

Un dia es féu una claror d'albada
i del fons de la tomba més glaçada
fremí una veu novella el cant dels cants:

—Foc nou, baixa del cel i torna a prendre.
Ja ha sonat l'hora d'esventar la cendra,
oh Pàtria de les tombes flamejants!

JOSEP MARIA DE SAGARRA

1894

Joan de l'Ós

Joan de l'Ós passava pel camí:
s'asseu, i escalfa al sol les dues mans
que estiraven les barbes dels gegants.
I se n'arrenca un brot de romaní,
i li diu: «Romaní, bon romaní,

per aquella virtut que Déu t'ha dat,
no em diries on és el goig perdut,
tu que ho saps tot i ets ple d'humilitat?»
Joan de l'Ós és vell i geperut
i es decanta a la font per veure's bé,
i tot esgarrifat s'hi mira, i crida
la força que no té,
i li sembla mentida.
Joan de l'Ós camina dropament
i vol fer veure encara que és valent.

Joan de l'Ós ja té la veu obscura
i fins tremola de sentir el seu cant:
la bona voluntat encara hi dura,
però la llengua és tota vacil·lant.

Veu una casa blanca i s'hi detura.
A la porta rosseja l'aviram
i una pagesa tranquil·la i madura.
—Deu-me menjar, que estic morint de fam!
—Joan de l'Ós, per la pelada via
com passes tan caigut?
—Ja ho veus, amb tanta força que tenia,
ara vaig geperut.
—Jo quan era una noia molt petita
sentia a dir que eres el més valent,
i a la paraula del teu nom, sols dita,
ja se'ns omplia tot d'esverament.
Tot el de nostra cuina t'ho menjaves,
i cap al bosc que no el deixaves mai,
i fins que te n'anaves
no passava l'esglai.
Tenia tres germanes més menudes,
i els parlaven de tu per fer-los por,
quan al llit despullades i ajegudes
no podia adormir-les la cançó.
Però jo m'hi tombava molt contenta,
i m'entrava un repòs de cap a peus,

i pensava en ta barba tan lluenta
com el pelatge bru de les guineus.
—Quin temps aquell! La trena escabellada
tota aromada de perfum boscà,
jo em ficava ben sol a la porxada
de la casa embruixada,
tot content com si anés a folgar
a l'hostal de la malmaridada.
I encenia fogaina, i canta i canta
per desfer tots els mals encantaments,
quan sortia el gegant de millor planta,
i si acàs deia: «—A mi tots els valents!»,
jo l'envestia, i no se n'adonava
que la boca i el nas li sanguejava
i li feia saltar totes les dents!
—D'aquestes coses n'era ple tothom,
i per les grans nevades
les bruixes maleïen el teu nom
dins les teules trencades.
—Ja han fugit, i mai més no tornaran
a emportar-se'n els bous i les arades,
i a malmirar l'infant;
ni amargaran la llet de les ovelles.
I quan sigueu al llit
no vindran a xiular-vos les orelles
mentre ronca el marit.
Quin desfer boires amb les mans alçades!
I quan eren ja foscos els camins
i la lluna rient per les teulades,
jo caminava cap als pins.
Ai com són lluny aquelles primaveres
càlides en el freu i en el tossal!
Com t'has podrit, ma jaça de falgueres!
Ja no és per mi la molsa del penyal!
Em persegueix tothora la basarda,
ja no em fa goig el caminar de nit,
i entre el bruc i el bedoll i l'olivarda
va ronsejant mon cos agemolit.

Ai! tu, que ets rossa i ets encara fresca
i tens fills que comencen a ser grans,
ara que el temps em guanya la juguesca,
no em donaràs l'almoina de tes mans?
No em donaràs, tu que fores valenta,
i vas ser un dia a sopar al meu costat,
una miqueta de palla, calenta
del baf del ramat?
Deixa'm el cavall blanc o bé l'arada,
que encar que m'arrossegui pel camí,
no tinc la mà gamada
i encara puc fer via amb el mantí.
O sols deixa'm la teva criatura
que la pugui bressar;
deixa'm seure al pedrís, que el sol hi dura
i hi fa de bon estar.—

I la dona pietosa se'l mirava
quan va sortir el marit.
Ai! el marit la porta li barrava!
Joan de l'Ós, tothom te té avorrit!
Joan de l'Ós fa nosa,
Joan de l'Ós se'n va,
i la dona, si gosa si no gosa,
li allarga un tros de pa.
I ell l'agafa amb les dues mans alçades
i ran de boca se li veu lluir,
i els pardals de les branques despullades
van recollint les molles del camí.

Joan de l'Ós troba la nit
pel camí de la fageda;
dins la gorga com un llit
s'ha dormit la lluna freda.
—Bona nit, bon picot de cua verda;
bona nit, bon picot del bec llarg;
bona nit, bell cucut de bec eixut;
bona nit, mare garsa baladrera,

i el gaig brillant que les cries esvera,
i el reietó menut.
—Joan de l'Ós, qui t'ho diria,
el més gran i el més valent,
que t'han tret de la masia
sense dar-te acolliment!

Joan de l'Ós ja s'ha perdut de vista,
la Mort el va guiant en son camí.
Ai! dins el cor d'aquella selva trista,
ja no s'hi sent l'olor del romaní!

La lluna nova a penes si s'obira,
Joan de l'Ós reposa vora un pi;
i Pare Llop al seu davant se'l mira;
escolteu què van dir:
—Germà llop, tots dos érem infants;
vam ser els amics millors;
tu em llepaves les mans,
jo et mirava amorós.
Cada nit ens trobàvem i ens dèiem bona nit,
i quants cops el menjar ens hem partit!
—Joan de l'Ós, l'amor que jo et tenia
te'l guardo ben sencer.
—La bona voluntat que en tu hi havia
encara deus haver.
Però, mira, germà, jo sóc molt vell
i ara vaig a morir;
quan sentis la fredor damunt ma pell,
enterra'm a la soca d'aquell pi,
i no empaitis si acàs ve algun ocell
a refilar per mi.
Germà llop, he sentit una cançó:
Joan de l'Ós, qui t'ho diria,
el més gran i el més valent,
que t'han tret de la masia
sense dar-te acolliment!
—Joan de l'Ós, t'han tret de la masia

i dins la selva vas cercant la mort;
ai dissortat del qui no t'acollia!
ai la pagesa quan camini a l'hort!
—Oh, germà llop, com ta paraula és dura!
No fereixis en va,
que la pagesa tranquil·la i madura
va dar-me un tros de pa.
Oh, germà llop, perdonaràs a aquells
que m'han ofès i que m'han avorrit;
no tornaràs amb els morros vermells
a rentar-te a la font com cada nit.
Per les herbes amargues i primes,
fes-me'n serment; pel vent rebel,
i per la lluna clara que t'estimes
i la gerra de la mel;
pel caminar de nits, que és cosa brava,
i perquè un jorn vares llepar les mans
del Joan de l'Ós! Que el braç se li cansava
d'empaitar tantes bruixes i gegants,
i la pagesa una cançó en cantava
tot adormint els seus infants.—

I en dir això Joan de l'Ós es va estremir,
i Pare Llop el palpa, i diu: «Ja és mort!»
Ai! dins el pit salvatge ja finí
de bategar-hi el cor.
I Pare Llop passà per la masia
i al poble va arribar,
i truca al campaner que dormia,
i el campaner respon: —Qui hi ha?
—Só Pare Llop, desperta't, campaner.
—Què vols i a qui demanes?
—Que t'enfilis al cloquer
i repiquis les campanes.
I els batalls, tremolant dins la nit freda,
que no es cansin de dir:
Pel Joan de l'Ós, que al cor de la pineda
s'acaba de morir!

El Mal Caçador

III

Toca amb el dit a totes les parpelles
perquè cap ull no se'l pogués mirar.
Tria després l'Elvira de companya
i li jeu al costat com un espòs;
comença dolçament la feina estranya
de deslligar-li l'ànima del cos...
I després se n'allunya, però encara
els qui vetllen Elvira, no han provat
res de nou; de moment guaiten la cara,
li veuen el color més apagat.
I ella vol fer tres batzegades vives;
li percudeix el cos un tremolí:
es gira d'ulls, li cruixen les genives,
i cau boca-badada pel coixí.

Novembre

Amb la fredor agemolint la tartana,
oh com és dolç arribar al camp obert!
Veure que el camp de tardor us encomana
aquella gran melangia de verd.

I ja de nit, entrar dins la masia
i vora el foc sopar ben aviat,
sentir amb el vent com la porta cruixia,
sentir el gemec del baldó mal posat.

Pujar a la cambra ben ampla i ben neta,
on tot ressona i on tot us ve gran,
sortir al balcó i meditar una miqueta:
veure una estrella i un núvol plorant.

I ja després enfilar-se a l'altura
del llit enorme i colgar-hi bé el cos,

el llit és fred i la màrfega és dura,
però és tot ell amarat de repòs.

I quan veieu el bell somni que us guanya,
us serà grat, poc abans de dormir,
sentir com entra la pau de muntanya,
i anar pensant que demà de matí,

quan les finestres haureu desbaldades,
i l'aigua salti pel rostre calent,
ja obirareu pollancredes daurades
i vols d'ocells escampats sota el vent.

Cançó de mariner

Dorm, criatura, dorm,
amb els deu dits sobre la neu
de la camisa blanca.
Dorm, criatura, dorm,
amb la rosa de neu a les entranyes.
No tinguis por de res,
que el mar pentina el coral
en el fons del fons de l'aigua.

Riu, criatura, riu,
i ensenya bé totes les dents
petites i esmolades.
Riu, criatura, riu,
amb la gran vermellor sense esperança!
No tinguis por de res,
que el mar gronxa sobre el cor
les princeses ofegades.

Cau, criatura, cau,
sense cinyell, sense vestit,
dins la petxina de nacre.
Cau, criatura, cau!

Abraça't contra el pit ben despullada!
No tinguis por de res,
que el mar ja porta aquell blau,
que el mar porta aquell blau de les batalles!

El poema de Nadal

...ALGUN cop, caminant per les collades,
aquells dies de fred, quan tot respira
un aire d'argelagues que s'adormen
amb una fina castedat de gebre,
i quatre ocells a la mateixa branca
no s'atreveixen ni a cantar ni a moure's,
quan despullat de la pintada angúnia
al vostre cor el ritme li escasseja,
com si comptés les perles del silenci
i el bategar tranquil de la muntanya,
¿no heu sentit aleshores, que la terra
era tota habitada per un somni?
I caminant, ¿no heu vist la senderola,
el caminet guarnit amb herbes clares,
amb pedra d'ull de serp verda de molsa
i amb galcerans atapeïts, que ensenyen
les gotetes de sang entre la fulla?
I no heu pensat en res? ¿No us acudia
cap cosa de cançó, o bé de paraules
que lligués amb els nervis d'un misteri,
d'un record, d'una estrella i d'una cova,
i d'un xai degollat sobre l'espatlla,
del pastor més valent que fa de guia?...
El camí de Betlem! L'únic, el vostre,
aquell que cadascú porta a les venes,
encara que no vulgui, ¿no seria
igual que aquell camí dalt la muntanya,
ensopegat només, perquè el silenci,
perquè els ocells, perquè les herbes castes,
van agafar tots els colors d'un somni?

JOSEP MARIA DE SAGARRA

Cançó de Taverna

AL meu pare li vaig dir,
que em cerqués una fadrina,
que em vingués justa per mi,
ni molt aspra ni molt fina;
perquè em feia galdiró
i estar sol m'era malura;
sortint de missa major,
el mal aviat se'm cura.
Això rai!
El casament és un ai.

I ja em teniu festejant,
i les velles se n'alarmen;
la mossa m'agrada tant
que no poden separar-me'n.
Em torno magre del cos
i se'm fa l'ànima prima,
quan al llit cerco repòs,
el seu record se m'arrima.
Això rai!
Que és ben dolç aquest desmai.

M'he donat a l'aiguardent;
la mossa plora que plora,
li faig el primer present,
no hi tocava de cap vora;
quan li he dut el collaret
del neguit era malalta;
ja no em fa calor ni fred
les besades a la galta.
Això rai!
La beguda em dóna esplai.

Ella té el color marcit
com una rosa que es passa,

el pare s'ha enfellonit,
el germà és tot amenaça.
De casa em treuen els dos,
i el despit és qui em governa;
cues baixes com un gos,
me n'anava a la taverna.
    Això rai!
Amb el vi s'adorm l'esglai.

Ara ha trobat un fadrí
de molt bona companyia;
si no es recorda de mi
jo que hi penso nit i dia.
Companys de tavernejar
que veuen les meves penes
em diuen: —Si et va deixar
te'n queden moltes dotzenes.
    Això rai!
I l'enyoro més que mai!

Record de Solsona

Fa una lluna clara i una nit serena.
Jo m'estic a la plaça de Sant Joan;
damunt les finestres cau la lluna plena,
cau damunt la pica que la fa brillant.
Aquesta plaça és tota recollida,
tan aquietadora i tan suau,
que sembla un replanet d'una altra vida
on s'anés a abeurar-hi un glop de pau.
Jo no sé pas per què jo aquí voldria
estar-hi llarga estona quietament,
amb una noia sols per companyia
sens besar-la ni dir-li cap lament.
Veure el tresor que d'aquí estant s'obira
sense esflorar-li el seu cabell gentil,
sols sentir-la a la vora com respira...
I respirar aquest aire tan tranquil.

J. V. FOIX

1894

Sol, i de dol

Jo tem la nit, però la nit m'emporta
ert, pels verals, vora la mar sutjosa;
en llum morent la cobla es sent, confosa,
em trob amb mi, tot sol, i això em conforta.

Negres carbons esbossen la mar morta,
l'escàs pujol i la rosta pinosa,
però jo hi veig una selva frondosa,
i en erm desert imagín una porta.

La fosca nit m'aparenta pissarra
i, com l'infant, hi dibuix rares testes,
un món novell i el feu que el desig narra.

Me'n meravell, i tem—oh nit que afines
astres i seny!— La mar omples de vestes,
i una veu diu: «Plou sang a les codines.»

•

¿Qui em viu en tu amb joia inseparable
que em trob més sol quan, de ta forma esclau,
de mar i llum i atzur faig el palau
que als ulls de tots és jaç grosser i establa?

¿Qui en mi et gaudeix i al teu misteri atansa
com si jo fos, absent, pelló i clofoll
d'un fruit secret ocult en auri boll
o lleu parrac d'un cos sense esperança?

En camp gebrat som càlida sorgent
graner petjat per un déu evident,
solc immortal d'una estranya semença;

i quan ma carn al teu desig s'avença
som, en el joc, astral pressentiment
d'ésser els lliberts de l'Etern Permanent.

Les irreals omegues

III

En un penyal d'aiguadolç el pintor Sunyer i jo, en un migdia de març, intentàvem d'aturar un vol de gavinots. Hauríem volgut ésser soldats, però les banderes del nostre regiment havien estat arrestades.

Si el braç ens arribés a l'altra riba!
Els burgesos hi tenen llurs tendres amants
dalt d'un vaixell, vestides d'uniforme
entre llargues estibes de saques captives
amb passius antillans i balanços bosníacs.
Llurs cossos de quinze anys, docents i dehiscents,
intemperants, i purs amb clarors d'hemisferi
són manolls defallents de violes silvestres
i ens fan senyals estranys de codis diferits.

(L'illot és un escull, no puc aparellar;
veig armes radiants i, ençà de la ribera,
les cuirasses solars de la host punitiva.
La llum m'aombra i puny, qui gosa forçar el pas?)

Erren els muls pel sorral i el canyís
i un vol d'ocells de mar per l'eixut de les dunes.
Hissem a tots tres pals reials senyeres!
Percudim les timbales per les coves!
Quin tors de déu antic enllà les Roques Altes
ens ullprèn com un far en nit coberta?
Quina brasa fumera ens embriaga,
purifica la ment i abat el cos?

S'esquerden els cristalls de les mars primitives,
es fon la sal de tantes mans obertes
pels garrofers frescals i els gira-sols dels fars;
és tot tan clar que ni sabem parlar-nos.
Escrivim versos nous amb signes fòssils!
Pintem en fulls arcaics nueses immatures!

Brolls de sang i vinagre fan florir els estigmes;
els soldats, peu descalç, se'n van per la carena
amb noies per trofeu i flèbil cantadissa,
sense dir-nos adéu, les banderes plegades,
l'ull enyorat d'un món sense capvespres.

Del Temps lliberts i jerarques del Nombre,
mercaders delinqüents d'astrals manufactures,
amb els braços en creu, a les maternes vinyes,
som fantasmes marçals i saó d'atzavares.

IV

Passàvem per corriols nocturns amb gavetes al cap curulles d'inútils ciments. Ens miràvem i no ens coneixíem. Elles també hi eren, al peu de les fonts estroncades.

Dalejàvem la mort per fosques travesseres
amb els braços alçats. I dèiem: Tu, qui ets?
I aquell? Puix que érem molts, moreus, hi érem tots.
Mireu: elles també, opulentament nues
amb els braços enlaire i moreues, al caire
dels abismes vesprals, en errívols trencalls,
collint de l'Arbre Intacte el fruit iridescent
o amb frèjols fils de nit, teixint malla secreta.

Dalejàvem la mort per burgs arborescents.

Érem cors calcinats a l'octubrer viratge
que arribàvem vençuts als suburbis tardans;
gustàvem barbullents els beuratges novells
i ens vèiem transparents, i, torbats, ens miràvem

quan l'or dels àlbers mor i neixen les estrelles.
Ens escoltàvem sords al bleix dels blats, plaent,
ensumàvem les pells i ens tocàvem, carnals
vora els frèvols mallols d'una mar que fumeja:

Dalejàvem l'amor en els molls clandestins.

Dalejàvem fondals amb aigualls i fullaca
i planyívoles fonts en nocturns santmarçals
braços enlaire. I dèiem: Tu, qui ets? I aquell?
—L'espantall de cad'u a la plaça sense armes,
bouers d'ull avetós plantats a la carena
per senyalar el camí d'impúbers penitents,
anònims ceretans amb fòssils a les mans
inscrits, elles també!, als almanacs de pedra—.

Dalejàvem la mar i érem troncs i érem brancs.

Érem tots, braç alçat, herois sense llegenda.
Matinada i crepuscle del dia indistint.
Caminàvem balmats; ens aturàvem, erts,
reculàvem: I tu? I aquells? I qui són elles?
(Vessàvem olis purs als patis mil·lenaris.)
En la gran nit comuna érem somni de tots:
Ombres d'ombres en creu, — murmuris convergents!
Damunt un mur de mar sense fossats ni portes.

Dalejàvem plegats pels quers del Cap de Creus.

V.

Vam arribar en aquell poble i no hi havia ningú, però per places i passatges sentíem la fressa dels qui foren i de llurs danses i les esquerdes dels murs esbossaven la faç dels qui vindran. Una llegenda clandestina gravada al peu d'unes figures que imitaven, rústegues, uns mísers infants, deia: "Sempre som en existència d'altri." Vam fugir pel coll fronterer vestits amb pells primitives i carregats de llibres.

No tinguis por, les ombres són de pedra;
llindes endins remoregen fontanes
i el vent fullós virolai dels espectres.
Per cambra i clasta sento veus i passos
i cants de nit en llargues foradades
sota els vinyars amb clarors europees.

A les parets, als batents de finestra
i als horts murats veig les cares pintades
dels qui van viure, vidents, en els segles,
dels qui vindran,—franques lluors futures!
Hi som tu i jo, la testa decantada,
amb colors crus i de ratlla estremosa.

Pertot, ah las!, els veires delectables:
escrits antics camperols i purpuris,
naus boreals a la lloia votiva,
voris vexats amb empremtes divines,
calcs d'En Miró amb alfabets rupestres
—verds i grocs lents en naufragi de tintes.

Sota el pont vell amagàvem les armes
i riu avall se'n van les salzeredes
i llur embruix, les corol·les nocturnes,
pàl·lids icons i confuses roselles.
Oh missatger, núvol alat, oratge:
—Aombra el mar amb àcides parpelles!

Al bardissar hi ha una toia esfullada
amb rous secrets i ceres clandestines
de quan olfacte i ull eren dolls d'aigua
cascadejant en un verger de laques
i l'home era home en una selva d'homes;
marfils en creu coberts amb gases rosa!

—Aixeca el braç, sagnosos els estigmes!
I toca el cel, oh blancors deslligades!
Nacres solars del Diví Simulacre,
amb gels ocults que delaten el pòrfir
i sots pregons amb sidèries polpes:
Venci el blau pur i brolli la semença!

Al celler musc amb frescors molineres
sentim, oh hisops pasquals!, música nova
i balls d'avui, complantes enyorades
(aspres besars en ponents adriàtics,
do de tots dos en albergs albanesos).
Però els hostes no hi són i els llibres ens fan nosa!

Caminarem descalços per les pedres
flairós el pit dels èxodes herbosos,
el llavi clos a les pairals rondalles,
el front marcat amb sang de les senyeres,
els ulls perduts als brulls de falses Medes
amb fars i freus a les cales adverses.

Veiem el mar entre parets calentes,
ceps cimejants i arbòries fumeres.
—Dem-nos les mans i desxifrem els signes!
El cercle pur prolonga llums sonores
al pur desert, hivernacle de perles;
ens parlem baix en una llengua estranya.

Heu'sací el bar i allà la barberia.
Al Pla de Dalt amb farigoles tendres
el dolmen, nu, gravat amb els horòscops.
I al peu del mas, a l'ombrosa comella,
testes de sants entre bidons i rodes.
Oh voluntat de foc que empeny la brisa!

Tornarem sols per la isarda drecera
que no sé on duu, darrera la duana,
coberts de pells, corbats pels incunables

i els cossos balbs:
—*No miris endarrera!*
Una barca s'emporta les campanes
i hem escampat els vidres per la platja!

VIII

Els falsos gratacels badaven llurs obertures al mar. Ella i jo passàvem per una insòlita vorera alçada a molts metres de la calçada. En les foscors d'aquella nit cercàvem l'astre del nostre destí. Les branques dels arbres que endevinàvem perduts entre llaguts i barcasses cedien al doll de les neus tardanes. Ens volíem dir adéu, però una mà invisible ens va tapar la boca.

Al vesprejar d'invisibles palmeres
entre llaguts i veles desmaiades
s'obren, secrets, els esguards i les timbes
escumejants a l'encís dels aiguatges.

Claregen cels llunyans a les alcoves,
els ors ocults als paviments pirates,
els coralls somnolents de les mestisses,
els ventres púbers als miralls murals.

Tu i jo passem per l'estranya sendera
—aquesta nit i l'altra nit i l'altra—
arran de falls ferejants i cingleres,
nous i florents a flocs tardans desclosos,
els ulls tancats per no perdre la ruta,
el peu descalç a l'encalç del silenci,
el nom balder pintat damunt la vesta
notariat amb lletres malforjades.

Callen els cors i tot d'arbres s'esfullen
als sorramolls amb remoreigs salobres;
calla la ment i defalleix un astre.

Al call pedrós, a les amples porxades,
a les negrors d'immarcessibles malles
—en fer-nos nit en nit profunda oberta
a l'albaneix de la Nit Immutable—
som espiats per cares ignorades
—ahir i avui, en aquest segle i l'altre—.

I quan el son desclou la flor exclusiva
en prats trements i espurnejants pinedes,
en empordans i en ordals i llurs nèctars
—blats regalats i ermites solelloses—,
a l'arenell braceja la basarda.

Dolços gemecs germinen a la broixa
i el cel s'encén amb guspireigs d'escata:
càlides mans, manyagues, ens acotxen
amb tremolors de pol·len sense antera
rou i sement de delirants captaires.

Tu i jo ens perdem en irresolta escorça
entre ombra i murs travats, a la drecera
del carrer clos que cercàvem sense esma.

XIII

Ens havíem banyat a la cativa i, a sol colgant, contemplàvem, després d'haver fullejat una vella crònica nacional, com tot de reis antics amb amples capes vermelles tenien llur assemblea al serrat de Cap Gros.

Mar vital quan floreja l'aurora; i obscura
en els horts cirerers de l'ocellós crepuscle
quan tornen els velers, vetusts, i el port llumeja.
Oh mar de tots, sense dofins reials
amb creus imperatius i els quatre pals

damunt l'or secular d'una estirp d'homes lliures.
Tancada; i secreta en els fraterns refugis
del dolç país esquiu, a la riba querosa
oh ments florals ronden el cos perfet
bell —absolut, immutable— total!
Astre pur esfullat en els torsos de sílex,
els paisatges antics amb llavors amagades
i els ullastres amb brancs pel qui venç i el qui dansa.
Púdic mirall del donzell remorós
que petja el temps i ombreja olimps, alat;
de meduses llisquents en peixeres celestes
portadores de cors amb esquema i consignes,
del cometa precís, de les ombres proscrites.
Pèlag fullat per atlas tardorals
amb focs pregons i plomissols extrems.
Llit d'herois destructors de les vides descloses
en els olis, els vins i les fruites melades
a la claror dels pins, a l'aurora ametllera.
(Corsaris i croats en negre i blanc:
papers desats als calaixos goluts.)

Per platja i ports, esquerps, els savis i els profetes
cavalquen l'unicorn; i els pelegrins erístics
que esbranquen els llorers i consagren la pítia
quan nega els déus, i la llar, i el qui és,
i en foc advers crema flors ancestrals.
Nosaltres, ull novell, per alzinar i fageda
invoquem noms terrals i llur bròfega fronda
les franqueses i els furs, les llibertats alades
i el que és per a qui és i allò que és just
davant les creus que brollen dels sembrats.

Ungeixin cabells d'ors becs aquàtics benignes!

Una fosa d'esguards fa tremir les salines:
—Quina pedra vital s'escalfa i s'estructura
en el mòbil desert de les fosses estèrils?

On són els murs paterns, perns i mandrons,
i el més enllà diürn amb sals intactes?
Quin joc ens fa vidents, sideral, i balbuços
quan vinyars i olivars, i el mas, es purifiquen
al vesprejar joncós de l'hora conjurada?
Què hi fan, jacents, en tos penyals extrems
els èfors embruixats amb litúrgics plomalls?
La teva claredat, jaç de guerrers ullpresos
(ni quan l'alba boscana crema, i castanyera,
amb la flama dels dits difícils papallones),
no ens deixa veure la llum.

JOAN SALVAT-PAPASSEIT

1894-1924

Omega

L'HORA floreix
rosa
vermella
roja i escarlata—
jo sé la noia que es daleix
i l'hora passa
dansa que dansa—
el meu rellotge té un panteig
sageta d'or i plom a la vegada.

*

L'hora floreix
i és el meu cor com l'esponja espremuda—
ara una esponja que raja d'escreix
(algú emborratxa
amagat
les agulles).
Cada minut cau com l'aigua de neu
llà on és l'amiga—
i a prop meu cau com l'espurna
la ferida.

Nadal

SENTO el fred de la nit
i la simbomba fosca.
Així el grup d'homes joves que ara passa cantant.
Sento el carro dels apis
que l'empedrat recolza
i els altres qui l'avencen tots d'adreça el mercat.

Els de casa a la cuina,
prop del braser que crema,
amb el gas tot encès han enllestit el gall.
Ara esguardo la lluna que m'apar lluna plena
i els recullen les plomes
i ja enyoren demà.

Demà posats a taula oblidarem els pobres
—i tan pobres com som—.
Jesús ja serà nat.
Ens mirarà un moment a l'hora de les postres
i després de mirar-nos
arrencarà a plorar.

Pantalons llargs

CAMPANETA daurada del meu carret de fira,
cavallet de cartró de mig pam, tot pintat;
havem caminat tant pels camins sense ira
que ara ens cal reposar, i agrair nostre fat.

Ja no tornaré més fent osque!, osque!, corrent,
a carregar amb palets el teu quadrant de fusta:
Campaneta daurada tu em sabies content.
Ara em mena la gent i tot-hora tinc justa:

i sóc infant encara, i no puc fer-ne esment.
Cavallet de cartró tu em sabies la joia:
si ara jugués a córrer, què diria la gent...
Trobaran molt millor que estimi alguna noia,

tant si és bella com no — cavallet tot pintat,
campaneta daurada — i que us deixi al terrat.

Tot l'enyor de demà

Ara que estic al llit
malalt,
estic força content.
—Demà m'aixecaré
potser,
i heus aquí el que m'espera:

Unes places lluentes de claror
i unes tanques amb flors
sota el sol,
sota la lluna al vespre;
i la noia que porta la llet
que té un capet lleuger
i duu un davantalet
amb unes vores fetes de punta de coixí,
i una rialla fresca.

I encara aquell vailet qui cridarà el diari,
i que puja als tramvies
i els baixa
tot corrent.

I el carter
que si passa i no em deixa cap lletra m'angoixa,
perquè no sé el secret
de les altres que porta.

I també l'aeroplà
que em fa aixecar el cap
el mateix que em cridés una veu d'un terrat.

I les dones del barri
matineres,
que travessen en direcció al mercat,
amb sengles cistells grocs,
i retornen
que sobreeïxen les cols,
i a vegades la carn,
i d'un altre cireres vermelles.

I després l'adroguer
qui treu la torradora del cafè
i comença a rodar la maneta,
i qui crida les noies
i els diu: —Ja ho té tot?—
I les noies somriuen
amb un somriure clar,
que és el baume que surt de l'esfera que ell volta.

I tota la quitxalla del veïnat
que mourà tanta fressa perquè serà dijous,
i no anirà a l'escola.

I els cavalls assenyats,
i els carreters dormits
sota la vela amb punxa,
que dansa en el seguit de les roderes.

I el vi que de tants dies no he begut.

I el pa,
posat a taula.
I l'escudella rossa,
fumejant.

I vosaltres,
amics,
perquè em vindreu a veure
i ens mirarem feliços.

Tot això bé m'espera,
si m'aixeco,
demà.

Si no em puc aixecar,
mai més,
heus aquí el que m'espera:

—Vosaltres restareu,
per veure el bo que és tot:
i la Vida,
i la Mort.

Res no és mesquí

Res no és mesquí
ni cap hora és isarda,
ni és fosca la ventura de la nit.
I la rosa és clara
que el sol surt i s'ullprèn
i té delit del bany:
que s'emmiralla el llit de tota cosa feta.

Res no és mesquí,
i tot ric com el vi i la galta colrada.
I l'onada del mar sempre riu,
sinó un somriure fi
que es dispersa com grills de taronja.

Res no és mesquí
perquè la cançó canta en cada bri de cosa.
Avui, demà i ahir

s'esfullarà una rosa
i a la verge més jove li vindrà llet al pit.
Primavera d'hivern. — Primavera d'estiu.
I tot és Primavera:
i tota fulla verda eternament.

Res no és mesquí,
perquè els dies no passen;
i no arriba la mort ni si l'heu demanada.
I si l'heu demanada us dissimula un clot
perquè per tornar a néixer necessiteu morir.
I no som mai un plor,

El poema de la rosa als llavis

(Fragments)

Oh, el seu flanc rosa i argent
i la trena que es deslliga
volar d'oronella al vent!
cabell desfet de l'amiga.

Amiga del dolç turmell.
—Com una vela s'enfila
espitllera de l'ocell:
si jo llenço el braç vacil·la.

Vianant vora la mar
prega pels marins que arriben;
si veuen l'estel dansar
moren de tant que sospiren.

Vianant puja al meu bot
que és lliure de la sentida,
però no diguis ni un mot
si no vols perdre la vida.

Vianant no parlis, no,
que l'oreig l'acosta, i mira

que et pendrà l'amor senyor
—que el mariner ja sospira.

*

Perquè has vingut han florit els lilàs
i han dit llur joia
envejosa
a les roses:
mireu la noia que us guanya l'esclat,
bella i pubilla, i és bruna de rostre.

De tant que és jove enamora el seu pas
—qui no la sap quan la veu s'enamora.
Perquè has vingut jo ara torno a estimar:
diré el teu nom
i el cantarà l'alosa.

*

Ulls clucs
l'amor
sap que la vida sempre és una festa

una cançó
Déu se l'estima com la llàntia encesa

ulls clucs
l'amor
Déu li manava que es lligués la bena

passava jo
i ara es venjava fent que fossis meva:

xiula i feineja
fa ta cambreta.

*

I quan confiats els arbres es vesteixen
ignoren els seus ulls
nit dia sol estelada plena
i les rodes de la fortuna de la seva sina

i el misteri de la rosa vermella dels seus colzes

ignoren el seu ventre
damunt la cripta ufana
que flameja el seu cos
vas de l'amor
llet i mel en son clos
flor d'atzabeja:
—quan confiats els arbres es vesteixen
Ella és la Primavera.

*

Com una fletxa el seu mentó
quan besa
—com una fletxa els seus braços alçats

la seva sina com una sageta
—una sageta el seu gest marxant

fletxa
arc
sageta
sagrari de carn:

i la joguina com la més tallant

*

La carn fa carn
el vi fa sang—
com és segura
l'ombra d'Islam!

A l'ombra mate dels meus pruners
l'amiga em renta i em besa els peus.
Oli d'ametlles
oli d'arrels—
naixien ales als meus turmells.
—M'estreny l'amada contra els seus béns.

Àmfora plena
del vi més clar,
del vi més negre
que ha fermentat.

Cap llavi crema com els vermells
de l'amor meva quan dóna el bes.
Tan fina és Ella que em dicta el vers.
—Prenc els seus musles i el seu coll tens
com una pruna que ara caigués.

S'ou la musica
de cent llaüts
clara i divina
sota els seus rulls.

Terra l'Aràbia, terra corser
d'alta crinera, bridall desfet.
El sol l'encalça, l'amor molt més:
amiga, amiga, no reposem
—un floc ma vida en el teu cabell.

La lluna és bella
si feia el ple:
a ta vorera
no ho fóra gens.

Copa vessada, veire roent
com la pregària de Mohammed
la meva amada, si el goig la pren
sota les tendes dels meus pruners.
—I el seu somriure, tremir d'estel.

Voltes de marbre
dels seus dos pits,
mesquita blanca
del meu delit.

Nocturn per a acordió

HEU's aquí: jo he guardat fusta al moll.
Vosaltres no sabeu
    què és
        guardar fusta al moll:

però jo he vist la pluja
a barrals
sobre els bots,
i dessota els taulons arraulir-se el preu fet de l'angoixa;
sota els flandes
i els melis,
sota els cedres sagrats.

Quan els mossos d'esquadra espiaven la nit
i la volta del cel era una foradada
sense llums als vagons:
i he fet un foc d'estelles dins la gola del llop.
Vosaltres no sabeu
                    què és
                              guardar fusta al moll:
però totes les mans de tots els trinxeraires
com una farandola
feien un jurament al redós del meu foc.
I era com un miracle
que estirava les mans que eren balbes.
I en la boira es perdia el trepig.
Vosaltres no sabeu
                    què és
                              guardar fusta al moll.
Ni sabeu l'oració dels fanals dels vaixells
—que són de tants colors
com la mar sota el sol:
que no li calen veles.

Ballet

El sol
          traint la sesta
folga amb el rostre encès la cortina adormida.

Així com una anguila quan és presa
s'esmuny la meva amada a ma follia:

—però el seu llavi és vermell
com el llum que duu el tren
i el banderol
                i el disc
                                i el senyal de la via:
així com una anguila quan és presa
son cabell
            com l'instint
                                cau damunt la carn viva.

Oh, quin pler   una gota de sang
viatgera del coll a la sina.
Així com una anguila quan és presa
es caragola
de cop
        la cortina.

Arquer d'amor

Si et veia la sina
veia dos fitons;
oh, deixa'm, amiga,
que provi el meu pols.

Si un pit et sagnava
beuria ta sang;
si et sagnava l'altre
amb les dues mans.

Obre ben bé els braços
i acluca bé els ulls:
si la carn no es bada
la vida s'esmuny.

Quan sentis ma boca
aguanta l'alè—

t'estremiràs tota,
i és quan jo et prendré.

Amiga, la vida
és una cançó;
jo canto ta sina,
arqueret d'amor.

AGUSTÍ ESCLASANS

1895

Ritmes

49

Precís i concís, monument d'una dura victòria,
tot ell ajegut al damunt de les amples espatlles,
un home somriu al repòs i a la joia més pura.
Finida la fosca agonia. Dispersa la lenta
musica terrible dels mots en panteix de deliris.
Truncada la lluita letal. Una llum de calvari
s'apaga en la cara sublim, com un ritme de força
vençuda. Coixí perfumat, llit de pau de la testa,
la mort li cenyia corones de roses morades...
Quin puny, quina ment ha menat la fatal imminència?
Cadàver, carcassa de gel, veritat absoluta!
La comba del front poderós, tèbia encar dels indòmits
incendis del verb, sembla fer-se més dura i la blana
rossor dels cabells que floreixen l'abim de les temples
s'anima amb l'alè besador d'un oreig tenuíssim.
Bon son, oh poeta difunt! Que l'imperi de l'ombra
no et sigui una estada severa i la pompa daurada
no esborri l'or viu de la teva vital reialesa!
Volies crear la bellesa? Reposa i no temis.
Avui ella et crea, bellesa tu sol, i per sempre...
Damunt l'ampla onada suau de la seda que en blanca

claror de llençols escumeja fent plecs de profunda
puresa, descansa el cos fred, despullat i magnífic.
Quin mur d'escultura més viu, la desferra d'un home!
Flameja el migdia finestres enllà, i el somriure
dringant de la llum tremolosa en la pedra daurada
no em sembla tan dens de puixança i de marques eternes
com l'alta bellesa marmòria d'aquesta divina
mortalla de membres. El pit ben combat, i la branca
nuosa dels braços, i el pont de les cuixes, columnes
de carn ben musclada, i els peus delicats, de la forma
més pura, i la coma del ventre que es fon en declivis
on dorm, com un ceptre retut, la noblesa del sexe...
Despulles augustes! On és la feblesa caduca?
Per quines aurores, per quines blavors més serenes
s'encelen, nimbades d'aloses, les flames humanes?
Quin vent d'altre món timoneja les veus que al teu dintre
trenaven el joc alternat de la llum i les ombres?
Un home perfecte somnia en la seva suprema
beutat... Cel endins, com un glavi d'argent, s'insinua
la fina fugida gentil d'una trena d'estrelles.
Jo poso la mà dolçament damunt tu, cor immòbil...
La calma pertot. Calma clara. La pau i el silenci.
Jo poso els meus llavis al front i a les mans. Joia clara.
Per què la ploralla i el dol i la nit sense límits?
Oh mort, és al si de la llum on he vist ta grandesa!

194

AMOR, esperit de la llum enyorós en l'exili:
no em miris mai més amb l'esguard captador de l'acerba
cruel correntia del dol i la pena... Caigudes
les fines parpelles morades damunt la cansada
claror de les nines de jaspi, les joies es moren
llanguint sota el pes de llur pròpia tristesa serena.
Si tot és inútil, per què tanta flama divina
dispersa en la pau dels camins d'aquest cel sense núvols?
Per què l'esperança mesquina del cor desvetllant-se?
Si res mena a res, per què ens cal de l'impuls l'embranzida

que ens duu sense forces al cim? Quin desig d'il·lusoris
besars em menà fins a tu, si els teus llavis no senten
l'anhel de tendresa que apaga la set, i que enganya
la fam inefable, i que ajunta les boques sorrudes?
Amor, esperit de la pau retrobada: les hores
esfullen les roses de llum que ploraven rosada
llavors que la fe de l'aurora brollava silencis
ardents al faldar de l'espai... No em valdria la porta
tancada, ni el fum que s'esmuny pel teulat, on la lluna
dibuixa dels signes suaus del miracle la xarxa
d'espines d'estrelles, riells encantats de tenebra
glaçada que lluu. Dins el doll ressonant de ta viva
mirada llanguent, voluptat, serp de foc, orgullosa
t'he vist en ta fuga rabent. I el meu seny solitari,
poruc de l'engany, el repòs retrobava en el gràcil
reflex d'una rosa en les aigües del riu que s'allunya...

303

La blonda, serena senyora d'ulls blaus, ara és morta.
Floreixen els camps a la terra i els núvols divaguen
pel cel. Tota cosa somriu perquè ve primavera.
Serena, la blonda senyora somreia tranquil·la
tot just fa tres nits. Ara és morta. La joia que torna
no troba la joia d'antany. Les espigues madures
brandaven amb pompa feixuga damunt els seus braços
en garbes de carn palpitant. Dos infants endolcien
la llar de la blonda senyora serena. La jove
puresa del viure matern es guarnia de flames
solars. Tot en ella era d'or: els cabells, el silenci,
la pau, els vestits, les cançons, el perfum, el somriure...
L'estreta d'amor fecundava de nou la carn forta
—combat de les mares!— i el cos refusava la lluita
cruel. Oh tempesta de sang de la vida que malda
per fer-se potent i s'abat amb sobtada feblesa...
Morí. L'han tancada al taüt, i al damunt de la sina
portava la filla mort-nada. La pedra dels somnis
posava carícies d'oblit en la imatge difunta.
Bon son, mare i filla vençudes, ja pedra per sempre!...

439

ADÉU, President!... Sota un arc de banderes retudes
te'n vas pels camins del no-res a la pau infinita
i ens deixes al camp de combat amb les armes alçades
davant l'enemic. Abrigat amb la llum dolorosa
del cel nuvolós del matí de Nadal, la serena
bondat del teu front decantaves, lassat de les lluites
estèrils, tranquil en l'augusta noblesa del somni
més alt que dins tu germinà. La República lliure
té avui pel teu nom el millor dels trofeus. Del silenci
reculls la victòria més bella, cabdill sense tares.
Adéu, President!... Follament les gentades adustes
es baten encara, per calls i carrers, les revoltes
absurdes covant amb enuig infantil, d'anarquistes
follies imbècils tornant-se pastura. Somreia
la mort al capçal del teu llit, gairebé com germana
de pau, vetlladora suau, maternal en la muda
fadiga d'espera. La veies, i tu, sens temença,
també li somreies. Callaven al lluny les confuses
converses dels homes mancats d'esperit. L'hora trista,
tranquil·la de veure't serè, fou més breu que les altres.
Adéu, President!... Has fugit pels camins que no tornen
enrera. Mai més no et veurem. Per les vies més dures
nosaltres demà marcarem les petjades cansades.
Mai més no seràs el menaire del poble que aviva
l'estel tremolós en la nit per clavar-lo per sempre
damunt la bandera barrada, i el veu com s'allunya
tenebres endins, i altra volta segueix les ombroses
cruïlles dels passos heroics. En l'aguant de ta destra
mai més no tindrem el repòs de l'infant que confia
les seves temences al pare, que en ell no hi ha dubtes.
Adéu, President!... El matí de Nadal era tètric
com mai, sota el vel del cel gris. Dolçament, tu mories
damunt el llit blanc, testa blanca, puresa senyora,
subtil cavaller de la gran pulcritud impol·luta.
Ploraven les gents a l'entorn del Palau, i planaven
les onze cruels batallades, sanglots en fugida

del vell campanar de la Seu, entre l'aire i la boira
i el fred del desembre fatal. L'esperit del silenci
sentia la folla fiblada, de carn que s'esquinça,
de vincle que es trenca, de força que es fon com un núvol.
Adéu, President!... Una pompa de flames revoltes,
flotar de banderes en iris, ardent homenatge,
s'abat a mig pal en record de la gran augustesa
de l'ànima clara que fuig per les voltes supremes
dels amples espais sense fi. La República lliure
recull el teu cos, President!, i en les pires heroiques
en fa sacrifici sublim, d'una pàtria més alta
captant la difícil comesa. Les joves corrues
et reten l'honor més excels. Vés en pau. Nit endintre
nosaltres passem. Tot és res. Catalunya és eterna.

MARIÀ MANENT

1898

L'ombra

TRISTESA perfumada, rossinyol de la nit:
amb sospirs, al meu son vas fent una corona.
El coixí feia olor de taronger florit,
oh rossinyol, colgat d'estrelles i d'aromes!

Però, si em desvetllava, he vist que era de neu
el jardí, i aquella Ombra hi venia daurada:
i es glaçava un somriure entre sa boca lleu,
com l'aigua de la nit dins una rosa amarga.

Diuen: la mar és trista...

DIUEN: la mar és trista. Quin trepig
fa cada onada, quan s'esberla!
I veig una mar trista, però, al mig,
tu, com una perla.

Diuen: la terra és trista. Quin trepig
fa cada fulla! Mig no gosa.
I veig la terra trista, però, al mig,
tu, com una rosa.

Sentint per primera vegada l'olor dels til·lers florits

Aroma dels tíl·lers florits, ben nova i dolça
per mi! No desvetllaves cap mica de record.
El passat no traspua en aquesta ombra d'or:
només viu el teu somni, arbreda dolça.

És lluny el vostre bleix, roses, glicines blaves,
tan ple de mi, tan càlid de secrets.
Tu, perfum sense ahir, com d'oblit m'abrigaves,
entre aquests arbres tendres i dolçament abstrets.

Matí

Ets eixida del son com del mar. Tota humida,
somriu encar ta boca als somnis, dolçament.
Brilla el sol a les herbes, però tu veus l'argent
de la lluna, entre l'aigua adormida.

Una llum de maragda mig emboira els teus ulls;
té perfums d'aquell mar ta delicada argila;
i dus una gran perla pàl.lida sota els rulls,
ondulats com una alga tranquil.la.

Cançó

Amigueta, el turmell
dus humit de rosada:
cervatell, cervatell,
cervatell vora l'aigua.

T'ha quedat a la pell
el color de l'albada:
cervatell, cervatell,
cervatell vora l'aigua.

La cançó d'un ocell
t'ha entristit la mirada:
cervatell, cervatell,
cervatell vora l'aigua.

Cançó àvida

Pomera daurada
que rius vora meu:
no cerco la fruita,
sinó l'ombra lleu.

Fonteta perduda
al cor de la pau:
no em cal l'aigua fresca,
sinó el cant suau.

Estrella encantada
damunt de la nit:
no et vull per guiatge,
sinó per neguit.

Diàleg

De rou ja brillava
la flor, si la culls.
Veuré la nit blava.
—No. Mira'm els ulls.

—Són flama lleugera
d'un foc més pregon.
La nit ja m'espera.
—No. Mira'm el front.

—Doncs dô'm una vida
d'amor i d'enuig:
ai, boca florida!
—No. Besa'm, i fuig.

A una oreneta que em desvetllà a trenc d'alba

Què saps, dolça amiga de seda,
quan l'alba es comença a daurar,
què saps de l'ombrívola cleda,
del meu insomni humà?

El liquen, humit d'ombra blava,
ja es deu aclarir vora el niu:
però ta cançó m'allunyava
la Son — ocell esquiu.

No saps la inquieta palpebra,
ni el front al coixí massa ardent,
ni el llit ennegrit de tenebra,
tu, entre l'alba i el vent.

Albada

És trist, nit amarga, el meu somni:
no hi cremen les roses d'argent.
La mar és fosca i no sé com ni
quan eixiria del vent.

Però l'alba pura s'inclina
i et deixen vora el meu neguit,
oh blanca, olorosa Petxina!,
les platges de la nit.

MARIÀ MANENT

La dama

Joncs d'aiguamoll, verda flama,
sovint s'ajupen al vent.
He vist que hi passa una dama,
dolça a la llum de ponent.

L'aigua és negrosa i esquiva,
però hi ha el lotus florit.
La dama, dreta, a la riba
s'està voltada de nit.

La son no em ve a la parpella,
aquesta nit resplendent:
igual que un jonc, prima i bella,
veig que ella es gronxa lleument.

He clos els ulls, però encara,
damunt el llac de la nit,
sa gorja veig, fina i clara,
igual que un lotus florit.

L'ocell perdut

Ai, ponent, corona vermella,
    or mig esvaït!
Ja veig la lluna, amb una estrella,
    al front blau de la nit.

Tinc la finestra, tota franca,
    oberta a l'aire pur:
vull que es mulli de lluna blanca
    el meu cabell obscur.

Em du secrets aquesta brisa,
    secrets d'un lotus blau.

De tant en tant el salze frisa
i la rosada cau.

Tinc una cítara daurada,
ben dòcil als meus dits:
ningú no escolta la tonada,
i els morts són adormits.

L'ocell esquerp, a trenc de dia,
se'n porta el vent sorrut;
i, en ser de nit, ja recollia
al cor, l'ocell perdut.

La plugeta

Quin seny tan fi, plugeta lleu! Ja la llavor t'espera;
dus al quintar cremat de sol frescors de primavera.
Vas néixer fosa al cor del vent, alguna nit estranya:
els solcs s'amaren del teu plor, i és verda la muntanya.

Ahir molts núvols abrandats pel cel feien corrua,
i cada llum dels mariners era una estrella nua.
Avui tot són colors frescals i papallons i merles:
ai, quina olor, jardí del Rei, brodat amb tantes perles!

Nit d'estiu

Ara aquesta rosada és tan pura
com l'aigua tardoral.
Un oratge lleuger torna la nit frescal.
Vora el llac, a l'atzar, l'herba tendra murmura.

Els nenúfars vermells, d'un perfum tot humit,
a l'altra illa s'estan, pels volts de la ribera.
És lluny el meu germà: hi penso dia i nit.
Aquí, de tota cosa em sento forastera.
Ai, clarins del castell, quina angoixa, en la nit!
Em cauen tot de llàgrimes al damunt del vestit.

PERE QUART

1899

Infinita fortuna de la sang

INFINITA fortuna de la sang,
Amor, aquesta gràcia imperiosa
que es refà, com el mar, en les tempestes.
Miracle, glòria, servitud del fang,
dolcesa furiosa
dels ulls, dels llavis, de les sines testes.

Sospirs amb pauses de cançó,
desig del gaudi, gaudi de l'espera,
tumult, victòria i abandó.
Amor, veu poderosa i mentidera,
palau dels somnis resplendents i estança
penombrosa del plany i la recança.

Tot el verí d'aquesta mel,
d'aquest sangprès la coïssor suprema,
la revessa metgia d'aquest fel
i aquella set que l'aigua fresca exalta,
¿qui no els sofreix, qui no els voldria esprémer
i ben xuclar-los, aprimant la galta?

I la tendresa, ventijol humit
—ales de la tendresa—,
polsim d'amor i fina embriaguesa;
el sentiment a mitges i el sentit;
coixí de pètals sota la rosada,
secret vespral en innocent albada.

L'amor dels somnis, tanmateix!
Aquella força plena i sense minva
que crea com un déu la seva fama,

el gaudiment que el peix,
la corona que el nimba,
la veu innumerable que l'aclama.

Per als mortals un altre amor
de flama o brasa que s'ablama encara,
demà ja trista, vers l'enyor
i vers el frau i la pobresa avara
i la memòria altiva
—corrent amarg que ve de l'altra riba.

Però hi ha el temps, Senyor, aquell temps
quan els sentits acorruats s'avesen
a tants plaers extrems
i a tants prodigis de rosada argila
dintre miralls mig entelats on besen
els amorosos de flagrant pupil·la.

I, sota el cel, aquell voler, convex
clavell de tendra porcellana,
cristall pel bleix, micròfon pels batecs.
Branda bleït de febre vana
i amb l'ombra secreteja
d'ocells carnals, que fan enveja.

La cambra de l'amor serà la nit.
Amarà les molleses i les brises,
l'esclavitud, l'oblit.
Els llacs d'aigües submises,
el trèvol i la gespa de les prades,
les branques dels fruiters mig decantades.

És aquesta la nostra eternitat!
Déu vetlla el breu camí, l'hora fecunda
i el mal àngel els sembra de pecat.
S'empara la follia vagabunda
d'instants que el goig afua i accelera
i el pensament eixampla com l'esfera.

Miracle, glòria, servitud del fang,
dolcesa furiosa
dels ulls, dels llavis, de les sines testes.
Infinita fortuna de la sang,
Amor, aquesta gràcia imperiosa
que es refà, com la mar, en les tempestes.

El Freu

ENCARA s'esbadellen les albes lluny de mi
en el país feliç a on mena
un paorós camí,
sense rodera ni petjada lleu,
com d'aigua tèrbola i serena?

Jo, mentrestant, travesso el freu,
peu nu dins una barca que s'emplena
d'aigua tenyida per la sang
dels que sofriren sense pensament
d'amor ni d'odi la darrera pena,
guerrers de rostre blanc
entre l'atzar i l'espavent,
només amb l'arma del lament.

Tota la nit dintre mos ulls oberts
a estels inerts, a llunes foses,
a sols extints camí d'albes moroses,
a inferns glaçats temps ha deserts,
a tanta nit, a tanta llum nonada,
a tanta mort a nova mort damnada.

Les ombres moren i reculen vers
l'ombra les clares vides.

Oh blau, oh blau pretès
vivent només en les humanes crides,
indeleble i suau com el no-res!

TOMÀS GARCÉS

1901

El somni

Blanca venies en la nit. La seda
era cinyell de la teva beutat.
Afeixugaves un braçat
de roses damunt de la seda.

Hi havia en els teus cabells
ombres i lluors amagades.
Dues estrelles atiades
enfosqueïen tos cabells.

Blanc i rosat era el teu cos,
amada, dins la nit encesa.
Com sentia l'embriaguesa
de les cent roses tendres del teu cos!

O somni llunyà! T'esvaïes,
boira desfeta, vel morat.
Amb la primera claredat
de l'alba, somni, t'esvaïes.

Aquella gràcia fugitiva
deixà entre flames mon cor pres:
ai, que no mor la sentor de les roses
i duc als llavis el record d'un bes,
talment la pols daurada d'un ala fugitiva!

Viatge

Les violes s'esborren en el verd de la font
i en un cel esvaït es retalla la clina.
Dringa la tarda, fulla d'or.
Oh, mon amor, la llum de la muntanya ens crida.

La terra, enllà, s'ondula amb tebior de carn
i com un pit enyoradís alena.
Caminem, i diríem que per sabê'ns el pas
el cel acosta al viarany l'orella.

Una cabana, flor del cim,
sabrem trobar, que els somnis aixopluga.
Oh, mon amor, el viatge finí:
a la fageda les ombres maduren.

Joc

Si veiessis el blau fumerol
adormit a la vella teulada,
¿em diries quants rostres hi ha
en el clar borrissol de la flama?

Si un vaixell, en el trèmul matí,
de les lloses del moll es separa,
¿no sabries per l'ombra que es mou,
els adéus que bateguen en l'aire?

I si un trot fugitiu deixondí
els camins esvaïts de la tarda,
per l'espurna que fan els cavalls
endevines els ulls de la dama?

Clariana

Sóc un infant que somia sota un verd llençol transparent.
El silenci és aquí un lleu murmuri sense pauses.
Oh, prestigi d'un cel només endevinat!
Soledat impossible!
A dalt dels arbres pengen les veus dels carboners.

TOMÀS GARCÉS

Cerdanya

A la llinda del bosc
s'esgarria la passa.
Ara vèiem, del cim,
els jardins de la plana.

Les esquelles només
el silenci trencaven.
Les crineres al vent,
el galop de l'eugada.
Llibertat, llibertat,
llibertat adorable.
Però passen els bous,
processó de la tasca.
Entre l'euga i el bou,
la mesura i el pacte.

Ah, quin aire més fi!
ah, quina aigua més clara!
Collirem l'aranyó,
la pometa boscana;
com un sol, brillarà
la carlina daurada.
Però em sento els batecs
i la tarda s'apaga
i la truita s'esmuny
riu amunt, pigallada.

JOAN LLACUNA

1905

Se'ns muden, Aurora...

SE'NS muden, Aurora,
els ulls amb els anys.

Tu, que els tens tan negres,
te'ls veuràs castanys.

—Patera, patum,
les banyes de fum.

Els sàtirs vindran
i se'ls enduran.

—Patera, patam,
les banyes de fang.

Els tritons, ondina,
es fiquen al blanc
de la teranyina.

Veig com s'exalten

VEIG com s'exalten
les flames dintre
la teva cambra,
on aixoplugues,
oh soltereta,
plors i miralls.

Adéu, coixins
de blonda, llit

blanc amb cistells
de flors daurades,
decorat (àngels,
cintes, ocells)
rosa, dofins
brillants d'escata!

Les brases gronxen
oquetes rosses,
aigües de plata.
La cendra escampa:

Ai, ai, ai, sí
que es corroeixen
les ales fràgils,
els flonjos cèrcols
dels teus molins
de vent!
Ai, ai, ai, sí!

—Adéu, bruseta
d'organdí lila,
faldilla blau
cel que em duran
dos cignes nuvis
la nit de Sant
Joan Baptista!

Les brases gronxen
aneguets grisos,
aigües morades.
La cendra escampa:

Ai, ai, ai, sí
que s'esvorellen
les parets brunes
i les vermelles
dels teus jardins
de roses!
Ai, ai, ai, sí!

Xucla el silenci

XUCLA el silenci
nocturn
sense empassar-te
estrelletes.

—Xuclo el silenci
nocturn,
i al tros més tendre
del cor se'm claven
les estrelletes.

—Abraça't amb
el lleonet
del picaportes
de casa,
abans no vagis
al llit.

—Copejaré
el lleonet
del picaportes
de casa teva,
perquè et despertis
d'un cop.

Aquesta nit

AQUESTA nit
el teu trepig
ressona dintre
meu, amiga.

Aquesta nit.

JOAN LLACUNA

—Aquesta nit
el teu alè
m'emboira els rulls,
la veu, amic.

Aquesta nit.

—La teva mà
fruita tendrors
de moll de jonc,
amiga.

La teva mà.

—La teva mà
fruita escalfor
de balma, amic.

La teva mà.

A la cintura,
hi tens flonjors
de rosa, amiga.

A la cintura.

—A la cintura
hi tens fluixell
dels meus coixins,
amic.

A la cintura.

—La teva boca
em crema el pèl
moixí d'arran
de llavis...

—La teva boca...

(No sé si som
al Xipreret
o a la riera
d'Odena.)

Amic... Amor...

—Amor... Orèade...

AGUSTÍ BARTRA

1910

Als llavis del silenci

I

Dolça hereva del dia, alta torre d'espigues,
oh captiva d'estrelles i de solars vencills:
els meus braços t'allunyen de segues enemigues
i a tos peus vinc a ajeure'm com la cançó dels grills.

En ton ànim plora l'estrella de la tarda,
a ton flanc duus clavada una dalla d'ocells.
Jo et llevaré del pit els núvols de basarda
i, fet pluja i rosella, besaré els teus turmells.

A les teves mans brilla l'ampla pau de les eres,
el meu amor d'avui ha deixat ses roderes
en ton cos estival de raïm i de nard.

Però ara que la lluna a ta falda s'atura,
em sentiràs lleuger, com herba que murmura
el seu càntic a l'ombra del teu arbori esguard.

II

Dir la brusca sorpresa d'un record de gavina.
Naufragar dolçament en sensibles esculls
de temps i llunyania. Quina claror llatina
celebra i canta el déu que dormia en mos ulls!

Rialla de la vela: àmfora en blava testa!
Oh les trenes salobres esbadiant-se al pit
immòbil de la terra vestida de ginesta!
Als llavis de l'escuma mor i neix l'infinit.

Espera del meu ésser, com roca extasiada
per un somni futur de proa il·luminada
que escolarà el murmuri innúmer de l'atzar.

Oh la sirga diàfana dins l'abís de tenebra,
l'assalt de l'ona tèbia que s'enduu tot el gebre!
Dir que en mi vetlla el cor profund del mar, del mar...

Davant el mar a Center Island

Mira i recorda. Encimbella aquest mai
del moment que t'assalta. Oh, batega, mirada,
i contempla, cor meu, aquesta aigua ajaçada
dessota tant d'espai!

Mira i recorda. Emporta't aquest vent
llatzerat de gavina,
aquesta llum que ajeu sos esquelets d'argent
dintre trèmuls sepulcres d'algues i sorra fina.

Mira i recorda. El sol deixa en la neu
els seus esclops vermells, una barca deixonda
un somni d'au i fronda,
i passen núvols blancs... Tot roman i és adéu!

Oh, sobretot recorda! Viu per la teva estela.
Car la flama és senzilla, com senzilla és la vela.

ROSA LEVERONI

1910

Neguit

XII

SENSE illes voluptat, sense riberes,
fúries candents i roses trepitjades...
Sols a la fi l'inútil gloriar-se
i la cendra i el llast de l'hora morta.

XIV

He dit estel i perfum de besades,
cançó de rossinyol i ales angèliques,
i als braços m'he trobat com a resposta
la melangia de la carn inútil.

Joia

I

OH joia omnipotent! Dur-te callada
dintre dels ulls, només per a mi sola,
gràvid secret, quan fortament voldria
a tots els vents cridar que jo l'estimo.

II

Podran florir els estels, florir les roses
i el món espurnejar de meravelles,
i sols ho copsaré dins els teus braços:
jo veig el món en la teva pupil·la.

IV

Una boca i un bes que mai s'acaba.
Un record que esdevé al·lucinant.

La rosa, de tan blanca es torna roja.
El rossinyol no sap sinó cantar.

V

Paraules sense dir, cossos en pugna,
llavis només, deixades les recances.
En la tarda d'hivern enfredorida,
has fet florir la meva primavera.

VII

Ni vela ni perfums, ni el mar en calma,
han aixecat en mi rastre de somnis.
El somni l'has dut tu quan m'oferies
el dolç descobriment de l'hora nua.

X

Has fet un collaret amb les paraules
per a ornament manyac de ma nuesa.
I m'has posat al pit gemma escollida,
aquella que de temps era esperada.

XV

Per què paraules, si el verger del somni
ha tret florida de besars immòbils?
Per què paraules, quan podem trobar-nos
en illes verges, xopes de silencis?

Absència

VII

Em pren la calma dels camps
quan l'hora esdevé rogenca.
I la quietud del mar
quan els vents dormen la sesta.

I mentre vola l'ocell
l'ànima esdevé lleugera...
Saber-te lluny sense dol
em fa ressò de miracle.
Ara, però, veig el món
amb la claror que m'encanta
de tenir-te dintre meu,
que fa que no em cal pensar-te.

JOAN TEIXIDOR

1913

Enllà

Prou he sentit en un moment escàs
l'afany d'un cos teu, meu, que tèrbol s'estenia
cap a un tot lligat. I en aquest llaç
august i taciturn, l'ànim al vol s'obria
de l'esperança, com si, dolç, l'abraç
fos fort per ofegar la nostra melangia.

Però quan s'esllangueix en el meu pit
el teu front que es sotmet a un somni que arriba,
em trobo sol en la mateixa nit
que ens acollí propícia i aixoplugà en sa riba.
Al meu davant, un camí resseguit
en nau tempestejada, al meu govern esquiva.

El que he tingut del teu somrís mortal
fou àngel pressentint la llum que ens és defesa;
l'esclat més poderós era malalt;
descompartits, els caps, en l'hora més encesa
presagiaven, impotents, el mal
de la deu de l'amor, que és pols en sa escomesa.

Qui sap si morts traspassarem el clos
que ens feia dos estranys! Avui, cap hora blana

mitigarà la febre del meu cos,
quan el teu front tan bell somia i s'agermana
a la lluor d'un món que em deixa exclòs;
massa pur i feliç per a ma fúria vana.

BARTOMEU ROSSELLÓ-PÓRCEL

1913-1938

Sonet

Gelós de les paraules i els afanys
—caprici en cigne de blancs tremolosos
vull lliurar l'agonia dels nous planys
—record pàl·lid de llums i cristalls fosos.

Amb ferides cruels de tots els danys,
obscur, afamegat dels enyorosos
reflexos dels ahirs en els enguanys,
penso en tresors brillants i neguitosos.

I després, al matí de la nit sens conhort,
quan el front torna ple de tristes veritats,
quin deixondir-se de frisances decebudes,

quin inútil cercar de consols i d'ajudes,
plor inepte i terrible entre les soledats,
sabent en la penombra la nostra faç de mort!

Inici de campana

Inici de campana
efímer entre els arbres
—fora porta — de tarda.
La pols dels blats apaga
un or trèmul en punxes

blanquinoses de plana.
L'àmbit vincla i perdura
comiats d'enyorances
d'avui mateix. Desvari
de vies solitàries.
Argila i calç. Finestres
de la casa tancada
quan torno, d'hora baixa,
girant-me adesiara.

Noça

Petits tambors toquen, toquen
damunt la pell de l'ase.
Entre les taules polides
cortesies de la randa.

Deu ciris cremen davant
Nostra Dona de la Grada.

Conjura l'alcova l'aire
feixuc de les abraçades.

El rellotge parla, viva
màquina de mort, fantasma.

—Aixecaràs la cortina,
la duràs a l'altra cambra
i et traurà sang per la boca
a la primera besada.

El nuvi cau desmaiat,
més blanc que la porcellana.

Indecisa, rara, nova...

INDECISA, rara, nova,
ara comença la rosa.

—Dama lleugera, ofrenada
sou al rei.

Entre focs i violins
d'artifici,
les llums, triomfals i fortes.

—Com sabré que la promesa
és aquesta dama tímida?
Contra el matí que la volta
no troba l'aire, no gosa,
la rosa.

Compliment a Mercedes

ELS clavells s'incendien,
per imitar-te, quan
tu passes per davant.

I, per felicitar-te,
les pluges ploren, fan
damunt els vidres, vidre,
damunt el vidre, cant.

El carrer de Montcada,
el dia del teu sant,
t'abraci, vell, galant.

Per brodar-te la gràcia
no trobo diamant.

BARTOMEU ROSSELLÓ-PÓRCEL

Auca

Retorno a les festes llunyanes,
quan la muralla de ponent
plena d'estàtues blanques sobre el mar
incendia la Catedral amb palmeres polsoses,
i pedres dins el xarol, diumenge de la Portella,
la primera vegada, cosins, amb marineres blaves.
Mira com es tanquen els vidres i dins la cambra la tarda,
la tarda es clou, la tarda damunt d'un llit d'agost, pots mirar-ho
des de qualsevol magraner;
sorprèn els recons del jardí i sabràs el secret de les vànoves,
dels *sillons* amb roba de llengos antiga, de les columnes entor-
vés al jardí al costat de la marededeueta, [cillades;
del safareig cansat de bressar les mateixes fulles,
hi ha les finestres que tenen el record del suïcida
i del Boig que el va veure penjat i perdia la boca rient-se'n,
amb els ulls tacats amb ombres com botons,
com els botons grocs de les margarides de la feixina,
a la Riera, més avall del Pont de Sant Pere,
on la Muralla no té canons sobre la Plana.
Jo n'hi he posats i enfonsaré els vaixells del port.
Els peixos es mengen el Jaume I davant la Farola.
El Pare Vidal, endolat, s'ho mira des de la Riba.
El Pare Vidal Taüt crida els cuirassats anglesos.
Jaume I, t'ho dic, torna a sortir vestit de blanc,
i jo et faré portar sobre una tauleta d'eben
a la sala de rebre de can Robert Massanet,
i passaràs per l'entrada amb capitells jònics i pluja,
—una casa de senyors, una casa bona, amb criades;
estaràs dins una botella verda de vi de Benisalem,
Rei Jaume amb un matalàs d'arena!
El rei En Jaume I amb un llençol de pols grisa
entra per la Llotja! Boters, atureu els martells,
canteu la cançó de Carmen Flores al Líric.
Ara passa el Jaume I pel carrer de la Mar.

Quadreu-vos,

carrabiners, saludeu el Capità amb la pistola!
Capità a la Glorieta dispara sobre la multitud
com si fossis el Polvorí que va esclatar amb el tro més gran
[de la terra
(no n'han sentit mai de més fort ni aquí ni fora Mallorca;
totes les vinyes s'aturaren i el vent es cenyia a les soques,
els pits de les noies fremien llur defensa blana,
i el Seminari masturba si Virgili les solituds
torna la lira renglera de canyes xiulets i bellveures,
cossiols de clavells al terrat i l'estampa més grassa).
Darrera la persiana sé el moment del cos al mirall·
i espio el munt de la roba vora la flassada blanca.
Vaixell, trenca els arcs, els quioscs, les lleones.
El passeig està fart de mirades,
i encara no ha après el peu ni la cuixa sota la falda.
Si vas a la Rambla, vaixell, trenca el verd de les Caputxines.
Llança el teu fum sobre la mòmia de sor Tomasa.
—Sor Tomasa, que balla amb el cardenal Despuig vestit de
[diable—.
Sor Tomaseta, el vaixell vol tirar-vos dins un pou;
arri, cavallet, camina, vola per la carretera,
menja la coca de mel dins la maneta de l'àngel.
Portes la santa que sap com repiquen les campanes.
La Nit es posa a vetllar dins els ullets de ma mare.
Ma mare, fadrina, canta al carrer de l'Om i broda.
Tambor, tamboret, tambor, broda, broda per la noça,
la noça demà passat, només amb una galera,
i tots a peu i, després, els tarongerars de Sòller.
Aquí pots nedar, vaixell: el Brollador t'acarona.
És un braç inacabable a la teva quilla negra.

Rellotge, calla, i no diguis que l'infant s'acosta.
Serà espasa i trencarà totes les cadenes;
les grises rengleres d'arbres li ensenyaran arts de bruixes;
el seu cap serà penjat a la Porta Pintada
i el guardaran a la nit perquè no parli.

BARTOMEU ROSSELLÓ-PÓRCEL

A Mallorca, durant la guerra civil

Verdegen encara aquells camps
i duren aquelles arbredes
i damunt del mateix atzur
es retallen les meves muntanyes.
Allí les pedres invoquen sempre
la pluja difícil, la pluja blava
que ve de tu, cadena clara,
serra, plaer, claror meva!
Sóc avar de la llum que em resta dins els ulls
i que em fa tremolar quan et recordo!
Ara els jardins hi són com músiques
i em torben, em fatiguen com en un tedi lent.
El cor de la tardor ja s'hi marceix,
concertat amb fumeres delicades.
I les herbes es cremen a turons
de cacera, entre somnis de setembre
i boires entintades de capvespre.

Tota la meva vida es lliga a tu,
com en la nit les flames a la fosca.

Ronda amb fantasmes

Les filles del silenci present i vigilant
em porten sempre a la perversa llunyania,
saben el meu espant, el meu instant d'espant,
d'isolament, malenconia i agonia.

Oh ciutat dels terrors! Entre les avingudes
estèrils —arbres lívids de la tardor!— viuré
l'hora impura de les aspres angúnies mudes
amb la por de morir tot sol en el carrer.

Terror entre les sales buides quan veig el llit
amb el mort, viu entre els llençols, i serenades
a la plaça, i remor de ganivets, enfora,

més terrible per tantes coses endevinades
durant la fuga, per les fosques, allà on plora
l'esquelet mossegat pels gossos de la nit.

Només un arbre, a la vorera, porta...

Només un arbre, a la vorera, porta
el tremolor del mar, i el frec de fulles
retorna el benefici de les ones.
Les roques mortes en arenes mortes
viuen només uns brins d'herba poruga.
Mar foll de gris i verd i força d'aire:
trenca cristalls sobre la costa blana!
Aprèn l'ombra llunyana, blava i blanca,
dels núvols plens de vent i pròdigs d'ales.
Només en mi pots créixer més i estendre
més pura sal, més amagada pedra,
i encara retrobar-te en camins foscos
per balenes remotes i algues velles.
Però jo m'he perdut en les planúries
que han oblidat la dansa, el crit de l'aigua,
entre alzines i roures, entre llunes
sense rius, sense pous, sense ones altes.

Escolto la secreta...

Escolto la secreta
harmonia de l'aire
i l'ardor que tremola
d'unes grans aigües lliures.

Ales i dansa! Déus
que ara passen i canten
altes músiques! Llum
dels ulls sagrats i verges!

Estic sol en aquestes
ombres i sento caure
ones de sang, enmig
d'una alba trista i aspra.

En la meva mort

Estic cansat de tu, domini fosc
i tempestat de flama.
M'exaltaré damunt els horitzons
i trauré les banderes al desert
de la darrera cavalcada.
Reina d'aquestes hores, ara véns
tota brillant, armada.
Inútil desesper del vespre! L'alba
s'acosta ja amb l'espasa,
i l'ardor temerari que m'encén
allunya les estrelles.

NEW POETS SINCE 1939

MÀRIUS TORRES

1910–1942

A la llacuna...

A la llacuna
la nit sembla més àvida
d'ombres, de gèrmens.
L'aigua bat en silenci;
la meva ànima és aigua.

Arbor Mortis

Al punt que hom naix comença de morir e morint creix, e creixent mor tot dia.

PERE MARCH

DÉU, al primer batec de cada cor que neix,
sembra dues llavors en una sola argila:
la vida remorosa que cada instant s'esfila,
la mort silenciosa que cada instant s'acreix.

En l'estança més closa de la nostra existència,
allà on només habiten l'esperança o l'horror,
viu l'Arbre de la Mort; i creix, interior,
de tot el que es marceix en la nostra vivència.

Quan ve, tumultuós, el gran vent del destí,
el seu brancatge, nu com un esquelet, vibra.
Arbre, en la primavera que tu trauràs de mi,

estreny, amb les arrels, el meu cos fibra a fibra.
Faran les teves fulles una ombra de repòs,
i un aspre perfum d'ànima vindrà a les teves flors.

¿Qui sabrà mai els anys...?

¿QUI sabrà mai els anys del somriure del món?
Alada, sobre un fang amargament pregon,

la primavera, verge nova d'amor, avança.
O temps mesclat d'enyorament i d'esperança

que arribes com una ala fins al fons del meu cor!
Però les nits tan vastes, on regna el vent del nord,

porten un bes d'hivern a cada branca nua
i les arrels es corben a l'ombra blava i crua

dels capvespres, profunds com els ulls d'un infant!
Ara que tot reviu sense records, si l'aire

pogués, com una boira més, endur-se enlaire
totes les primaveres que fan vell el meu cant!

L'abisme de llum

QUAN seguim àgilment, amb un cor que no es cansa,
qualsevol cosa viva dins nostre o en el món
—flama o ocell, temps de turment o d'esperança—
fins als termes suprems on tota boira es fon,

una sagrada esgarrifor, de mort o crisma,
ens pren, de veure allò, com nosaltres vivent,
tornar-se gra de pols que es perd en un abisme
enllà dels nostres ulls i de la nostra ment.

Com un espai, profunditat vertiginosa,
tu ets per ella, cenyint la vida tremolosa,
renaixement de tot morir, nord de tot rumb.

Claredat massa vasta per la nostra mirada!
Alegria de l'ànima que sent, enlluernada,
Déu entorn nostre, com un abisme de llum!

SALVADOR ESPRIU

Al vespre

Com una ofrena dolorosa,
Vespre, a l'hora del teu retorn,
et porto, en una almosta, fosa
tota la cendra del meu jorn.

Cendra de flor, cendra d'espina,
d'haver cregut, d'haver estimat;
per a moldre aquesta farina
cada instant fou un gra de blat.

Freda i feixuga, no la irisa
cap joc de llum o d'esperit.
És una pols amarga i grisa
que s'endurà el vent de la nit.

Vine a impregnar-la del teu hàlit,
Vespre, rei dels perfums serens!
Crema-hi, encara, amb un bes pàl·lid,
un impalpable àtom d'encens

que ungeixi la trèmula conca
i la cendra a punt de volar,
mentre el foc que mai no s'estronca
incinera ja per demà.

SALVADOR ESPRIU

1913

Cementiri de Sinera

II

Quina petita pàtria
encercla el cementiri!
Aquesta mar, Sinera,
turons de pins i vinya,

pols de rials. No estimo
res més, excepte l'ombra
viatgera d'un núvol
i el lent record dels dies
que són passats per sempre.

III

Sense cap nom ni símbol,
ran dels xiprers, dessota
un poc de pols sorrenca
endurida de pluges.
O que l'oratge escampi
la cendra per les barques
i els solcs dibuixadíssims
i la llum de Sinera.
Claror d'abril, de pàtria
que mor amb mi, quan miro
els anys i el pas: viatge
al llarg de quiets crepuscles.

IV

Els meus ulls ja no saben
sinó contemplar dies
i sols perduts. Com sento
rodar velles tartanes
pels rials de Sinera!
Al meu record arriben
olors de mar vetllada
per clars estius. Perdura
en els meus dits la rosa
que vaig collir. I als llavis,
oratge, foc, paraules
esdevingudes cendra.

Presa segura

Pas de caçador.
Sento com s'atansa
per sols de tardor.

Lentament, d'aquesta
font d'aigua glaçada
he begut. Després,
he mirat enlaire.

Volaven falcons
damunt la certesa
de la meva mort.

Sagitari

Ahir passà, vetlla estremida, i torna
avui l'arquer tot nu,
amb l'arc i l'alba.

—Que fredament t'allunyo
per la terra d'enlloc, on pot només seguir-te
la teva solitud sense paraules!
Dolor o fum? El meu agut somriure
traspassa l'altivesa del teu càntic.

Et perds, germà difícil
de la rosa i el foc, per la secreta
llei del camí que uneix l'arrel amb l'ala.
Ja el cor i els ulls no saben
qui fores tu.

Matrimoni

Tanca el ponent a fora,
tot l'estiu, la parada
fatiga de suburbi,
gerani i falzies.

Tens ordenada i neta
i a punt la nostra casa,
veritat? De seguida
començarem a dir-nos,
potser, velles paraules.
Te'n riuràs, però sento
dintre, de sobte, rares
veus de Déu i manubris,
set de gos i missatge
de lents records que es perden
part enllà d'un pont fràgil.
I tu portes la tassa
de malalt i en silenci
t'asseus, mentre ens condemnen
els anys, els morts, l'enorme
balcó roent del vespre.

Arpa de les tenebres

D'UN vell color de plata
jo voldria que fossin
els meus versos: d'un noble,
antic color de plata.

Davant la mort, que porta
secrets senyals del rostre
que jo veig en mirar-me,
cerco amb ells extingides
veus del mar, pas de núvol,
les distants primaveres.

Trist i lliure, camino,
davant la mort que em mira,
a la llum, per la plata
antiga dels meus versos.

Després dels arbres

Quan ja no pugui perdre'm
més en la neu i vegi
llums i cel de sortida
damunt l'esglai dels boscos,
sentiré la fatiga
del caminant pel somni
de la font i la casa,
benigna olor de terres
i pa llescat a taula.
Aleshores, ben lliure
d'espera i de temença,
m'adormiré per sempre,
escoltant cops d'aixades
molt lentes als camps amples,
remor de vespre als pàmpols.

JOAN VINYOLI

1914

El vell parc

El vespre apaga el crit innumerable,
metàl·lic, gris, de la ciutat i deixa
sentir-se en l'ombra l'amorosa queixa
dels purs amants que torben l'immutable,

melangiós interior: perduts
són ara els límits, vagament perdura
un so planyent entre les quietuds:
alba de lluna als roserars fulgura.

Flonjos parterres amb quiet respir
ple de sentors volten els marbres;
passen les barques com un lleu sospir;
tot és immòbil: la foscor dels arbres

anyencs, les aigües, el suau pradell.
Dures poncelles en secret esclaten
com màgics focs i llur perfum dilaten,
i plora o crida, en soledat, l'ocell.

L'aire nocturn expira dins les frondes,
i s'obren i es cobegen les boques i les flors;
al més ocult s'estrenyen ombres fondes,
mots que somnien vessen d'un cos a un altre cos.

Fi de tardor

Sóc la tardor, com un núvol em fonc,
enrera veig, encara plens de fulles,
arbres, avui sols rígides despulles,
i un plor reté, ja corglaçat, el tronc,
garfint l'espai amb branques desvalgudes.
Ja el dia es pon amb llangorós calfred,
el pàl·lid cel té llunyanies mudes,
la serra mostra una blavor de fred.

D'una terra

III

Remor llunyana dels camins que llisquen
vers la ciutat incendiada al vespre,
flaire boscana al pas dels carboners
que retornen del fons de les muntanyes:
encara us sento i em tremola el cor,
i veig la llum sedosa de les tardes,
omplint la vall, a l'hora en què la vida
canta en el pit i s'expandeix per l'àmbit
crepuscular i dolçament declina
el dia alegre alegrement viscut.

Oh vida!, les abelles que brunzien
al bosc ombriu, el serpenteig quiet

del rierol, transfigurat pel simple
record d'un peu de nimfa o la petjada
del bou calmós, quedaven ja per sempre,
llum en el cor, clarificant-lo.
Pures,
rosses abelles matinals, alegres
missatgeres de vida i romanins fragants,
voleu, creixeu encara en el meu cor, un dia
tan vinculat al vostre viure pur.

Oh estrènyer les mans, on batega...

Oh estrènyer les mans, on batega,
amb la més noble sang, la més pura,
la més trista, la més agitada,
la més encesa i ardent, —oferint-se,
la plenitud d'un cor!

Ai, aquest doll, aquest vessar d'amor
que es perd en l'aire i en les coses!
Tant que voldria el cercle
tancar: de tu a mi, de jo a tu cloent-se
la vida i res ja no es perdria
d'aquest immens, insadollable anhel!

XAVIER CASP

1915

Jo sense tu

Jo sense tu. Quin trist silenci
fan els sentits
afeixugant-me cada passa
sobre l'ahir!

XAVIER CASP

Que bé que et mire
cap el record!
Estàs exacta,
tu, nit en lluna, dia en sol.
Però ara et mire
amb un cansanci sense nord...

Jo sense tu, a l'ombra inútil
d'un pensament,
llance la xàrcia
del meu després
sobre les hores
revirescents.

I és una pesca peresosa,
sense retorn...
Sota l'estil de cada vela
hi ha un trastorn
esbiaixant per cada borda
la solitud del pescador.
Pesca d'afectes que agonitzen
trets de la mar del teu amor!

Jo sense tu. Quin gros solatge
manté la sang
a to dels polsos
del meu passat?
Encara alena la teua carn
—com una flama
massa lleial—

per la tempesta d'aturar-me
al vol dels ulls
des d'aquest jo felic per fàcil,
jo sense tu!

JOSEP PALAU

1917

Autoretrat

No m'exhaureixis, rostre, forma, llum,
ull poderós, vivent miratge d'home.
Deixa els meus ulls vagar — a contrallum
de tu: Sahara sense ombres.

Lluito amb ton ull i sempre ets vencedor.
El teu esguard m'anul·la, m'anhila.
Cloc les parpelles per trobar claror
lluny de l'excés que el teu ull irradia.

Mos ulls són orbs de tu, astre diürn.
Potser voldries que no t'esguardéssim,
i prens un aire esquerp: gran taciturn,
feixuc guerrer del regne del silenci.

En la mort de Rabindranath Tagore

Et sabia d'infant, i ara ja t'oblidava:
—la teva barba blanca, la teva ànima blava,

els teus anys vora el foc d'innumerables llars,
avi de tants d'infants, enllà de tots els mars...

Jo tenia, com tu, blanca la cabellera,
i ma barba invisible voleiava lleugera

al grat del vent més fi. Com la del gran Ramon,
ma barba embarbesclada d'haver petjat pel món,

era plena de somnis, de peixos i marines,
de contes i de fades i de faules divines

—la barba que em venia de tants i tants passats
que ara en mi, mig vius, mig ofegats...—

l'espolsava i filava i en tenia gran cura:
qui té la barba blanca té l'ànima segura.

Només pel que sé d'ella jo puc saber de tu,
puix que em plora la barba; mes no ho veurà ningú.

I la sento que em pesa, més llarga que altres dies...
I és el pes de la teva. I és saber que et mories.

Sonet escrit de cara a la mort

En els cercles concèntrics del teu iris,
com en l'aigua agitada per un roc,
jo veig la meva imatge entre deliris,
segur només d'haver arribat a enlloc.

La diminuta arena dels martiris
i les pedres brillants de gel i foc
encenen les ciutats de cementiris
que habiten les fondàries d'aquest lloc.

El dia que es farà l'aigua quieta
i el teu ull serà net com un espill
contemplaré la meva faç perfeta.

I després del moment del gran perill,
amb la boca negada, i capgirat,
vindré a raure al teu fons d'eternitat.

Sol

A voltes, en llevar-se, l'home sol
sent fred al cor, una dent que el mossega
a causa de no haver sota el llençol,
durant la nit, un cos per a la brega.

I es mou feixuc, amb la recança oberta
d'abandonar un lligam que desconeix,
i mira el llit de nou i empal·lideix
veient la companyia tan deserta.

Viu amb el pensament alatrencat,
com si tot l'univers mudés de ruta
i no trobés una esfera segura.

I va tot sol i sent nosa al costat:
algú que en el flanc dret se li detura
fent-li present la seva vida eixuta.

L'Aventura

Sensation

PAR *les soirs bleus d'été, j'irai dans les sentiers,*
Picoté par les blés, fouler l'herbe menue:
Rêveur, j'en sentirai la fraîcheur à mes pieds.
Ja laisserai le vent baigner ma tête nue.

Je ne parlerai pas, je ne penserai rien:
Mais l'amour infini me montera dans l'âme,
Et j'irai loin, bien loin, comme un bohémien,
Par la Nature, —heureux comme avec une femme.

JEAN-ARTHUR RIMBAUD

Sensació

I

PELS vespres blaus d'estiu aniré pels conreus,
picotejat pels blats, sollant l'herba menuda.
Somniós, sentiré la frescor sota els peus,
deixaré el lliure vent banyar ma testa nua.

No pensaré en res, no parlaré per res.
Mes l'amor infinit m'inundarà l'entranya.
I aniré lluny, ben lluny, de mi mateix desprès,
feliç, per la Natura —com amb una companya.

II

Pels vespres blaus i verds aniré pels conreus,
esgarrinxat pels blats i petjant l'herba fresca.
Sentiré palpitar la terra sota els peus
com si una dona nua s'oferís a ma destra.

Sens parlar, ni pensar, ni enyorar-me de res,
l'ample vent m'ompliria els narius i l'entranya.
I aniré lluny, molt lluny: allí on és defès
—tot sol, amb mi mateix— com amb una companya.

III

Pels vespres blaus de verd aniré al groc de l'aire
amb les cames ferides per espases de blat.
Sentiré sota els peus aquell ventre apagat
que les bèsties oloren amb un desig minaire.

I emmudit —el cap nu— irremeiablement,
em donaré amb furor al gran desig de l'aire,
i em deixaré bressar com una lleu sement
que fecunda una flor —altiva o solitària.

IV

En els blaus i en els verds, a l'estiu, prop de l'aire,
fecundat per llavors que prodigava el vent,
aniré, sense nord, com una rel dansaire,
per la muntanya amunt, cercant el meu ponent.

Vegetal —o animal— i sens bri de raó,
confós amb la natura ardent i solitària,
seré el pol·len que duu el vent de la tardor,
quan la tempesta brunz i s'alça l'alimària.

V

Sense blaus, sense verds, perdut en mi mateix,
conqueriré l'altura que el sol llaura.
Sense fred, sense vent, madura d'un sol bleix,
l'antiga terra encara trepitja Minotaure.

Si la font ni la flor no troben la paraula,
la pedra la dirà com el meu front.
En el desig del vent restà la vella faula.
El front, la pedra, occeixen. —Resta el desig pregon.

JOSEP ROMEU

1917

Sonet

Avui, creada en mi només per la mirada
quan, les mans presoneres i el cos, el tacte és va
i la ment s'adelita en la forma i et fa,
pels ulls, tan sols imatge viva en la meva estada,

puc refer-te senyora de silencis i roses
—oh l'alta majestat del teu cos i del flanc,
tan dòcils al meu goig com a l'empremta el fang,
coneguda tan pura i tan nua de noses!—

i entre rosa i silenci, i entre el foc de la ment,
t'amaré rediviva encara que miratge
únicament em sigui la sang que el meu turment

aboqui en ta figura per fer-la, més que imatge
i fal·lera del somni i ombra del pensament,
Eva carnal i forta, guia d'incert viatge.

Sonet

És com si t'invoqués, Àngel, claror,
i fos La Sense Nom qui pel gran aire
d'una imatge vingués, de mi no gaire
llunyana ni del somni o del dolor.

Com si et demanés llum clara i estesa,
els ulls girats a tu en súplica greu,

oh font que no s'acaba com un déu
prodigant-se en callada amor encesa!

Blanquíssim d'ala i ploma: no ets pas tu
qui jo cercava un jorn per vies llargues,
ni el teu perfecte cos d'un gest segur,

sinó aquest infinit que ara m'allargues
només amb el teu càlid bes tan nu
sense greuges ni súpliques amargues.

El Mal Caçador

(Fragment)

HUMIDA i roja terra caigués, dura,
damunt la meva carn, i verms i arrels
fessin del cos inert casa i pastura,
nodriment de saó i sabes fidels.
Visquessin dels meus ulls aspres ortigues
en els llavis immòbils verds rosers
vida xuclessin, àvides formigues
fessin mos ossos blancs, rels de xiprers
es lliguessin als membres i a les venes
que em portaren amb ímpetu ahir,
com xarxes inclements, ferotges, plenes
i exaltades de sang, plenes de mi.
¡Ah, la fam d'un sepulcre i d'una terra
cobrint-me pietosa en llarga nit,
de nou sembrada, oferta la desferra
del cos al fang que em treia de l'oblit!...

JOAN BARAT

1918

Any Nou

MITJA nit, cendra
i epíleg d'un tros de mi

i del temps: reprendre
una sang i un camí
etern, sense comprendre.

Per invocar Sant Jordi

ORFE País, desavesat de mites,
amb tos fills exhaurint-se
en un pàl·lid dolor. Massa medites
sàviament en un vague futur... ¡Oh, endinsa
en els ulls del crepuscle la llança roent
perquè es desvetlli la carn eixarreïda
i els que ara pugen només tinguin esment
que fou un somni aquest bocí de vida
que, a poc a poc, supura en nostre cor,
talment el temps fos una ardent ferida!

JOAN PERUCHO

1920

Els amants

ESTIMAVEN una lloança,
diminuta i cruel,
sota cada mirada.
Estimaven les lentes tardes arrecerades,
amb temorosos llavis,
quan la innocència és com una flor
corrompuda
que torna delicada la ignomínia.
Estimaven les besades furtives,
l'abocar-se a un cel desesperat
perquè el desig
exasperadament clama en els cossos,
invencible i segur.
Estimaven, estimaven.

Creien en llurs aurores martiritzades
o en un agònic impuls
que els isolava de la llum dels homes,
dels esforçats somriures
davant de rostres púdicament perversos.
Renovaven un amor o un mite
perquè ignoraven
que una vida cobeja sempre una altra
vida
com una mort cobeja sempre una altra
mort.
I encara endevinaven una glòria.
Però dura i cruel
la vergonya del món els perseguia.
No estimaven llurs cossos;
estimaven una obscura i mesquina victòria
sobre veus abatudes,
sobre records que viuen
en segles de misèria i d'infortuni.

Llavors mentien un amor,
un oblit impossible, en la nit silenciosa.

Els anys són com fulles

VEU, tenebra,
sorral amplíssim on es neguen les llàgrimes,
lletra d'amor probable,
aquella infantil pruïja que ordenava els
destins
així com la divina joventut atresorada,
¿què foren sinó graciosa creença,
una inútil mentida
per tal de congriar el dolor que empresona?
El vent, a voltes, tusta una porta
o delicadament desvetlla una consciència,
però els anys són com fulles
que el mateix vent s'emporta

per camins caducs o sinistres.
No intenteu, doncs, la vida;
intentareu tan sols un vell record.

La morta

Lívidament s'escola el teu astut desig.
Areny de ma ventura, no retrobares rostre
per on sotjar la veu que ara s'allunya.
Només el foc, la ira.

No cercaré ta pau en els versos antics,
car tu no habitaràs les cambres solellades
i la feblesa meva és a mi que em pertany.
Però digues, rosa o verm o pedra sebollida,
per a qui la memòria és una ombra en el vent
i la mà més petita absoldrà les mirades;
digues, digues, si pots, la torxa o el terror
d'aquesta veu impura que degota en ma nit
com un plor o una lira.

Ara jo resto sol a la terra dels homes,
un batec mineral rígidament s'esmuny
entorn d'aquest silenci, enllà d'aquest silenci.
El silenci és un mur que endola el teu lament.

Amarga memòria

La gràcia amenaçant,
el mur clos, sense estels, enderrocant-se,
la rialla, la ira, la grandesa
ignorarem per les coses més pures:
per la senzilla branca,
per un infant que plori
sota un cel ventejat d'averanys.
Furtivament la mort ens sotja.
La galta contra galta,
el llavi contra sang,

la destrucció més íntima com el foc que
retorna
tot s'abandona a la terra,
a l'entranya fecunda,
a la terra que occeix amb un somriure
quan hom dreça la vida com un temple
amb esguards amorosos
perquè sent una joia immarcessible.

Delicada, extenuada primavera,
defugiré l'enganyadora veu que em crida,
amb amarga memòria,
per intentar la llibertat que ignoro,
la sola llibertat que ara desitjo.

Aurora per vosaltres

Una boca o una flor,
la mínima delícia que les hores atura,
la vesprada sordament remorosa
per on un cor abasta la vida cada dia,
cada dia us invita
amb gracioses sofrences
a la més dura pulcritud lloada,
a una mort que és la vostra,
a un cel on els somriures són benignes.

Els homes, però, ombrívols,
en cofurnes eixorques i en tempestes d'ira,
quan la llum decandeix a llurs mans de misèria
blasmen astorades paraules,
símbols de reverència
o divina grandesa
amb odi caut i angoixa posseïda
mentre vetllen llurs somnis
com si encara l'amor fes rutilar algun rostre.

Quina victòria us cerca
sorrudes llàgrimes, afamades rancúnies?

JOAN TRIADÚ

Si quan la vida s'obre,
dolç infant, blanca veu,
ja designis obscurs arrabassen les mares
abocades a uns ulls
que conegueren la pròpia defallença,
per ventura podríeu
ignorar la mentida més cruel i envilida?

Un jou, però, us espanta.
No us espanta la terra
como no us espanta el núvol,
ni tan sols el deliciós terror de la sang que vigila;
però terra i sang dicten
la llibertat perduda,
aquesta llibertat que defensàreu
com un ultratge a la casa dels amos.

I si els fronts desemparen
la memòria del déu,
del país que intentàreu com una rosa antiga
deshabiteu llur infamant paraula,
llur púrria maleïda,
perquè una aurora vindrà pròxima i forta:
l'aurora per vosaltres,
la que espera,
la que sempre heu cregut que haurà de néixer.

JOAN TRIADÚ (1)

1921

Endimió

Trist deixaré l'esforç a una altra espatlla,
perquè em trobin els ulls d'eternitat
i una herba nova senti el pes de l'aire,
on em reposen cada dia els peus.

[1] The following three poems have been inserted at the request of the Editor.

L'espai poblarà d'ombres el seguici
dels morts mal abraçats, fosos amb mi
com un record. Les pedres en obrir-se,
em somriuran fins al centre del cor,
i no desitjo pluges, ni l'antiga
creació del món, sinó el jardí
vora la llosa clara, terra humida,
perenne de respir i estranya al dol
dels germans, on es recull el silenci
de tots els crits, el manament dels mots,
l'extrem espill de l'aigua navegada,
on vénen mars a plorar els seus ocells
i gelosa la vida ens desempara.

*

La forma sospitada m'escomet
ara, al bell mig de les altes sorpreses,
i sóc la mà del vent damunt el mar
quan s'apaga l'onada i el somriure
abans de pondre's l'innocent destí
tan lluny de llunyanies. Sols l'empremta
trobarà Déu en el seu son precís
i la sabrà fidel, que fou segura,
tota silenci de suavitats.
Mentre obeeixo, vénen els miratges,
l'horror rebel que és sentir-me tot sol
i no saber crear la companyia,
sinó doldre'm, obscur, cara als sentits
del cor, sempre amb l'engany hostil que lluita
al centre de la vida avarament,
on reposa sembrada l'esperança.

Aquest estiu

El vent es penedeix de no tornar.
El blat que fuig, el riu, l'antiga cria
de l'oreneta, no ens esperen demà.
Vivim sobre el pendís de cada dia...

CÈSAR NOGUÉS

1922

Pels camins que trenquen França

CENTAURE fi damunt la prada verda de França.
Cavall blanc, cavall blanc!

La Loire s'ha adormit amb la cançó de la
boira inconsútil.

Debussy, cos avall, sàtir divertit, dibuixa
una claror més palpable.

I tot s'endevina i fuig, tot es posseeix i
s'esmuny.

Hi ha un no sé què de cosa tremolosa
que fa semblar la terra cel i el cel desesperança.

I la nit perseguint la nit encara és verda
de l'herba de la tarda.

I els ulls estan desperts de verd. Els ulls
per als quals ja tot s'ha donat.

Cavall blanc, cavall blanc!

Oh, centaure de plata damunt el jaç verinós
del camp verd, no estiguis més fressós,
que amb la Loire tots els rius de França s'han adormit.

S'han ensomniat entre el gris i el verd,
la broma i el cel, la desesperança i la terra.

Gris

M'HE embegut de l'hora tèrbola.
I he xuclat, ben mut, el vent ombrívol.
Les ales se m'han quedat plegades en la pluja
aturada de la gàbia.
El pensament encantat, l'ànima ajaçada.
Porteu-me un catre d'escuma blanca!
Vull anar-me'n en una tarda de fulles caminades!
Ací hi ha la meva mà. Ben cega de mal.
I davant meu un altre, tan exacte a mi!
Tot resseguit de Mort!

La pluja de la nit...

LA pluja de la nit ha nevat l'acàcia
de verda carícia humida.
I el vent perfilat de març l'ha orfenat
dels seus fràgils, orientals estels.
Oh, besa'm en els ulls, estranya,
pura, inoblidable amant!
Que en els teus cabells es moren,
entrenuades, les meves mans.

JORDI SARSANEDAS

1924

Goigs fragmentaris de Barcelona nostra

BLANC i daurat en pedra marinera,
nacrat al nimbe en ales de coloms,
se'ns ha clos el goig vell de Barcelona.

Vènia per parlar;
els oficis de Barcelona, poden començar?

JORDI SARSANEDAS

De les grues solars amb caramells d'albada,
pel xiscle d'esmolet als vidres dels carrers,
el fosc treball estès com una boira,
com un ample salut que s'anés responent.

Si jo fos manyà,
lladrucs de la llima,
guspires de foc,
a la mà tindria.

Si paleta fos,
dalt de la bastida,
maons i maons
al cel posaria.

Si fos mariner,
me'n vaig a la Xina!
Tot arreu del món
amics hi tindria.

El blanc de la bugada es cansa en les façanes.
Abans de la vorera de poruc ja s'ha post.
Ara direm els pobles en el blau de la feina,
de ribera al serrat,
els pobles blaus,
la primera o darrera Barcelona.

Juny, en el caire encès de la collita,
juga l'amor a promesa i record.
El seu cos olorós de mare jove,
ciutat com dona, nostra, nostra.

Com ha passat la sang!

Posaré el meu amor, que és tan llarg com les venes,
a la boca cendrosa d'aquell infant esquerp
entre la pau humil de les darreres cabres.
Vull besar aquella fam que li afina la passa
i posar un somni lleu en el crani rapat
i el reflex darrer de la nostra mimosa.

Adéu, la palmera
—al meu cor la palmera—,
adéu, palmera d'Horta, la gràcia marcida,
plomell dels Tres Tombs!

Jo t'estimo, ciutat, en ta cendra de boscos,
en el teu herbei ras.
Santa, santa, santa.
El pit et llagrimeja, i canten les campanes.

Trista

Ai, amor, et coneixia blanca
i no sabia la vida lleu,
la vida, la teva pell,
sobre una greu mar calenta
i negra amb la pols d'estels
baixant lleugera.

Abans,
la nit tèbia, suau, on grans vents silenciosos
emporten lentament boirina lluminosa,
en la gràcia insegura de ta cintura en gest
la coneixia;
aquesta nit al teu si,
promesa de pau i vida.
—La nit, entre tu i jo,
un frèvol ventall de randes—.

Has fugit pels teus camins
—silenci al camí de l'aigua—
i darrera l'alta nit
ha caigut la teva absència.

JORDI SARSANEDAS

Per a Maria Rosa

He perdut el desert com les roses amigues,
he perdut el matí frisós de veles,
de cases i fullam.

Quan la sang de basalt ens ompli el cor, germana,
tu i jo tornarem a la casa dels pares,
al plàtan ple de sol, al balcó ple de pàmpols.

He vist al bosc una garsa clavada
en creu, al tronc d'un pi,
i porto poms rodons de grans jonquilles dobles.

Paisatge malalt

El cor petja la fusta,
el cor tot qualsevol perdut entre la pluja,
xipollejant pels sons dels taulons a la platja.

Llarg és el riu
que murmura els ocells a la gira de l'aigua.

Les gavines, els corbs pugen de xiscle a plor
pel calfred de llur cel de mímica febrosa.

Passa de blau a blanc l'atonia de l'aire
el riu retut.

No pot, per recordar,
una mà de cristalls vibrant d'íntima llum
esvair el fum amarg d'un foc secret de ferro.

I si vingués la nit?
Ja ve la nit, ja passa.

Però les mateixes boires pesen damunt del riu.

JORDI COTS

1927

Viure amb fe cada hora santa...

VIURE amb fe cada hora santa,
com si l'endemà partíssim
cap a un país estranger,
sense comiats l'hora nostra.

I arrencar del cel la pluja,
i el temps dels teus ulls, amiga,
ocell, flor de neu, per mirar-te.

Oh el ritme greu de la mort,
la mort en els meus cabells,
segura com una rosa!

Res no serà que avui no sigui

RES no serà que avui no sigui.
I sempre aquest plor que somou
l'amant, sense una oració,
el dolor i la joia en un crit!
Avui les banderes plegades
al meu braç, en una ferida,
i en rostres estranys un silenci
com d'orats o de noia santa.
Però han de trobar-me despert
les cançons i els amics feliços,
les mans esquinçades de flors.
Cap veu, llavors, dins el meu cor,
no confondrà el seu cant,
ni serà estrany un record amable.

JORDI COTS

Ploraré sobre els teus cabells

PLORARÉ sobre els teus cabells.
No m'és donat de mirar sense un plor,
i he de torbar la teva pau
que, com una llei, em sorprèn,
perquè temo el teu dolor
i no trobo flors per donar-te.

Ploraré sobre els teus cabells,
amiga: no sé posar-te un nom.
No posseiré la paraula!
Potser serà un dia en la tempesta,
i en un rar moment sentiràs
el meu cant. Llavors partiré
com de tu, sense juraments.

Ara vindrà la mort...

ARA vindrà la mort com un ponent,
i els noms que hem donat a les coses
es faran estranys, inconeguts,
com després d'una lluita suprema.

Sols restaran fidels els amants
que avui no s'han trobat encara.
I és en va que diem el dolor:
ningú no sap la nostra joia.

Silenci

QUI sap per quina gran joia el meu plor?
Que és el silenci com si un estranger
ens ensenyés les cançons, quan tu calles.

I és com si avui en aquest dolç país
d'on ve el silenci, la música, els somnis,
algú es jugués la seva eternitat

per tu i per mi, que hem après a mirar-nos.
Oh aquest corrent de les aigües, silenci!

Quan jo et parlo...

Quan jo et parlo, una vall a dins se m'obre
per endur-se'ns vessant-se com una aigua,
que, en mirar-te, no ve de mi aquest càntic.

Es fa meva la llum que neix de tu
i dels dies que són com rius per sempre:
així em viuen als braços els espais
que travesso amb el pit, mes per romandre
en l'altura on la mort no és cap misteri.

ALBERT MANENT

1930

Lúcid esguard de la tardor...

Lúcid esguard de la tardor que em mira
i m'aclareix camins envers l'altura.
Albiro amb goig, com un infant en una fira,
el foc madur, la lluor pura.

He perdonat el vent, el capvespre esvaït;
tots dos em seguiran, fidels llebrers, quan hagi
de traspassar l'enllà d'aquestes cimes,
un matí, quan el rou bastirà cel·les primes.
Ara m'alço en la llum. Després, talment en un naufragi,
seré llançat cap a l'imperi de la nit.

Altra aurora de la mort

ÀLIGA de la llum, llançada contra mi
un dia qualsevol, ara que em trobo alçat
en l'abisme i és Déu qui mesura el meu dir,
amb lenta veu intacta, nodrint-me en el combat,
vetllaré fins que em vegi reflectit en l'espill
del teu gest emboirat i el teu parlar senzill.

En el llindar de l'àngel

EN la boira sóc hoste
de l'ònix i del quars.
La lluna ja s'acosta
duent l'albor de l'arç.
Un horitzó de cignes,
assossegats i dignes,
als ulls em brillaria?
Sóc sol. Ell, pur i fort,
entre el nard i la mort,
vaixell de llum, espia.

BIOGRAPHICAL AND BIBLIOGRAPHICAL INDEX

Agelet i Garriga, Jaume

Born in Lleida in 1888. Has spent most of his life abroad, as a diplomat, and although a frequent visitor to Catalonia he now lives in Paris. Poetic works: *Domassos al sol* (1924), *La tarda oberta* (1927), *Hostal de núvols* (1931), *Els fanals del meu sant* (1935), and *Rosada i celístia* (Lleida, 1949). Cf. p. 252.

Alcover, Joan

Born in Palma de Mallorca in 1854, died there in 1926. Read law in Barcelona, and achieved a considerable reputation as a public speaker. His earlier works were written in Castilian, and it was only from 1902 onwards that he concentrated solely upon Catalan poetry. Lived in Mallorca, where the literary circle over which he presided became famous. The tragic death of his son was extremely significant in his poetic development. Poetic works: *Cap al tard* (1909), *Poemes bíblics* (1918), and *Poesies* in the year of his death. Complete works published in three volumes by Il·lustració Catalana (Barcelona, 1928), and his poetic works have appeared in a single volume of the «Biblioteca Selecta», with a prologue by Miquel Ferrà. Cf. pp. LXV-LXVII, 167-79.

Arderiu, Clementina

Born in Barcelona in 1893. Wife of Carles Riba (q. v.); her first book of poetry, *Cançons i elegies*, was published in 1916, the year of her marriage. It was followed by *L'alta llibertat* (1921), *Poemes*, *Cant i paraules* (awarded the Folguera Prize in 1938), and most recently by *Sempre i ara*, published in a limited edition in Barcelona in 1948. Cf. pp. LXXVII, 268-71.

Aribau, Bonaventura Carles

Born in Barcelona in 1798, died there in 1862. Wrote few poems in Catalan other than *La pàtria*, whose appearance is deemed to mark the beginning of the Renaixença. Lived in Madrid; his separation from Catalonia was responsible for the writing of *La pàtria*, which was published in the Barcelona periodical «El Vapor» on the 24th of August 1833. It was dedicated to the banker in whose firm he worked. The text we publish is the one definitively established by Carles Riba. Cf. pp. XX, LVI-LVIII, 112-4.

Bartra, Agustí

Born in 1910. Has published short stories, poems, a novel, and critical articles in various periodicals. His first volume of poetry, *Cant corporal*, was published in Barcelona (1938). Has published in exile *L'arbre de foc* (Mexico, 1946), *Màrsias* (Mexico, 1946), and other poems like *Oda Atlàntica* (1951), *Pau Casals* (1950), which was translated into English by Lloyd Frankenberg. Won the «Flor Natural» in the Jocs Florals held in New York, 1951. Cf. pp. 323-4.

Barat, Joan

Born in Barcelona in 1918. His earliest published poems appeared in «Poesia», edited by Josep Palau Fabre (q. v.), in 1944 and 1945; his volume *Poemes* was published in 1947. Cf. pp. 354-5.

Cançoner Anònim

The *Cançoner Anònim* or *Romancer* is the generic term applied to the corpus of popular ballad literature. This was first brought to light and evaluated by Manuel Milà i Fontanals, who collected and published over six hundred ballads and songs in 1853 (revised edition, 1882). F. Pelai i Briz continued his work with the five volumes of *Cançons de la terra* (1866-1877), which was followed by Marian Aguiló's *Cançoner popular*. The task was then taken over by the «Obra del Cançoner Popular de Catalunya», organized by the Institut Patxot, but publication was interrupted by the Spanish Civil War and has not yet been resumed. Francesc de B. Moll has also published *Cançons populars mallorquines*: I (Palma de Mallorca, 1934). The representative selection published in this anthology is based on the texts of Milà i Fontanals and Aguiló, revised by Josep Romeu i Figueres (q. v.), who has established the definitive texts and their chronology. Josep Romeu is preparing a definitive edition of the *Cançoner* for the Editorial Barcino of Barcelona. Cf. pp. xx, LIV-V, 97-112.

Carner, Josep

Born in Barcelona in 1884. Has lived most of his life abroad as a member of the consular service. His writings in both prose and verse are extensive, and he is as influential as a journalist as he is as a poet. Most important poetic publications: *Els fruits saborosos* (1906), *Bella terra, bella gent* (1918), *La inútil ofrena* (1924), *El cor quiet* (1925), and *Nabí* (1946). Publication of complete works interrupted by the outbreak of the Spanish Civil War in 1936, and he was obliged to go into exile when it ended in 1939. Has continued writing in exile. Cf. pp. LXXIII, 238-46.

Casp, Xavier

Born in Carlet (Valencia) in 1915. A leading influence on the younger generation of Valencian poets, to which he belongs, ever since his first book of poetry appeared in 1943; founded and edits «Esclat» and a series of books by new poets called «L'Espiga». Lives in Valencia. Poetic works: *Volar* (1943), *La inquietud en calma* (1945), *Jo sense tu* (1948) which is his most significant book to date, *On vaig, Senyor?* (1949), *Aires de cançó* (1950), *Proses en carn* (1952). Cf. pp. LXI, 347-8.

Costa i Llobera, Miquel

Born in Pollensa (Mallorca) in 1854, died whilst delivering a sermon in Palma de Mallorca in 1922. A canon of Palma cathedral. His most important publications were *Poesies ca-*

talanes (1895) and *Horacianes* (1906). Complete works first published by Il·lustració Catalana (Barcelona, 1923); recently re-edited by Editorial Selecta in «Biblioteca Perenne» (Barcelona, 1947). Cf. pp. LXV-LXVI, 147-67.

Cots, Jordi

Born in Barcelona in 1927, where he read law. Was one of the young university poets first brought to the notice of the public by the *Antologia poètica universitària 1949*. His volume *Fidelitat* appeared in the same year. Cf. pp. 366-8.

Esclasans, Agustí

Born in Barcelona in 1895. Studied in France and Barcelona. Besides his poetry, has published novels and plays, and a number of books of short stories, literary criticism, and translations. His *Sistema de ritmologia* formulates the theories underlying his most important poetic contribution: the thousand *Ritmes* (published in several separate volumes). Has also published volumes of sonnets, elegies, and odes. His fervent patriotism is often mirrored in his poetry. Was temporarily imprisoned after the end of the Spanish Civil War; now lives in Barcelona, where he is engaged in preparing his complete poetic works for the press. Cf. pp. LXXIV, 303-7.

Espriu, Salvador

Born in Santa Coloma de Farners, in 1913. Read history and law in Barcelona, where he is a practising lawyer. Poetic works: *Cementiri de Sinera* (1946), *Les cançons d'Ariadna* (1949), and *Les hores* and *Mrs. Death* (both unpublished). Cf. pp. LXXVIII, 341-5.

Ferrà, Miquel

Born in Palma de Mallorca in 1885, died there in 1948. Once Librarian at the University of Barcelona. In 1917 he published *Cançó d'ahir*. His most important volume of poems is *A mig camí* (1926). Published studies on Alcover and Costa i Llobera; influential upon the younger Majorcan poets of the past twenty years. Cf. pp. LXVII, LXXII, 247.

Foix, J. V.

Born in Sarrià, now a suburb of Barcelona, in 1894. In contact with painters and sculptors in the years preceding and following the first world war; has constantly exerted a guiding influence on his fellow poets, contributing towards the discovery of fresh poetic values. Has never indulged in critical writing. Works: *Gertrudis* (1927), *KRTU* (1932), *Sol, i de dol* (1948), *Les irreals omegues* (1949), and *No mor qui mor* (unpublished). Cf. pp. LXXIV-LXXVI, 283-92.

Folguera, Joaquim

Born in Sabadell, an industrial town near Barcelona, in 1894, and died in Barcelona during the influenza epidemic of 1919. Published *Poemes de neguit* (1915), *El poema espars* (1917), and a volume of criticism called *Les noves valors de la poesia catalana* (1919). Complete works published by La Revista in four volumes (Barcelona, 1919-21). The most important award for poetry in Catalonia, the Premi Folguera, was named after him when it was established in 1931. Cf. pp. LXXIV, 271-2.

Garcés, Tomàs

Born in Barcelona in 1901. Read philosophy and law, and is a practising lawyer. Founded the literary magazines «Mar vella» and «Quaderns de poesia». Has published several volumes of critical and other articles. His first book of poetry, *Vint cançons* (1922), has been frequently reprinted, and set to music by the leading Catalan composers. Published *A l'ombra del lledoner* (1924), *El somni* (1927), *Paradís* (1931), *El senyal* (1935), and *El caçador* (1947), which marked the end of a long period of silence following the Spanish Civil War, and he has since republished most of his earlier works. Cf. pp. LXXVII, 316-8.

Gassol, Ventura

Born in La Selva del Camp in 1894. A Catalan politician, has been in exile more than once. Has published two plays and many articles. Poetic works: *Amfora* (1917), *La nau* (1920), *Les tombes flamejants* (1923) which is his best work yet, *Tardoral* and *Mirra*; has also published a volume of French poetry called *Fleurs*, in the «Cahiers du Rhône». Cf. pp. LXXII, 272.

Leveroni, Rosa

Born in Barcelona in 1910. Studied librarianship from 1930 to 1933, and was appointed to the Library of the University of Barcelona in 1934; held this post until the University ceased to be autonomous, at the end of the Spanish Civil War. Published *Epigrames i cançons* (1938), now incorporated into a new volume of poems *Presència i record* (1952). Cf. pp. 325-7.

"Liost, Guerau de"

Pseudonym of Jaume Bofill i Mates: born in Olot, at the foot of the Pyrenees, in 1878; died in Barcelona in 1933. Divided his time between family estates, in the mountainous region of Montseny, and Barcelona, where he was very active in politics and achieved a considerable reputation as a public speaker. His life on Montseny lies behind the poetic vision of the Catalan countryside presented in *La muntanya d'ametistes* (1908, revised edition 1933), whilst residence in the capital provoked *La ciutat d'ivori* (1918). Remaining poetic works: *Somnis* (1913), *Ofrena rural* (1926), *Sàtires* (1928), and a number of previously unpublished poems also incorporated in the edition of his *Obra poètica* by Editorial Selecta (Barcelona, 1948). This also contains a critical introduction by Jaume Bofill i Ferro. Cf. pp. LXXIII, 218-36.

Llacuna, Joan

Born in Igualada, in the district of Anoia, in 1905. Published works: *Onix i níquel* (1934), and *Aurora de l'Aragall* (1948). His brief production reflects the very essence of his experience. He lives in Rubí, near Barcelona, where he works as an insurance agent. Cf. pp. LXXVIII, 319-23.

Lleonart, Josep

Born in Barcelona in 1880. Studied in Germany. Nephew of Maragall (q. v.), whose example inspired him to begin writing poetry at eighteen. Published *Elegies germàniques* in 1910 and subsequently translated Goethe's *Faust*; most significant subsequent productions: *La merla i altres cants* (1914), *Tres poemes* (1920), *Les elegies i els jardins* (1937), and *La ciutat somniada* (unpublished). Has also published plays, novels, essays, biographies, and numerous translations. Cf. pp. LXXII, 236-8.

Llorente, Teodor

Born in Valencia in 1836, died there in 1911. Wrote in Castilian as well as Catalan, and published translations as well as original poetry. His *Llibret de versos* (1885) belongs wholly to the Renaixença. He founded the Jocs Florals of Valencia, in conjunction with other prominent writers who combined to form the society of «Lo Rat Penat», which was to prove so important for future literary developments in Valencia. Republished his *Llibret de versos* in 1909. Cf. pp. LX-LXI, 116-7.

Llull, Ramon

Born in Palma de Mallorca, most probably in 1233; traditionally supposed to have died there in 1315, from injuries received in Tunis when stoned by the Mohammedan mob. Wrote in Catalan, Latin and Arabic; some two hundred and forty authenticated works of his survive, of which most are in prose. His personal poems, together with some extracts from the didactic works which he wrote in verse, have been published by Ramon d'Alòs-Moner as *Poesies* in the series «Els Nostres Clàssics» (Barcelona, 1928); his verse has twice been edited in its entirety. The *Libre d'amic e amat* (which forms Part V of his long didactic novel *Blanquerna*) was published in «Els Nostres Clàssics» in 1927 by Marçal Olivar and Mossen Salvador Galmés. Professor E. Allison Peers published an English translation of the *Libre d'amic e amat* in 1923, and a translation of *Blanquerna* in 1925. Cf. pp. XV, XXXII-XXXVII, 1-42.

López-Picó, Josep Maria

Born in Barcelona in 1886. His first volume of poetry, *Intermezzo galant*, appeared in 1910. As founder and editor of «La Revista», and sponsor of the editions published over that imprint, performed an extremely valuable task for the cause of Catalan literature. With the exception of his more recent writings, the bulk of his poetry was brought together in a single volume as *Obres completes*: *I*, published by Editorial Selecta (Barcelona, 1948). Cf. pp. LXXIII-LXXIV, 248-50.

Manent, Albert

Born in Sant Pere de Premià (Barcelona) in 1930. Son of Marià Manent (q. v.). Reading law. Contributed to the *Antologia poètica universitària 1949*; published *Hoste del vent* in the same year; his second book, *La nostra nit i altres poemes*, is still unpublished. Also writes articles and short stories. Cf. pp. 368-9.

Manent, Marià

Born in Barcelona in 1898. His *Versions de l'anglès* (1938) are famous, and have been responsible for a great deal of the interest in English poetry which has marked recent poetic developments in Catalonia. His first volume of original poetry was *La branca* (1918); *La collita en la boira* followed in 1920; his imitations from the Chinese vere published as *L'aire daurat* (1928), made under the influence of English translations, these deserve to be considered as original work. His most important book, *L'ombra i altres poemes*, appeared in 1931 (second edition, 1946). Has edited a number of periodicals, and holds an important post in a publishing firm. Cf. pp. LXXIV, LXXVII, 307-12.

Maragall, Joan

Born in Barcelona in 1860, died there in 1911. Read law, but joined the staff of the «Diari de Barcelona» (the first

Barcelona daily paper), on which he served until the death of his father gave him the economic independence required for him to be able to dedicate his life to literature. Continued to write for the press as well, and his articles and essays are second in importance only to his lyric poetry. Published five books of verse, now available in a single volume, and his dramatic poem *Nausica* was acted and published after his death. Complete works published three times: by Editorial Gili (Barcelona, 1913); revised by the author's sons (Barcelona, 1929-1932); and by Editorial Selecta in the «Biblioteca Perenne» (Barcelona, 1947). Cf. pp. LXVIII-LXXII, 180-215.

March, Ausiàs

Born in Gandia, near Valencia, in 1397; died in the Valencian capital in 1459. Nobleman, courtier and soldier in the service of Alfons III of Catalonia (IV of Aragon); took part in numerous military engagements in Italy and in the Mediterranean. Owned considerable lands and held a prominent position at Court. The greatest Catalan Renaissance poet. His poems are normally grouped into the *Cants d'amor*, *Cants de mort*, *Cants morals*, and the *Cant espiritual*. The standard edition is *Les obres d'Auziàs March*, of Amadeu Pagès (Barcelona, 1912-1914); a new edition, by Pere Bohigas, will shortly be appearing in the series «Els Nostres Clàssics». Cf. pp. XLI-XLVI, 53-87.

Masdovelles, Joan Berenguer de

Dates of birth and death unknown; flourished between 1438 and 1467. Nobleman and courtier; supporter of Joan II against the Prince of Viana, and later against the Generalitat. No fewer than one hundred and seventy-four of his poems have survived, more than those which we have of any other Catalan poet prior to the Renaixença. Cf. pp. XLVI, 87-8.

Nogués, Cèsar

Born in Barcelona in 1922; died there in 1950, aged twenty-eight. Published one book of poems, *Lassitud*, in 1949; his remaining works await a posthumous edition. Cf. pp. 361-2.

Palau Fabre, Josep

Born in Barcelona in 1917. Read philosophy in Barcelona. Founded a review called «Poesia»; edited a series of books by new poets called «La Sirena». Has lived in Paris since December 1945. Has recently given the collective title of *Poemes de l'alquimista* to the five books of poetry which he has written: *L'aprenent de poeta* (1945), *Imitació de Rosselló-Pòrcel* (1946), *Càncer* (1946), and *Laberint* and *Atzucac*. Cf. pp. LXXIX, 349-53.

Perucho, Joan

Born in Gràcia, a district of Barcelona, in 1920. Read law and is in practice as a lawyer and municipal magistrate. Published *Sota la sang* in 1947, and *Aurora per vosaltres* in 1951. Cf. pp. 355-9.

Pons, Josep Sebastià

Born in Illa de Tet (P. O.), Rousillon, in 1886. Poet, essayist, playwrigth. His most important volume of poetry, *Cantilena*, appeared in Barcelona in 1937; it was reprinted in Toulouse in 1949. His latest book is *Conversa del molí*. Cf. LXXII, 251-2.

Pons i Gallarza, Lluís

Born in Sant Andreu del Palomar, which is now part of the urban district of Barcelona, in 1823; died in Palma de Mallorca in 1894, having lived there the greater part of his life. Fully acclimatized in Mallorca, he became one of the founders of the island school. His poetry is small in quantity, but very significant in the history of the Renaixença. Published *Poesies* (Palma de Mallorca, 1892). Cf. pp. LIX, 114-6.

"Quart, Pere"

Pseudonym of Joan Oliver, who only uses it for poetry: born in Sabadell, an industrial town near Barcelona, in 1899. Also well-known for his short stories and his plays. Chiefly satirical, his published poetry consists of *Les decapitacions* (1934), *Bestiari* (1936), and *Saló de tardor* (1946). Went into exile in 1939, returning to Barcelona in 1948, where he republished the three previous volumes as *Poemes de Pere Quart* (Barcelona, 1949). Cf. pp. LXXVII-VIII, 313-5.

Riba, Carles

Born in Barcelona in 1893. Read law, but soon devoted himself entirely to the Classics. Professor of Greek in the autonomous University of Barcelona until 1939. Went into exile in France at the end of the Spanish Civil War. Returned to Catalonia in 1942; now chief adviser to the Fundació Bernat Metge, which exists to produce critical editions of the Classics. Has translated works of the Greek tragedians, Plutarch, and Homer, his most notable contribution in this field being his verse translation of the *Odyssey*. Has also engaged in literary criticism. Poetry: *Primer llibre d'estances* (1919); *Estances (llibre segon)* (1933); *Tres suites* (1937), which was produced during the Spanish Civil War; *Elegies de Bierville* (Buenos Aires, 1942; Santiago de Chile, 1949; revised and definitive edition, Barcelona, 1951), written in exile; *Del joc i del foc*, published in «Biblioteca Selecta» (Barcelona, 1947). Has brought out in 1952 a volume of sonnets, *Salvatge cor*. Cf. pp. LXXIV, LXXVI-VII, 253-68.

Rocaberti, Hug Bernat de

Born during the first quarter of the Fifteenth Century. Commander of the forces of Joan II in 1461. Ambassador to France, where he was detained and held captive by Louis XI. Took part in the war of the Roussillon and in the negotiations which followed it. Held a castle, belonging to his family, near the city of Amposta. Wrote *La comedia de la glòria d'amor*, a poem of over fifteen hundred lines, which has been published as *The Glòria d'Amor de Fra Rocaberti* by H. C. Heaton (New York, 1916). Cf. pp. XLVI-VII, 89.

Roiç de Corella, Joan

Born in the territory of Valencia, about the middle of the Fifteenth Century; believed to have died in 1500. It would seem that he was a Master of Divinity and a well-known preacher, but the identification is uncertain. Wrote both in prose and verse, combining both media in such a work as the *Tragèdia de Caldesa*. Complete works published as *Obres de J. Roiç de Corella*, edited by R. Miquel i Planas, in the «Biblioteca Catalana» (Barcelona, 1913). Cf. pp. XLVII-L, 90-5.

Romeu, Josep

Born in Òdena, near Igualada, in 1917. Doctor of the Faculty of Filosofia i Lletres of the University of Barcelona. Has concentrated on the study of Catalan folklore and, resident in Barcelona, is engaged on a definitive edition of the *Cançoner* (q. v.). Has published *Sonets* (1944), reprinted in one volume with *Elegia del mite* and *Nits més enllà del somni* (Óssa Menor, 1950), and *Aires de Llegenda* (1948). His poetical work, together with unpublished material, has been printed in «Biblioteca Selecta» (1951), with the title *Obra poètica*. Cf. pp. 353-4.

Rosselló-Pòrcel, Bartomeu

Born in Palma de Mallorca in 1913, died in Brull sanatorium on the northern slopes of Montseny early in 1938. Studied in Barcelona and Madrid; published numerous critical articles both in Mallorca and in «Mirador» (Barcelona). His first critical work was a study of Quevedo, still unpublished. Had already published *Nou poemes* and *Quadern de sonets*, both during the course of the Spanish Civil War; *Imitació del foc* appeared posthumously in 1938, and a volume containing his complete poetic works was printed by R. O. D. A. in Palma de Mallorca, in 1949. Cf. pp. LXXVII, 328-35.

Sagarra, Josep Maria de

Born in Barcelona in 1894. Read law with a view to entering the diplomatic service, but turned to writing and journalism. Was for a time a foreign correspondent in Berlin. Equally prolific in prose and verse. In addition to his journalistic articles, has written numerous plays, novels, a travel book, and Catalan translations of the *Divine Comedy* and all of Shakespeare's plays. *Primer llibre de poemes* (1914), *El mal caçador* (1916), and *Cançons de taverna i d'oblit* (1922) are the best of the eleven books of poetry which constitute the poetic output of his first twenty-five years as a writer, all of which have been republished in a single volume, *Obra poètica*, by Editorial Selecta (Barcelona, 1947). Went abroad during the Spanish Civil War, travelling extensively in Polynesia; his resultant *Entre l'equador i els tròpics* represents the first Catalan poetic reaction to the South Sea Islands. It is available in «Biblioteca Selecta», together with *El Comte Arnau* (a long poem of over ten thousand lines) and *Poema de Nadal*. A subsequent poem of sixteen thousand lines, *Montserrat*, is in course of publication. Cf. pp. LXXIV-V, 272-82.

Salvà, Maria Antònia

Born in Palma de Mallorca in 1869. Translator of Mistral and Manzoni. Lives in Lluchmajor (Mallorca), near one of the places most closely associated with Ramon Llull (q. v.). Her poetry has constantly been characterized by her intense consciousness of the soil, the landscape, and the people. Published *Espigues en flor* in 1927; the most important of her books of poetry is *El retorn*. Complete poetic works at present in course of publication. Cf. pp. LXVII, 215-8.

Salvat-Papasseit, Joan

Born in Barcelona in 1894; died there in 1922, after a long illness. Founded the periodical «Un enemic del poble» at seventeen (1911), and published *Contra els poetes en minúscula* in 1920. Published five books of poetry during his lifetime:

Poemes en ondes hertzianes (1919), illustrated by the well-known painter Torres-García; *L'irradiador del port i les gavines* (1921); *Les conspiracions* (1922); *La gesta dels estels* (1922); and *El poema de la rosa als llavis* (1923), his most important work. His *Óssa Menor* was published posthumously in 1925. His experience of suburban life in Barcelona and his knowledge of the docks formed the basis of much of his poetic inspiration, whilst a single visit to Madrid reinforced his ardent Catalanism, furnishing him with the themes for *Les conspiracions*. Cf. pp. LXXII, LXXIV-V, 292-303.

Sant Jordi, Jordi de

Born in the kingdom of Valencia (if not in the city itself) towards the end of the Fourteenth Century, possibly in 1395; probably died in 1430 in Valencia. Took part in various campaigns in Italy, in the service of Alfons III of Catalonia (IV of Aragon), being captured and held prisoner by Francesco Sforza. Wrote the *Enuigs* and some miscellaneous poems, and was co-poet of the *Passió d'amor*. The *Obres poètiques de Jordi de Sant Jordi* have been edited and published by J. Massó i Torrents (Barcelona, 1902). Cf. pp. XXXVIII-XLI, 43-53.

Sarsanedas, Jordi

Born in Barcelona in 1924. Grew up in France, studying at the University of Toulouse and at the Sorbonne. Lecturer in Catalan in the University of Glasgow, 1948-1949. Published *A trenc de serra* in Barcelona in 1948; a second book of his poetry is still unpublished. Has also written a volume of short stories entitled *Mites*, and critical articles on art and literary subjects. Cf. pp. 362-5.

Serafí, Pere

Dates of birth and death unknown, but still alive about 1563. Native of Barcelona, and a painter by profession. Described by Nicolau d'Olwer as a belated troubadour, but also deeply influenced both by Petrarch and Ausiàs March (q. v.), and by the Castilian poets of the Sixteenth Century Italianate school. At his best in his songs and sonnets. Poetic works first published in Barcelona in 1565. Edited by Rubió i Ors (Barcelona, 1840). Cf. pp. LII, 96-7.

Teixidor, Joan

Born in Olot in 1913. Read philosophy; writes and lectures both as a literary critic and as an art critic. Published three books of poetry before the end of the Spanish Civil War: *Poemes*, *Joc partit*, and *L'aventura fràgil*; and recently, after a prolonged silence. *Camí dels dies* (1948). Cf. 327-8.

Torres, Màrius

Born in Lleida in 1910, died of consumption in Puig d'Olena sanatorium in 1942. Poetical works published posthumously by his friends as *Poesies d'En Màrius Torres* (Coyoacan, Mexico, 1947); recently republished by Óssa Menor (Barcelona, 1950) with a prologue by Carles Cardó. Cf. pp. 339-41.

Torroella, Pere

Flourished in the second half of the Fifteenth Century and probably died after the beginning of the Sixteenth. His surviving works were all written between 1453 and 1490. Educated in Castile, lived at the court of Navarre with the Prince of Viana. Wrote a large part of his works in Castilian, under the name of Pedro Torrellas. Of his thirty-one surviving pieces in Catalan, the *Desconhort* (just under seven hundred lines in length) quotes twenty-nine poets in six different languages; others are brief love lyrics. *The Works of Pere Torroella* have been published by P. Bach i Rita (New York, 1930). Cf. pp. XLVII, LI, 95-6.

Triadú, Joan

Born in Ribes del Freser in 1921. Read Classics. Lecturer in Catalan in the University of Liverpool, 1948-1950. Has edited an *Antologia de contistes catalans* (1850-1950) and an *Antologia de la poesia catalana* (1900-1950) in the «Biblioteca Selecta».

Poetry: *Endimió* (Barcelona, 1948), and *Els límits del vivent* (unpublished). Editor and founder with Romeu and Palau Fabre of *Ariel, Revista de les Arts*. Cf. pp. 359-60.

Verdaguer, Jacint

Born in Folgueroles (Osona), a small village on the plain of Vic, some forty-five miles from Barcelona, in 1845; died in «Vil·la Joana», a country house at Vallvidrera in the hills near Barcelona, in 1902. Born of peasant stock; entered seminary at Vic and was ordained. His health gave way, and acting on doctor's advice he became a ship's chaplain in the pay of the Compañía Transatlántica. Also travelled extensively in Europe, going as far afield as Russia, and visited the Holy Land. Gained a prize at the Jocs Florals of Barcelona in 1865; awarded a prize by the Diputació Provincial for his first long epic poem, *L'Atlàntida*, in 1877; made «Mestre en Gai Saber» in 1880. Became almoner to the Marquis of Comillas, but differences with the Bishop of Vic, beginning in 1893, ultimately led to his suspension in 1895. His written retraction in 1898 led to reconciliation with the hierarchy; he was given a new benefice, but withdrew to «Vil·la Joana», where he died four years later. Wrote much, both in verse and in prose. Most important poetic works: *Idil·lis i cants místics* (1870), *L'Atlàntida* (1877), and *Canigó* (1886). First complete edition, 1905; revised edition begun by Llibreria Catalonia in 1929; third complete edition, in one volume, by Editorial Selecta (Barcelona, 1949). Cf. pp. XV, LXI-LXV, 117-46.

Vinyoli, Joan

Born in Barcelona in 1914. Lives in Barcelona and works for a publishing firm. Connoisseur of German poetry; translator of works by Goethe, Hölderlin, Nietzsche, Rilke, and Hoffman. Original poetry: *El primer desenllaç* (1937), *De vida i somni* (1948), *Les hores retrobades* (unpublished). Cf. pp. LXXVIII, 345-7.

INDEX OF FIRST LINES

www.ingramcontent.com/pod-product-compliance
Lightning Source LLC
Chambersburg PA
CBHW022009110726
47901CB00006B/1450
9780520349049